*Be Fruitful
and Multiply*

SOC
HB
871
F68

Be Fruitful and Multiply

Life at the limits of population

John Fremlin

Rupert Hart-Davis   London

Granada Publishing Limited
First published 1972 by Rupert Hart-Davis Ltd
3 Upper James Street London W1R 4BP

Copyright © 1972 by J H Fremlin

All rights reserved. No part of this publication
may be reproduced, stored in a retrieval system,
or transmitted, in any form or by any means,
electronic, mechanical, photocopying, recording or
otherwise, without the prior permission of
the publishers.

ISBN 0 246 10566 6
Printed in Great Britain by
Northumberland Press Ltd, Gateshead

Contents

Preface	vii
1 Be Fruitful and Multiply	1
2 The Natural Control of Population	10
3 The Defeat of Our Natural Limitations	37
4 Britain as it Could be in Eighty Years' Time	62
5 Armageddon?	91
6 Providing for the Multitudes	104
7 The Blazing Limit	126
8 Anticlimax	157
9 Traditional and Practical Means of Artificially Controlling our Numbers	174
10 Possible Solutions	186
Appendix I Population Growth and Age Structure	221
Appendix II Group Selection for Intelligence	231
Bibliography	233
Index	235

Preface

Within the last ten years the majority of thinking people have woken up to what a minority has always known; that the natural world around us is important as well as beautiful. As a result, increasing numbers of books on the future of humanity have appeared in the last few years and these have been increasingly gloomy, often indeed apocalyptic, in tone.

Many of these books have been written by authors of intelligence and insight, who have seen real dangers and have seen that these real dangers are really increasing at unprecedented speeds. You do not call the attention of your friends to real dangers in a whisper, so you give your message in a shout. But people are used to being shouted at, and few of us nowadays notice even a shout the first time – so you shout louder.

There is nothing so big or so bad that you cannot exaggerate its bigness or its badness, and it is my belief that many of the perfectly real and serious dangers have been very seriously exaggerated. This is an excellent way of attracting attention and has probably done a lot of good. But it is itself also dangerous. Suppose several people are walking along a path round a bog, and one of them is so perturbed by the neighbouring peril that he tells the others that if they so much as set foot off the path they will be swallowed up without trace. Possibly all of them are so impressed that they all stick to the path. Fine. But suppose that one or two thought it was all nonsense and stepped off the path. They do not get swallowed up; they merely get their shoes a bit muddy. So they decide it *is* all nonsense, and take a short cut straight across and get swallowed up.

I believe it to be rather important that there should be a warning that does not exaggerate and that cannot therefore be seemingly disproved by an experimental step off the path. I am just as sure of the reality of the dangers as are any of the prophets of imminent doom, but I am trying to give a warning which *cannot* be disproved by soothing Commissions of Enquiry.

Since this book was written, several important and relevant publications have appeared. Of these I would like to mention two: 'Blueprint for survival' which formed the whole of the January issue of *The Ecologist*, and *World Dynamics* by Jay W. Forrester. Each of these, in very different ways, underlines the importance and urgency of reducing our demand on the world's resources to a rate which can be permanently maintained.

It is a tragedy that the 'Blueprint' should have weakened its admirable general message by coupling this with a series of 'supporting' statements likely to alienate, by their lack of connection with the facts, the technically skilled minority who must be responsible for actually carrying out any major changes in our way of life.

An example is the statement that a slightly increased rate of mutation *reduces* the adaptability of a species.

Again, unlike many polemics on the dangers of the present rat race, the 'Blueprint' has made an attempt to outline changes in social and civic structure which could cure and not merely alleviate the human situation. Its proposals however have an unreality which leaves little chance of their adoption.

Thus the proposal that all big cities should be broken up into units of 5,000 people, each self-supporting in food and other essentials, could hardly be combined with another proposal to ban completely fresh road building. Furthermore, it would force us to retreat completely from mass-production of goods to small-scale production, and this could hardly make possible the complex variety of occupations which adds so much to the richness of life or the medical technology which has made it necessary in the first place. Nevertheless, the fact that the 'Blueprint' has the general support of a large number of eminent scientists – a group who are rarely found supporting unnecessary revolutions – goes a long way to prove that concern with ecological and population

Preface

problems is more than just a current fad, and the value of its impact may be considerable.

I have less faith in the value of *World Dynamics*. This is a detailed comparative study which extrapolates existing trends on a variety of sets of plausible assumptions – every one of which leads to a runaway world catastrophe after a few decades.

As the author says, further refinements of the detailed assumptions will be needed, but in fact these have been made with care and thought and detailed changes are unlikely to change the world picture. The absolutely basic assumption which Forrester has made, and which makes his method of analysis appropriate to atoms or ants or even apes, but not to human beings, is that the rate of change of anything, for example wealth or population or pollution, depends only on the absolute amounts of the others, and not on their rates of change, let alone on forecasts of their future values.

In fact, practically our entire response to population, pollution, or the exhaustions of the resources of the earth, to take but three of Forrester's very proper concerns, is due to their rate of change and to our theoretical extrapolations of the effects of these; not to the fact that we are now living in misery because of them. Plenty of people in the world *are* living in misery, but they are not the ones who are demanding a halt.

World Dynamics gives an excellent picture of what might happen if nobody had noticed what is happening – and if 'Blueprint for survival' and *World Dynamics* had not been written. Similarly if we walk towards a cliff top without noticing it, we shall go over the edge. But if we do notice it we shall not.

The dangers are exactly as stated and the dangers are real and approaching; but it does not help our chances to pretend that they are so large and so close as to be irresistible.

Many readers may regret my almost complete neglect of the utter destruction of all wild life and of our entire natural environment if we multiply for even a few generations more at our present rate. This is not lack of concern; my friends will know that concern for the rich variety of nature has been one of my main motives in writing this book. But two messages are less effective than one. I shall be delighted if by quoting my message others will strengthen theirs.

I have throughout used the metric system of measurements. All world statistics are given in this way, and it makes the arithmetic far easier for anyone who wishes to check my calculations. It should make no difference to those who do not want to do so. A metre is only a little bit more than a yard and a kilometre is nearly two-thirds of a mile. A metric ton is almost the same as a British ton, both being larger than an American ton, and a kilogramme is just over two pounds. A hectare is $2\frac{1}{4}$ acres, but exceedingly few townspeople nowadays would know which it was if you gave one to them on a football field.

I would like to thank my wife and various friends who have pointed out and helped me to correct mistakes and ambiguities; my secretary Mrs Denise Perkins who has shown a skill approaching clairvoyance in reading 90,000 words of appalling handwriting, and a great many school sixth forms whose original and penetrating questions have helped me enormously to clarify my arguments and to judge their relative importance.

One

Be Fruitful and Multiply

Introduction

Let us suppose that men have inhabited this planet for half a million years.

For most of this time we changed our way of life only slowly, and our numbers more slowly still. We are now increasing at about 2 per cent per year, but if we had been multiplying at even one-fiftieth of this rate throughout the whole half-million years, and had, improbably, started with but a single pair, the human race would now outweigh the visible universe. For an increase of 0.04 per cent each year means doubling our numbers every 1,700 years. In half a million years we would have doubled our numbers 294 times. If you want to check this result by straight multiplication, you will need a large piece of paper.

In fact we do not yet know how long we have existed, and in any case there can have been no definite moment at which the first man or woman was born. We live in groups, and evolved in groups. In the past, as now, an average group would have some unusually bright members and some very dull members. It is therefore likely that occasional individuals, with intelligence well within the present normal range, occurred sporadically while the average mentality of the species was far below the human level. One such bright individual could change materially the prospects of survival for his whole colony or troop, even though his genes dispersed among the rest produced no descendants in the human range for generations at a time. Nevertheless, in considering our actual past and potential future development, we have to start somewhere, and if we choose half a million years, we can hardly be wrong by a factor of three (that is, by three times too much, or three times too little).

For most of this time the world population must have been growing very slowly indeed; for much of it, perhaps, not growing at all. Hundreds of thousands of years may have been needed to reach a population of ten million people, and nearly the whole period of our existence to reach a thousand million. This figure was probably achieved about 1850 AD. The second thousand million however took perhaps ninety years – to 1940 – and the third twenty years to 1960. The fourth should be complete by 1975 – fifteen years for the fourth against the 499 thousand years for the first. Our evolution has adapted us to a stable world, and we are now in a changing one. It is not surprising that we find the times are out of joint.

The impact of the situation is not due directly and solely to our increase in numbers, great though this is. (If you read fairly quickly, there are now 100 more people in the world than there were when you read my first sentence.) The average density of the world population is still little over half that reached by England in the eighteenth century. If we had reached our present numbers by the gradual spread of peasant communities, developing, over thousands of years, the agricultural techniques appropriate to areas of the planet which are now uncultivated, we should be quite unconscious of a problem.

There are at least three major factors, which are more directly responsible for our present concern than are our unprecedentedly large absolute numbers.

The first and most obvious of these is the *rate* at which our numbers are changing. For most of recorded history, the old have considered that the world – and the people in it – have deteriorated in quality since their own youth. With the advantage of hindsight, we can see that the worldwide changes in a generation have, until the last couple of centuries, always been small, and perhaps more often than not for the better. But, for the first time, people now retired can remember actually living in a world with half as many people in it as there are today. A majority of western Europeans can see houses and shops on the open spaces where they used to play. Whether they remember the greenness and the sunshine, or the mud and the scarcity of shoes and meat, there has been a perfectly genuine and major change, which is not just a piece out of the history books, but is direct personal experience. The use of simple weapons to hunt large animals, and the development of agriculture, must each have permitted far larger increases than have characterized the human race in the last two hundred years, but the increases were slow. It is therefore unlikely that they were noticed at all at the time, however far reaching their ultimate effects.

The second major factor which has forced the situation on our notice, is the associated enormous rate of change of our way of life. The growth of the world's towns and the multiplication of its cars and television sets are faster by far even than of its population growth. The grandchildren of most of those in Europe or North America who were engaged in agriculture seventy years ago, are growing up in blocks of flats in the suburbs of great towns. Where in 1900 few healthy people would think of any other means than walking to visit relations or shops, or even to go to work a mile away, we are rebuilding whole cities to ensure that nobody will have to walk four hundred yards. The grandfathers of most of those who watch television today, will have thriftily denied themselves a daily newspaper, and have stoically accepted isolation from the news of the world until Sunday.

This change in the form and quality of life has penetrated the whole of the 'developed' world, and has affected deeply much of the world that materially has only begun to develop. I believe it to be the biggest of the factors which lead us to see and to concern ourselves with the other changes.

What makes it so important is that we have not really been prepared by our evolution for a changing world at all. We have evolved to have an unprecedented capacity for learning facts about, and learning to understand, the world around us during our extended youth, so that we can apply this knowledge and understanding to our advantage in our later lives. In a changing world the value of our youthful factual knowledge is much reduced. This can be illustrated by considering the learning of simpler animals than ourselves. A flock of sheep who have lived for generations in rough hill country are said to be 'hefted' (i.e. adapted) to their area or 'heaf'. They do not fall over the precipices, or get stuck in the bogs. When the snow falls, they are not caught in exposed places. Yet, moved to another area, they may succumb to very similar hazards. They behave as though they had acquired a special set of instincts, enabling them to avoid the particular hazards where, and only where, they grew up. In fact, they learn when young to avoid a precipice, not because they know they might be killed by falling over it, but because their mothers avoid it ... because generations back a sheep *did* fall over it, and ever after the others have stayed clear, without memory of the martyr or knowledge of the danger. Since there is no understanding, in a new area they may easily fall off a cliff, which they had never been taught to avoid. It is because of this that the destruction of his flock, at a threat of foot and mouth disease, is so serious for a hill sheep farmer. Compensation can buy him more sheep, but it can't repay him for the loss and trouble of the next few years, while his new flock is learning the hard way where not to go.

In a rapidly changing world, our old – and even middle-aged – people are like the sheep who have been hefted to one area but live in another. We have an advantage over the sheep in that we learn to *understand*. But this does not help us to evaluate the risks of extensive contrails from Concorde in the upper atmosphere, or of DDT in our children's fat.

This is not to say that all change is bad; the majority of the changes in my lifetime seem to be good. But it does mean that all big and rapid changes have an extra cost, which is not often counted in the balance, and would not be there if the changes were equally big but slow.

The third major factor, and the one which inspires most of those who are, perhaps unfairly, known as the prophets of doom, is our increasing impact upon our environment. In an important way, it is a very heartening thing that so little immediate harm to human beings has aroused so much concern. For the first time, we are crying before we are hurt. I am not by any means criticizing this – it is of course by far the most useful time to cry.

The spread of smoke and malnutrition during the nineteenth century, over a rapidly industrializing Britain, condemned huge numbers of our children to rickets, (over 80 per cent were affected among London and Durham school children as late as fifty years ago), and limited much of our industrial population to unhealthy lives and an early death. But this produced not a tithe of the protests now aroused by the spread of persistent insecticides, the use of which has saved tens of millions of lives.

Apart from the long-term biological risks, resulting from the world-wide spread of novel poisons, several other industrial activities are producing large-scale economic or physical effects on their environment. These result from the enormous increase in individual and national wealth over the last two generations. Not only are there more of us, but each one of us uses more power and more goods, takes more space to live in, and throws enormously more away. This means that, although in this century Far Eastern and tropical populations have increased faster than have European and North American, it is the latter which have produced by far the biggest effects. In the nineteenth century, the average American probably used only two or three times the amount of the world's resources that was used by an Indian or West African peasant. He now uses something more like fifty times as much. So, although India may have trebled her population while America has doubled hers, America will be using resources perhaps forty times as fast as before, against India's five or six times. Europe lags behind the USA, but not by more than a factor of two, and Holland and England in particular, with seventeen times the density of population of the United States, must be well ahead in a league table based on total usage of resources per hectare.

The effect on England itself, and to a lesser extent on the rest of Britain, is only too obvious. In 1970 we built only about eighty centimetres of new roads for each motor vehicle we put on to them, but we still used up a lot of land for their construction. The expansion of existing cities, and the building of several completely new large towns took up a great deal more. We thus have simultaneously a smaller amount of countryside, a larger number of people who want to visit it, and more leisure and more spare cash for each of them with which to do so.

Having pointed out the cost of wealth and of the drift to the cities, it is important to remind ourselves that these have a value as well as a cost. One of the difficulties of discussion of the subject, is that those who are most clearly and most greatly concerned about the cost, rarely discuss the value, and indeed often give the impression that the spread of cars and the growth of cities can only be the result of insanity or masochism among the citizens. It is neither insanity nor masochism that leads to the rapid and steady drift from the country to the towns, which is now going on in every country in the world. Individuals may indeed fail to foresee all the drawbacks, but there are real advantages in comfort and variety of life, which can be obtained only where people live together in very large numbers.

While many critics of our urban developments cannot see the value, the economists and others who have their eyes firmly fixed on productivity and the Gross National Product, rarely appreciate the cost. If we were changing slowly over generations, this would not matter, as both cost and value would be coming in small instalments, leaving plenty of time for re-evaluation as we went along. In fact something like half of the whole industrial output of the world's entire history has been produced during the last forty years and only part of the cost has been paid. The rest will have to be found by our children. More important still, we shall not be able to get the price returned if we don't like the goods.

To forecast population growth reliably is even more difficult than weather forecasting. Not only does it depend, like the weather, on a very large number of local factors, most of which we don't know, but it is also affected by a special factor similar to the uncertainty principle in physics. (This states that it is impossible to forecast the exact future motion of an atom, because, in making the measurements of its position and velocity on which the forecast is to be made, its motion is necessarily disturbed by the observer.) Thus, when Professor Paul Ehrlich makes a convincingly unpleasant forecast of our future, he may be taking everything else into account as well as can now be done, but he cannot make allowance for the effects of his own forecast on all the people who are impressed by it, and consequently do something that they'd previously never thought of doing.

I am not going to make any forecasts at all. In particular I am not going to follow the lead of the prophets of doom, who predict that Britain has no more than even chances of surviving to the year 2000, or that the whole atmosphere will soon become unbreathable, or that we shall all die of insecticide poisoning. This is not because I think it wrong to call attention to the disastrous possibilities of some of our large-scale mistakes and misdemeanours. I do not even think it is invariably wrong to exaggerate somewhat the imminence of these disasters. We are so used to overstated advertising, that we usually do not listen to anything less than a shout, and automatically discount four-fifths of the statements we hear. It is fair to allow for this. At the same time, it has a disadvantage. If we seriously exaggerate the imminence and magnitude of a number of dangers, none of them will develop as soon or as injuriously as was forecast. Even greater exaggeration, with a higher-powered loud speaker, is then needed to attract attention, and presently no attention can be attracted at all.

I am not saying that the dangers are not real and serious. There was a boy who cried 'Wolf! Wolf!' before the wolf's arrival. The seriousness of his mistake was not because no wolf existed. It was because there *was* a wolf that it led to disaster.

I believe that an unlimited rise in our numbers would indeed lead inevitably to utter and permanent catastrophe. But I do not think that I can prove this by pointing to horrible things that will happen if we make no sensible effort to avoid them. I shall try to show that, even if we foresee and forestall every one of the horrors that the most painstaking collector has assembled, and use the highest level of technical skill and intelligent co-operation that it is possible to conceive, we shall *still* come to disaster if we continue to multiply.

Some of my suggestions for postponing the ultimate débâcle will seem pretty improbable. They are, very. We should be much more likely to fight each other than to collaborate on the necessary scale. But I think my proposals are possible. Even if they were not, it would not affect the argument. If we could not use the other planets, for example, we should reach disaster sooner, but we should still reach disaster. If anyone can disprove a bit of the gospel of the prophets of doom, he can feel that perhaps the rest can also be disproved, and that all will yet be well. But if anyone can prove that anything I shall suggest is impossible, he will be proving only that catastrophe will come even sooner than I say. There is one way, and one way only of avoiding it, and that is not to go on multiplying. This is not the only thing we have to do. Even if our numbers remained as they are now, we should still have some urgent and difficult problems to solve, before we could bring the general standard of living up to the standard of the affluent minority. But we cannot make even a useful start on this until we have drastically reduced our rate of increase. Without this, all else is futile, and it is therefore the only thing with which this book is seriously concerned.

On the same principle of showing the best that we can hope for, I have tried not to show my improbable futures as miserable or desperate. I myself, and most comfortably-off people of this era, would find them unmitigatedly ghastly, but there is no reason to suppose that people brought up to them would do so. Global co-operation for centuries would be quite as unlikely as any of my technical solutions but it is *possible*, and would be more likely if at least the great majority were contented with their lot. And continuous worldwide co-operation would be essential, if we are to defer the wolf for the maximum time.

One more piece of explanation is necessary. Some readers, particularly the arts-educated ones, may think that I have given far too much technical detail, and at much too great a length. It is true that I could have described possible ways of life at different population densities, with a great deal less arithmetic and without any reference to the fundamental laws of the universe. I could have made *ex cathedra* statements implying that, since I am a physicist and most of my readers are not, they have no business to question my dicta. This I believe to be wrong, and also unnecessary. A lot of people dislike arithmetic, and if they do so, I do not mind in the slightest if they accept without check that I have done it right. But three-quarters of the arithmetic I have given consists simply of multiplying by two a rather large number of times: so that anyone who wants to check can do so. Similarly, people who do not know, and do not wish to know, any engineering, are welcome to skip the design details for the cities or for the ultimate buildings – I have indicated by subheadings the more technical sections. But if they care whether what I have said is right, they do not have to argue that I have a more or less technical-looking set of degrees than do my critics. They can get hold of a reference book and an A-level physicist or chemist and work it out.

Naturally the arguments given will not convince the real antiscientist, who believes in witchcraft, or has faith in miraculous intervention. I do not know what are the chances of miraculous intervention, either to clean up the messes we have made, or to write us off as a bad job. But I am writing this book because I believe that there is a serious risk that there will *not* be any miraculous intervention.

Some of the propositions which I shall discuss, for example the poisoning of the atmosphere or the entire chapter on 'Armageddon?' will – I hope – be unnecessary for most people. But, like the idea of miraculous intervention, they represent excuses for forgetting the long-term problems of population reduction. 'Eat, drink and be merry, for tomorrow we die' is not a stirring call for devoted hard work, and can lead to unavailing regrets for wasted time if tomorrow we do not die.

The main part of the book is divided into three parts. The next two chapters explain how it is that the problem has arisen. In Chapter Two the different limiting factors are discussed by means of which the populations of other creatures are prevented from indefinite expansion, and in Chapter Three it is shown how we have, one by one, learnt to evade all of these limits. In a further five chapters the results of unlimited expansion are examined, and the means of supporting such expansion to a succession of technological levels are followed up to a final and inescapable limit. In the last two chapters the artificial limits available to help us provide an alternative future are described, and the possible ways of encouraging their adoption are considered.

Two

The Natural Control of Population

The present growth of the human population is unprecedented, not only for human beings themselves, but for any living thing existing now or at any time in the whole history of our planet.

This is not just because we are increasing at 2 per cent per year, doubling our numbers every thirty-five years.* In good conditions some microorganisms can double their numbers every thirty-five minutes. It is not because there are 3,500 million of us. There are more bacteria than this in ten grammes of surface soil and as many roundworms in twenty metres square of pasture land.

The difference between us and the rest of the inhabitants of the world is that their numbers have established natural limitations, and ours have not. We used to be limited in much the same ways as the rest but one by one we have discovered these limits, disliked them, and taken effective steps to dispose of them. Unknown limits may be lying in wait, and might suddenly assume enormous importance. Confidence that such hidden limits *must* exist and will be impossible to overcome, would absolve us of all need to think about – or indeed to admit the existence of – a population problem. I am inclined myself to doubt whether there are any unsuspected limits, but if there are, I am rather confident that they will be ineffective. Coming up against a natural limit means that one's children die, or that young women die before they have their children, or that people are sufficiently stressed to make reproduction inefficient. We do not like these

---

* This relation is true only for a continuous steady growth rate. It is explained, and the effects of changing growth rate are demonstrated, in Appendix I.

The Natural Control of Population

things happening, and with the development of applied science we have not only learned how to get rid of the main remaining causes which used to kill our children but, of far deeper significance, we have learnt *how to find out* how to remove such causes.

Stability of Natural Numbers

Natural limitations are extraordinarily effective over long periods. As we saw in the first chapter, if human beings could have doubled their numbers every 1,700 years over a period of half a million years, they would by now outweigh the known universe. We do not know the average length of life of a species between origin and extinction but for the larger animals it may be from two to five million years and for the larger plants perhaps from ten to twenty million years. Some insects seem to have changed little in a hundred million years. The 'fossil ant' *Ponera coarctica*, living now, appears identical with a species occurring in Baltic amber thirty million years old.

If we consider a largish animal such as a man or a deer, about 200 million million of them would have standing room only over the whole ice-free land surface of the globe. It is quite certain that no single kind of large animal has ever reached such numbers, whether it has existed for two million years or five.

If we started with one pregnant individual and doubled the numbers ten times, we should have just over 1,000. If we doubled the numbers ten times more we should have a little over a million; twenty times more still and we would have over a million million. Altogether, to reach 200 million million we would have had to multiply by two just over forty-seven times. This means that if the population had grown *steadily* through two million years of existence, it could not have doubled its numbers oftener than once in 43,000 years. That represents an annual increase of 0.0015 per cent. Similarly a large species of a tree lasting twenty-five million years cannot have shown an average annual rate of change greater than about 0.0001 per cent while even an ant, of which one might put 100,000 on a square metre, could not have shown a steady growth over 100 million years of as much as 0.00004 per cent per year.

Of course, I am not suggesting for a moment that the total numbers of each kind of ant in the world in any one year cannot be more than 0.00004 per cent different from the number present the year before. In a good season following a really bad one there could well be 100 times multiplication in a single year. But large increases will be followed by falls and catastrophic falls will be followed by increases, so that the *average* rate of change over many generations remains almost unbelievably small. This cannot be due to the working of pure chance.

Careful records of the numbers of snowshoe hares killed in the Hudson Bay Watershed over 100 years or more showed regular fluctuations every ten years or so, from a few thousands to many tens of thousands. Thus the figures between 1905 and 1928 showed maxima and minima as follows: 1905, 20,000; 1912, 72,000; 1918, 10,000; 1923, 80,000; 1928, 2,000; etc. There is every reason to suppose that such variations have continued as long as hares have existed, but they have never reached zero or overflowed into the sea. This can not possibly be the result of random chance which at most from year to year could give a variation of only a few per cent. It *must* mean that when the numbers become very low the pressures become less so that life and reproduction are easier and numbers rise. When numbers are very large, on the other hand, the chance of survival and of leaving offspring must become smaller and numbers drop. This is a situation described by the engineer as due to 'negative feedback'. In the particular case of the Canadian hares, the chief element of negative feedback is known as a lynx. When hares are common the lynxes multiply; when the hares become rare the lynxes die.

Control by Living Space

Perhaps the simplest possible limit to living is just the room to live. As a temporary limitation in a small uniform area it is fairly common. For example, a small pond in spring may have a few fronds of duckweed scattered around on the surface of the water. By midsummer they may have multiplied to cover the entire pond, so that there is no room for even one more adult plant until another one dies. For a time then the numbers

The Natural Control of Population

remain very closely constant, any which die or are removed being quickly replaced. The steadiness of population however does not last; cold or being eaten will finally reduce their numbers again to a scattered few. Although it is unusual, such a simple limit does occasionally become permanent – at least while climate and general environment remain steady. For example, in Siberia continuous stands of a single species of conifer may cover large areas. Year after year their seeds are dropped but cannot develop under the continuous canopy of adult trees. Only when a tree dies of old age, or is struck by lightning and falls, does enough light strike through to the ground for seeds to germinate and grow. At once hundreds of young trees begin to grow, crowding each other in the vacant space. Any which grows a little faster than those around will get a trifle more than its share of the limited light and will grow a little faster still until on the average one alone survives and the forest becomes the same size as before.

Such examples are rare because they need rare characteristics in the plant or animal concerned. This must be significantly better at exploiting its habitat than any other species; it must have no natural enemies which can destroy it in any numbers or weaken it to the point where some other species can successfully compete, and it must be able to live indefinitely without important injury from its own excretions or from the accumulated remains of previous generations. Such a collection of requirements can never be satisfied in the tropics where the choice of both enemies and competitors is too great for any one species to have a chance of such pre-eminence. Even in circum-polar regions it is, as we have seen, extremely rare. It occurs only among plants or among animals such as mussels or corals which live sessile lives essentially similar to those of plants. When the right conditions do occur, the population of the area concerned does not oscillate like the hares mentioned above, but remains very closely constant, perhaps for immense periods of time.

At no time in the history of humanity have we been limited by shortage of physical space – by there being standing room only.

Control by Pollution

Very often the numbers of a fast-growing species in restricted regions are limited by the toxic effect of the species's own wastes. For example, yeasts growing on rotting fruit or in homemade wine excrete carbon dioxide which evaporates and alcohol which does not. When the alcohol concentration reaches a few per cent the growth of the yeast slows down and stops. Many bacterial cultures on limited substrates behave in similar ways. However, control of this kind occurs only rarely on a large scale.

Although we do not like living surrounded by our own excrement, and doing so may have dangerous side effects, our population has never been controlled by this. But many thoughtful people, with some reason, fear that we could soon be limited by our industrial waste products.

Control by Predation and Parasitism

A species can be limited by being the food of some other species; a plant, for example, attacked by caterpillars. The great variety of trees in tropical forests, as compared with temperate forests, is probably due to the fact that any tree which becomes common will form a source of food particularly easy to find. Then the insects which specialize in eating it will multiply to the point where they weaken conclusively its ability to compete for space with larger numbers of different and separately uncommon trees surrounding it. When it also becomes rare as a result, the great majority of its insect persecutors fail to find food and, being specialists unable to change their diet at short notice, drop to numbers which may still be troublesome in bad years but are no longer disastrous. Among common British plants which one can see being controlled in this way is the common yellow ragwort, which will multiply in rough pastures for several years until one year every plant over a large area will be eaten down to the ground by the black and yellow caterpillars of the Cinnabar moth. The plant is rarely completely exterminated from the area, but has to start again from very small numbers of survivors.

The Natural Control of Population

Many moths and butterflies have larvae which are protected by irritating hairs or by an unpleasant taste. This does not help the individual which is experimentally tasted by a young and inexperienced bird – but does help other similar larvae. In the absence of other enemies such a species would multiply till it had eaten itself out of house and home. But many such insects, though for practical purposes untouched by birds and animals, remain uncrowded and often even very rare. In such cases they are almost always limited by parasitic insects smaller than themselves.* The female of one of the parasites will find a larva of the larger host species and will lay perhaps fifty or more of her own eggs inside it. The larva will continue to feed and grow while inside it the young parasites feed on its internal food reserves and grow faster still. When the larva reaches its full size, the parasites begin to attack more vital parts and when they reach full growth and finally emerge through a hole bitten in the side there may be little left but an empty skin, the whole of the interior being eaten away.

An easily observed example is the common Large White butterfly, whose black-speckled grey and yellow caterpillars feed in colonies on our cabbages and nasturtiums. When full grown, each of these casts its final skin to become a grey-white chrysalis perhaps 3 cm. in length, and lashed by a silk thread round its waist to a wall or fence near the area where the caterpillar fed. These can easily be found with a little searching but among them will be many clumps of twenty or thirty much smaller yellow silken cocoons each a few millimetres long, and each clump still attached to the empty shrunken skin of the unfortunate caterpillar from which it came. These in due course will hatch into slim dark flies known as braconids. For the butterfly and this braconid, or for any similar pair of insects, there will be in theory an equilibrium situation in which the numbers could stay the same from year to year. Then each pair of butterflies will on the average have one pair of descendants in the next generation.

---

* The distinction between a parasite and a predator is a rather narrow one. In general, if you are killed and eaten by something of comparable size to yourself you are suffering predation, while if you are eaten – and especially if only part of you is eaten – by something much smaller than yourself, you are suffering parasitism.

Since each female butterfly lays some hundreds of eggs, this means that almost all of them must fall victims to the parasitic flies. On the other hand, these flies also must leave one pair of descendants per mother next year in order that equilibrium should be maintained. Since the female parasites too lay a large number of eggs, this means that a majority of these females must die before they find a suitable healthy butterfly caterpillar at all. There must at each stage be a lot more parasites than hosts and it is highly unlikely that so exact a balance could be maintained for long periods. If chance, or some change in the environment such as sudden use of a chemical spray, should reduce the number of butterfly caterpillars available to be parasitized, the proportion of these found by parasites will be increased but both will be very much reduced the following year. Each of the few caterpillars of next year's crop, however, will have far fewer braconid females hunting for it and will have a much bigger chance of survival. On the other hand the few braconid females will each have to search far longer to find a caterpillar and since even in good times most of them fail, an even bigger proportion of them than usual will fail. Hence their numbers next year will be smaller still, while the number of butterflies will be greater, though perhaps still not up to the equilibrium figure. In this second year, there will be a fair supply of caterpillars but very few parasites to take advantage of it. Hence the next year again, the third year from the chemical spray, there will be a large crop of butterflies and the caterpillars will reach plague proportions.

In this year the few surviving parasites will do very well indeed, and producing as they do fifty or so individuals for each caterpillar successfully parasitized, will, at latest in one further year, have cut the butterflies down to well below equilibrium. Such an oscillation may continue indefinitely, and indeed must be regarded as more normal than a continuous steady state. (If no other factors intervened, the oscillation would build up until one or both species became extinct. But the object of this detailed study has been to show why oscillations in numbers should occur at all – the way in which the oscillations themselves are prevented from getting too large is a more complex story with which I do not propose to deal.)

An interesting corollary to this kind of relationship is worth

The Natural Control of Population

mentioning. This is that although improved efficiency in the host is advantageous to both, there is no long-term advantage to the parasite in acquiring more than a very moderate competence. Suppose we had a host-parasite system in equilibrium, so that the number of hosts just kept level when 90 per cent of their offspring were eliminated each year by parasites, the remaining 10 per cent being enough to keep the population level in face of all other hazards. Then if the parasites suddenly become much more efficient they would at first increase themselves, but would also drastically reduce the number of hosts. A new equilibrium would eventually be established with the hosts so much rarer that even the more efficient parasites could find only 90 per cent of their larvae per generation. The numbers of both would then have dropped and the parasites, although the surviving individuals would be more efficient, would collectively be worse off than before.

It is unlikely that the human race has ever been limited in numbers directly by a simple parasite – host relation, with the humans acting the part either of the parasite or of the host, although there have been limited groups over limited periods which have come close to this. As predators rather than as parasites, the Eskimos have depended on the seals, and the North American Indians once depended on the bison, but although in each case the dependence represented a major limitation of numbers it was far from complete. It was nevertheless complete enough in each case to give a dramatic illustration of the proposition set out above – that it can be a long-term disadvantage to the predator or parasite to become too efficient. With the advent of the horse and the gun to North America the Indians were able enthusiastically to destroy the vast herds of bison on which their way of life depended. They were of course helped by European hunters as far as the relatively few of these were able, but they would doubtless have succeeded in cutting off the branch on which they sat even without this assistance. Again, the use of modern weapons by the Eskimos has enabled them dangerously to reduce the animals on which they depend, to the point where reindeer have had to be introduced as a previously unneeded source of food.

As hosts again, we have rarely had our numbers limited entirely by parasites – other than those which give rise to disease, which I shall treat separately.

Control by Hunger

We can distinguish two forms of control of numbers by food supply. In one case the food is fixed, or at least not affected by the activities of the consumer. (This is quite common among some of the simpler organisms, but as a sole limit it is not very common among the more complex ones.) Shortage of suitable food in winter is an important factor in limiting the population of many small birds in northern Europe, although there is no significant shortage for the rest of the year. The rapid explosion in numbers of small rodents in the spring suggests that their winter numbers also are controlled by food supplies, but this is not necessarily the main check on their population. Such insects as fruit flies or burying beetles however are often chiefly controlled in this way, as is shown by the immediate drop in their numbers when the food supply diminishes.

In other cases the supply is itself controlled or affected in a major way by the activities of the consumer. Thus the case of the common ragwort, controlled in numbers by the activities of the Cinnabar moth, could equally be considered a situation in which the numbers of the Cinnabars are periodically limited by shortage of ragwort. Most predators are largely controlled by the numbers of the birds or animals on which they prey; which in turn are controlled by the attacks of their predators. As in the cases of the large white butterfly, or of the Canadian hares, it is unlikely that such a situation will lead to steady populations at the equilibrium level. This would be a highly unstable situation and would rapidly go over to a series of oscillations.

Control by Disease

The last physical factor capable of acting alone as a primary means of control is disease. This can be regarded as a limiting case of the host-parasite relation already discussed. As we go through the series: tapeworm, hookworm, liverfluke, trigonella, bilharzia, malaria, syphilis, tuberculosis and typhoid, we start with what everyone would call a parasite and finish with what everyone would call a disease, but the point at which the dividing line is to be drawn is none too clear. Nevertheless there is enough in common between what are usually called diseases for it to be practically convenient to consider them separately.

Almost always the organisms responsible are extremely small. This has several important corollaries. For example, they are usually unicellular organisms capable of doubling their numbers in an hour or less – impossible for complex multicellular organisms. The viruses are smaller still and may be replicated ten or a hundred times in an hour. This means that, being comparable in size to, or smaller than, the cells of which we and other animal hosts are built, disease organisms can reach very large numbers – perhaps thousands of millions – in attacking a single victim, before they produce a major effect. In such numbers there will usually be several mutations and these, if advantageous to the attacking organism, may multiply to become an important proportion in the single host. A disease may therefore change its characteristics significantly – often in the direction of greater virulence – during a few transfers from one host to another in the course of a single epidemic.

But their small size also means the disease organisms have no structural defences and are open to chemical attack in the form of the immune reaction of their victim. When this reaction is fully developed, the invaders will usually be completely wiped out, and furthermore the host will generally retain the ability to destroy this particular organism, and so be temporarily or permanently immune to its attacks.

Disease is rarely the sole controlling factor in natural conditions for populations of the larger animals, but may often lie in wait to provide an effective emergency limit when a species has escaped the control of other agencies. Thus a population of small rodents such as field mice may remain in an oscillating equilibrium with various predators for a number of years, shortage of food in the autumn slowing down their growth in numbers to the point where the predators can catch up. In occasional years when their expansion starts early or that of the predators starts late, they may get well out of hand while there is still a large food supply available in a ripening cereal crop. Then, although they may do catastrophic damage, they rarely reach the point at which they have eaten everything available and have begun to starve; more often a lethal epidemic* will start when their population reaches a critical density and their numbers will be reduced in a few days to far below their normal value for the time of year.

The mechanism for this – somewhat simplified – is as follows. When an animal is rare in the sense that individuals or members of one band will only very occasionally come in contact with members of any other band, the organisms causing any really lethal and infectious disease will rapidly disappear, dying with their victims before having the chance to infect others.

This will still be true, even if, without killing the victim, an attack of the disease is sufficient to produce a long period of immunity. From the point of view of the invading organisms, an immune host is the same as no host at all. Highly infectious, but only occasionally lethal diseases, such as measles, will spread rapidly through a small, close-knit community, leaving every individual immune, and will then die out. New babies born to the community will be susceptible, but cannot be infected until a new case makes contact with the community from outside. Only if the community is so large that new victims are born at an adequate rate, can the disease persist. For measles the minimum size of community is around 300,000. Measles, which has no alternative animal host, could not have evolved therefore until settled agriculture based on irrigation had made it possible for

---

* Pedants prefer to use the terms epizootic for animals, epiphytic for plants and presumably epimycotic for fungi, but this has several disadvantages. First, one has three or four words where one will do; and secondly, most non-specialists won't understand them. This may be just why the pedants prefer to use them, particularly as they are defended in depth from being rumbled by the ignorant. (If you look any of these words up in a dictionary, you are liable to find an entirely different meaning). Thirdly, if one is going to insist that demos was Greek for people, not animals, one should remember that it applied to the common people only and that it is impossible for an aristocracy to have anything but an epiaristic. Animals are afflicted in just the same way as we are and sometimes as a result of attack by the same organisms. The English language is simplified if we use the word epidemic, independently of its origin, to cover all victims alike.

The Natural Control of Population

permanent intercommunicating populations of this order of size to exist.

Only those diseases which can regularly (not necessarily invariably) persist for long periods in their hosts, without seriously decreasing the host's efficiency, will survive; perhaps isolated in regions of the body where they do not provoke, or are protected from, any immune response. Even the rarest of animals must come in contact with other members of their species occasionally, so that these mild or latent strains will occasionally get passed on and, if they remain mild, will survive. Occasional virulent mutants will of course occur, but will wipe themselves out. But if the animal becomes commoner, the chance increases for virulent populations to infect another victim before they die themselves. If the host is common enough, they may infect several new victims before their first host dies. We can easily put this in a quantitative form. Suppose that on the average each infected host passes on the infection to a number, G, of further hosts before it itself dies (or gets well), where G is the growth factor for the disease. The condition for an epidemic, in any population whether animal or human, is that G should be greater than 1 – that is, that the chance of transmitting the disease to at least one other person is better than evens. (It is interesting to note that exactly the same theory must be used to show whether a 'chain reaction' will proceed in a nuclear reactor or an atomic bomb, or whether a joke or a rumour will spread.) The value of the growth factor G will depend on the density of population, which controls how many infective contacts can be made by a sick individual. Contact may be indirect; thus if the disease is spread by fleas, rather than by direct transfer of germs, G may be large in a thin population with plenty of fleas but may be small or even zero in a far denser population free from fleas.

Among the mice mentioned above, the population may remain for years below the density at which $G=1$, affected by various mild disease, but free of any risk of epidemic. As soon as it rises above the level at which $G=1$ it is at risk. It is unlikely that a suitably virulent strain of disease will develop at the instant $G=1$; frequently G may have reached 2 or more before its appearance, with correspondingly catastrophic results.

Mathematically, then, the *prevention* as distinct from the *cure*, of epidemics consists simply in finding a way to keep the growth factor below 1. To ensure an epidemic in a population of pests, we have merely to ensure that G is well above 1 for some promisingly lethal complaint, and wait. Unfortunately we rarely know how to measure G before an epidemic occurs and so far as I know very little attempt has ever been made to change it.

Disease has undoubtedly been one of the important limiting factors for human populations. While we were rare animals mainly controlled by being eaten or by not finding enough to eat, conditions for lethal epidemic diseases were unfavourable; that is to say G was much less than 1. Since the development of agriculture, conditions for disease have been only too favourable, especially in the tropics.

Multiple Controls

The separate physical forms of control – predation, disease, etc. – rarely operate separately. The immensely stable coexistence for long periods of roughly constant numbers of each of a huge collection of species is usually the effect of the interaction of several different factors for each species.

Thus for example the Canadian hares, given good conditions, can multiply faster than the lynxes. In the absence of any other factor they would multiply indefinitely while the lynxes, though themselves multiplying faster and faster, would follow ever further behind. The multiplication of the hares must begin to slow down for some other reason, although once this slowing has started the lynxes, which have not slowed, soon catch up and are certainly responsible for the ensuing population crash. The preliminary slowing could be due to an epidemic breaking out once the population reached critical density. This is not, however, likely, as the numbers normally show a reduced rate of rise rather than the sudden catastrophic drop which an epidemic would produce. It is more likely that the cause is an approaching shortage of food. This might either directly affect the reproduction rate, or alternatively might force the hares to search for food in new areas in which they were exposed to the attack of some other predator such as minks (which may kill for pleasure far

The Natural Control of Population

more than they can eat) or hawks, from which they were protected in their normal environment.

It seems clear that for most animal or plant species, in a stable environment, there is one obvious major factor controlling numbers, but also a kind of natural defence in depth, so that if this factor fails another one will become operative. Man's interference with the natural balance has shown us plenty of examples of this.

For long ages the Kaibab plateau of Arizona had a rich fauna. This included some thousands of deer with an apparently unlimited food supply, themselves forming the main food of a smaller population of wolves and mountain lions. No doubt both populations showed periodic fluctuations but always within a limited range.

Over quite a short time, a few decades ago, the predators were exterminated by hunters. If the deer had understood what was going on, they would presumably have given this unqualified support. As a result, they increased rapidly to an enormously larger population. But the situation was no longer stable. They began to eat faster than their food plants could recover and in a very few years the whole area was reduced – as far as the plants which the deer could reach were concerned – to a near desert. Huge numbers of deer died of starvation and the survivors live difficult lives in small groups. As each group multiplies and finishes off the patch of vegetation on which it develops, it can leave descendants only if a few animals can find a regenerating patch of vegetation elsewhere.

Behind the limitation by predators, therefore, there lay in reserve a second limitation by starvation. An interesting point is that the second limit is by no means necessarily higher than the first. The final population of deer on the plateau is much smaller and in far worse condition than the population preyed on by wolves and mountain lions.

A still more striking example is one in which man helped a plant species to escape its most effective natural controls. We disliked the new natural limit which it found for itself; and finally set up a fresh quasi-natural limit which suited us, if not the plant, better. This was the case of a cactus, the prickly pear, of which several species were introduced into Australia from

America. They were brought in mainly as ornamental plants, beginning as long ago as 1788. They escaped from cultivation and spread rapidly. (The ancestor of every single individual of the most troublesome species, *Opuntia inermis*, was a single pot plant brought from Brazil in 1839.) In their original habitat these were controlled, like the other plants around them, by a hundred or more different kinds of insect and other parasites. No important parasites were, however, brought to Australia with the plants. The conditions of life in Queensland and New South Wales suited the prickly pears extremely well and by 1870 several species were spreading with no significant natural enemies, out of control.

By 1926 some twenty-four million hectares were thickly infested. Over half this area, the plants had reached their new natural limit – space in which to grow. With an estimated live weight of 1,200-2,000 tons per hectare, they had, like the Siberian conifers, choked out all competing herbage. There seemed to be a serious prospect that a quite novel limitation to human numbers had developed. This distasteful outcome was avoided by the introduction of controlling agents from the original home of the prickly pears. Of these the ultimate major success was a small moth from the Argentine, *Cactoblastis cactorum*. Like all adult moths or butterflies, these do no harm themselves to the plant, but their eggs hatch into larvae which burrow into the thick fleshy 'leaves' of the cactus and eat them out from inside. Between 1926 and the end of 1927 more than nine million eggs were distributed; then more between 1928 and 1930. By 1933 the *Cactoblastis* larvae had eaten some fifteen thousand million tons of healthy undamaged plants; and by now (1972) the prickly pear is no longer of economic importance. It still exists, carrying a moderate population of *Cactoblastis* in a gently oscillating equilibrium. Without further human interaction it is under a biological control which is of an entirely natural type.

This episode illustrates many features of the control of populations. It shows just how a population from which the original limits are removed can expand exponentially till it approaches a new limit. The plants taken from their stable, parasite-controlled native lands to a favourable new habitat, expanded to a new limit at which they settled down again to a new stability.

Cactoblastis behaved in a similar way. It came from an area in which it was limited by the wide dispersion of its food plants and by predators and parasites of its own. It entered an area entirely free of enemies, and with vast and concentrated supplies of food. It too expanded exponentially to a peak which must have been a thousand to a million times greater than could ever have occurred if both *Cactoblastis* and cactus had been present together from the first. It then crashed but in spite of the catastrophic fall from heights unprecedented in nature, neither plant nor insect crashed to extinction. Both fell well below the equilibrium value in 1931-2 and there was a big regrowth of prickly pear, but by 1934 the insect had recovered and brought this regrowth under control. Since that one big swing, the oscillations have been small and random as in natural communities.

This example is particularly important in that we know, or at least we can be almost sure that we know, all of the important factors. In natural equilibriums, like that of the lynxes and hares in Canada, there is always a chance that there are major or even vital factors which we have not suspected; that for example one or both animals might be controlled by some disease organism. But the whole of the prickly-pear episode has been artificially produced in an alien area, whose indigenous creatures had no apparent effect on either of the main protagonists in the drama. The fact that with this simple pattern we get the same result as in the complex natural ones, gives us confidence that our understanding of the latter is basically sound. And, finally, although the ways in which our own population has been controlled in earlier times will be left to the next chapter, it is worth summarizing the effects on the people concerned.

In the first quarter of this century, the human population of that area of Australia was also expanding exponentially, having also moved into a favourable new environment without any effective controls. We then accidentally introduced an entirely novel control which could have set an equilibrium limit below the then existing population level. If our understanding of the situation had been no better than that of the insect or the plant, there would be fewer of us in the relevant area of Queensland now than in 1925. But we didn't like the limit and, unprecedented as it was, learned to understand it and get rid of it.

Control by Behaviour

As we have seen, physical controls require strong 'negative feedback', which may involve major oscillations. On every downswing of these, when the population is well below its norm, there is a far larger chance than usual of accidental extinction. Major oscillations are therefore better avoided. Broadly speaking, behavioural controls enable a species to keep some of its reproductive capacity in reserve in good times so that, by not multiplying as fast as it physically could, it avoids either the destructive increase of predators and parasites, or the depletion of food stocks. In bad times on the other hand, the reserves can be called on to maintain the population, or to enable it to recover more rapidly without ever falling too far. Big improvements in food-finding or hunting skill can then be safely evolved, with corresponding resilience in times of stress, without the disastrous reduction both in the sources of food and in their own numbers that we saw could occur in super-efficient parasites of insects, or in pathogenic micro-organisms controlled by physical factors alone.

The specific forms of behaviour leading to this maintenance of a reproductive reserve are very various. So far as I know, surgical termination of pregnancy is used by no creature other than man, but a surprising number of the ways which we now use, or have used in the past, to limit ourselves, have been employed by some animal species or other.

By far the most important of these is the establishment, usually by individuals or by mated pairs, of well-defined territories from which other members of the same species are excluded. The territories are chosen to provide food and shelter enough to maintain the individual and to raise a family. This pattern of life is general among the vertebrates from fishes upwards, wherever the species is not nomadic. It is common among the more advanced invertebrates.

Birds have been studied in more detail than mammals because they are easier to watch and have attracted a lot more observers. Perhaps the best known case is that of the red grouse.* This bird

---

* V. C. Wynne-Edwards. *Scientific American* Offprint No. 192.

The Natural Control of Population

lives on heather covered moors, feeding on and protected by the heather itself. During August and September the cocks endeavour to establish themselves as owners of territories or defined areas of the heather moor. Aggressive displays generally take the place of actual fighting. After a short time, as the boundaries of domains become defined, owners gain confidence and vigour, as though aware of having nine tenths of the law on their side, while intruders start without any such confidence and are usually quickly ejected. The area which each cock can win must depend on the length of perimeter he can defend, and this in turn must depend on his relative confidence. There will have been a strong selection pressure for generation after generation to ensure that the corresponding area can provide, with a comfortable margin, adequate food for the rearing of a family.

For the first two or three months the owners insist on their property rights only for an hour or so after dawn each morning, after which the moor becomes freely available again for the whole population to feed for the rest of the day. As winter comes on, however, the owners become more possessive, and more and more grouse are driven off the moor altogether. Some of these will be hens, but from February onwards the remaining hens will form individual pairs with the territory-owners, and all those which fail to do so, with the surviving landless cocks, will be finally driven from the moor. Since the area of the moor is constant, the number of territories and pairs of grouse will be much the same each year, so that if a normal number of chicks have grown to grousehood in the previous summer, there will be many birds for which no territories are available. The prospects for these are poor; they will be short of food, and without the protection of the heather from foxes or other predators. (Even though they may be slow to fly, the wedge-shaped grouse can run along the ground and dodge through the heather at a speed that a fox who has to jump over or push it aside can hardly match.) The dispossessed birds then, while they survive, form a reserve which can be useful to the landowning class in two ways. They are inhibited from breeding themselves, but if a casualty should occur among the landowners, they will at once provide a replacement. Furthermore, being easy meat, they reduce the pressure of predators on the better protected inhabitants of the moor. In spite of considerable losses during the winter, therefore, the breeding season starts with almost every territory filled and with much the same number of breeding pairs as the previous year.

By means of this behaviour pattern, the grouse can maintain a steady population close to the maximum that the moor can permanently carry. They run no risk of destroying their food supply as did the non-territorial deer of Arizona, even though their reproduction rate is far higher than the deer's, and is capable of bringing them back to equilibrium in a year or two after the most unusual and serious catastrophes.

A somewhat different territorial system operates among small song birds such as the robin.* Each cock robin will attempt to establish a more or less permanent territory of around one-third to one hectare of woodland. As the average expectation of life of a robin is perhaps fifteen months, there is a fairly rapid turnover. In the autumn a few hens will also establish similar territories, but the majority, probably accompanied by the excess males from the previous season, will migrate. Resident hens and returning migrants will form pairs with territorial bosses, and any territories left vacant will rapidly be taken up by fresh cocks (presumably returning migrants, since males without territories do not seem to be found as permanent residents). Each pair may rear a couple of broods in the year, but as with the grouse, the number of territory owners at the end of the season, however successful, will be much the same as at the beginning.

Unlike those of the grouse, the territories are firmly maintained throughout the year. More peculiarly, each territory is defended, with violence if necessary, only against a singing and threatening outsider. Strange robins are allowed to come in and feed so long as, like human trespassers who do not wish to be prosecuted, they leave quickly and quietly when requested to go. This is still true in late winter, when food is often short enough to cause some birds to starve, which has led Dr Lack to believe that the main value of territories to robins is their aid to pair-formation. He considers that the regularity with which the territories are filled is an effect rather than a cause of constancy of population, this being controlled by other factors yet to be dis-

---

* See *The Life of the Robin* by David Lack (Witherby).

covered. His view is reinforced by the fact that territories are very irregular in size and much larger than needed to produce the food required to rear a family of robins.

This last argument is not perhaps very strong since we do not know the factors which determine a robin's territory. Presumably these are based on critical features in the environment in which robins lived during the evolution of their behaviour. This may have been very different from the man-made English countryside in which Dr Lack made his observations.

The permissiveness in respect of feeding is a more serious argument, if it is to be believed that the territorial system has evolved to ensure a winter supply of food. There is not, however, necessarily an inconsistency. For the largely vegetarian grouse, the food supply is closely proportional to the area of moor, and indeed, Wynne-Edwards has recorded that the average size of territory goes down when the heather is growing more richly. For a mainly carnivorous bird such as the robin on the other hand, the food supply is much less directly connected with area of land, and the feeding areas which will be good in February may not be easily distinguishable in August. Even if the *average* territory is large enough, some territories may have far more food than necessary at the critical time of year, and some may have little or none. The simple territorial pattern therefore might save only a small fraction of the robins, each with much more food than it required, while the rest starved. A rigid demarcation in summer keeps the *average* density of robins per square kilometre to a suitable value, and this, followed by permissiveness at the critical time, gives a beautiful solution to a difficult problem. Certainly the advantage of permissiveness is to the group rather than to the individual, but a species does not remain uniformly interbred the whole time, and birds with large territories in specialized kinds of country will often form quite small semi-isolated populations. Hence, if a selfish and successful robin passed on his selfishness successfully, his selfish descendants would form the greater part of their local group. This would suffer big oscillations in number, and there would be a very large chance of the whole group being exterminated in a hard winter if all of the very few selfish and well-fed survivors happened to be eaten. They would then be replaced by more co-operative types from elsewhere which, being much more numerous, would be far less likely all to die in the same way.

Whatever the detailed mechanism, the important point for this chapter is that territorial behaviour is an important part of the robin's way of life, and helps to maintain steady numbers in face of very unsteady hazards.

Seabirds are naturally unable to mark out private fishing areas in the open sea, but nevertheless may establish a different type of territorial system, which serves the same function of preventing the population from overfishing the food supply, with a consequent periodic crash in numbers. This is done by limiting the area available for nesting rather than for fishing. There is for example a large colony of gannets in Cape St Mary, Newfoundland,* where, among several apparently similar rocky slopes, one only is used for nests. Within its boundaries, the entire area is covered by nesting gannets spread out no further than the reach of their beaks. In this case, pair-bonding can hardly be assisted, but does not appear to be in the least inhibited, by the presence of several thousand others. The limits of the area are closely defined, so that at the end of each season there will be a large number of newly adult birds for which there is no room in the 'town'. There is room within the colony at the beginning of the next season only for those required to fill spaces left by others who have died, or, occasionally, have been driven out. As a result there is a surplus of birds, which may be comparable in number to the total of nesting pairs. These form satellite colonies on the surrounding rocky slopes, but having no licence to do so from the local authority, they neither pair nor nest. As with the red grouse, they form a reserve pool of birds which will not multiply to produce an increasing drain on food supplies, but which can be called on at need to fill gaps in the stable breeding population.

Human numbers have only rarely been limited by the establishment of exclusive breeding territories. The best example known to me is that of rural Ireland. Here it has for long been normal for the eldest son to remain unmarried until he inherits his father's plot of land. Younger sons and the surplus young women must emigrate to get married at all.

* V. C. Wynne-Edwards. *Scientific American* Offprint No. 192.

The Natural Control of Population

In general, the smaller mammals do not maintain individual territories in the way that birds do. They may jealously keep intruders away from their burrows but they cannot escape from predators by flying, and so cannot afford the continuous and well-advertised patrolling which is needed to maintain control of an area large enough to provide food for a family. Hence the simple external physical controls, such as predation or epidemic disease which I have already discussed, and which give rise to periodic large oscillations, are much commoner among mammals than in birds which can control themselves. Nevertheless some animals have established behavioural systems which have similar effects in rejecting the excess when numbers threaten the food supply of all.

The black and yellow Norwegian lemmings give us the best known example. When the density of population is small, these behave much like other rodents; each animal lives its life within an extremely restricted area without any tendency to wander abroad. But when numbers rise above some critical density, controlled presumably either by availability of food or by frequency of contact between individuals, or by both, their behaviour changes completely, long before the food supply is actually exhausted. The huge majority abandon their homes and join in a mass emigration. Lemmings from any one area all go roughly the same way, but the directions of travel from different regions vary widely. The emigration continues across roads and rivers and is undeterred by predators or by wholesale slaughter. It is presumably possible for some to find satisfactory habitats but the vast majority die without issue, and from most of the area invaded, they will by next year have vanished without trace. The advantage accrues solely to the tiny minority of lemmings which did not emigrate at all but which have been saved from certain starvation by the exodus of the others. It is quite clear that the selection pressures leading to this result must have acted on groups; not individuals. Essentially all the individuals which have a strong instinct to emigrate will die, and those in whom it is weaker will survive. Nevertheless, any group which by selection of individuals builds up a majority without the instinct to emigrate will in due course starve itself out and become extinct. Only those groups in which most animals carry an individually dangerous instinct will survive at all.

Some of the largest and best-armed carnivores such as tigers or bears maintain individual or family territories (particularly important for the rarer ones in which big oscillations of population could take them dangerously close to extinction) but more of the herbivores and medium-sized carnivores live gregariously and maintain group territories. Some kinds of deer, wild dogs or wolves, monkeys and baboons are examples. Collectively their defensive capacity may be enough to deter a large carnivore or, as with monkeys, their agility in their natural habitat can protect them if warned in time, and a number together can afford sentinels and patrols over an area large enough in resources to support the group. Members of each group recognize individually all the other members and accept them, but drive out of their territory, with whatever level of violence is required, any member of all other groups.

An important and interesting point is that the amount of violence required is usually nil and almost never serious. Even such well-armed and efficient predators as wolves do not have the bloody battles that the uninitiated might expect. Normally wolves will allow themselves to be chased off the territory of others as soon as the owners appear, even when these are fewer, although as soon as they are back within their own territory they will stop and drive the others away in turn.

Even if two wolves are competing for a mate or for urgently needed food, they rarely injure each other seriously. A period of posturing, growling and snapping in the air will often enable them to tell which is the stronger; the weaker will then abandon the field without a fight at all. If they seem evenly matched and a fight does start, their bites mainly land on each others' jaws with much clashing of teeth but little injury. But the most striking phenomenon, graphically described by Konrad Lorenz in *King Solomon's Ring*, occurs when one feels itself weakening, or getting the worst of the fight. Suddenly it surrenders; turning away its head with its powerful jaws, and exposing its vulnerable throat to the victor. The victor gives every sign of being about to kill the other, which he could easily do with a single bite, but he appears to 'freeze' with his jaws barely a tooth-length from the other's jugular vein. He is completely inhibited from attacking another wolf in the 'surrendered' position and after some minutes of rigidity the vanquished one will be able to run away unharmed – but of course without the mate or the meat or the territory that the quarrel was about.

This inhibition against killing their own species, which enables fights to be resolved without death or even serious injury, is so common among the predators as to be regarded as normal, but it does not exist among species less well armed, which can inflict serious injury only slowly, so that a beaten individual has plenty of time to break off the fight and escape. If an alien dove is introduced into a caged group from which it cannot escape, it will be slowly and mercilessly pecked to death. In most predators the restraint is absolute, but as we shall see in the next chapter, when a species has few enemies and no effective competition such inhibitions may no longer be to its advantage.

The advantage does not lie only in the effective sharing out of scarce resources, without risk of death or injury to the landowners. Among practically all gregarious animals, the young adults, or at least the young males, indulge in a round of fights which establish an order of precedence. This order of precedence was first noticed among hens by Schjelderup-Ebbe and termed the 'peck-order'.* When this is fully developed, each hen of a flock has an established position in which she can peck with impunity any hen below her in the hierarchy, but must accept without retaliation pecks from those above her. It means that whenever food is limited, hens high in the peck-order can take the first turn, or the richest area, the lower-class sisters having to wait and hope that some will be left. The fights which led to this position are therefore of some importance to the combatants, and the inhibitions of the carnivores enable such groups as wild dogs or wolves to establish a similar order without a holocaust. But this is not simply a humane agreement: if all in a group shared equally when food was short, all would suffer from malnutrition, and in the limit all would starve. With the help of the 'peck-order', when food gets short, those at the top continue to get all the food they need and those at the bottom die. At the end of the shortage there is a smaller, but healthy and vigorous

---

* Murchison's *Handbook of Social Psychology*, chapter 20, Clark University Press, Worcester, Mass.

population, instead of no population at all. The inhibitions of the stronger members of a wolf pack do not necessarily save the lives of the weaker members in the long run, but they do lead to an organized and systematic unfairness, which gives the best result for the species as a whole with the minimum of fuss.

The same behaviour as among permanently gregarious species, is seen among the many kinds of birds which search for food in flocks in winter when food is short, but spread out individually in the summer when it is plentiful. With an established peck order, each high ranking individual then gets not only the food it finds itself, but may demand and get attractive items found by lower ranking individuals nearby. The advantage to these latter is nil. The greater safety from predators in the middle of a flock may partially or even wholly compensate for these losses most of the time, but in bad winters when many starve – all of them low-ranking individuals – these would seem to have a better likelihood of survival if they searched on their own and took a chance on the predators. The advantage to the high-ranking birds is obviously high, and since *all* of the survivors have gained from the flocking and the peck-order, and since none of the losers have survived, the flocking instinct is positively selected for, and would still be selected for, even if it had no advantages in respect of predators at all.

The final behavioural system which can limit a population and which I want to discuss is the much-quoted – perhaps over-quoted – way of life of overcrowded rats. The basic experiments to be described were done by Dr John B. Calhoun.* His first investigation was based on the behaviour of a colony of wild Norway rats in an enclosure of about one-tenth of a hectare. These were given unlimited food and protected from predators. After twenty-seven months at the initial rate of reproduction, some 5,000 adults might have been expected. In fact there were 150, and at this figure the number remained. The reason appeared to be a very high infant mortality, so Dr Calhoun set up a series of similar experiments in more controlled conditions, using a domesticated albino strain of the same species. Watching these made it possible not only to find out how the high infantile mortality arose, but

* J. B. Calhoun. *Scientific American* 206 (2), No. 139.

The Natural Control of Population

to observe several kinds of abnormal behaviour which developed at the same time.

The infant mortality turned out to be due mainly to derangements of the normal behaviour of the mothers. These, under the stress of constant contact with other rats, especially the constant harassment by males, made less and less satisfactory nests – eventually none at all. As a result their babies suffered from cold. Secondly, in moving their young from one place to another as rats often do, they would drop some on the way and put the rest in different places so that more than half might get lost and die – when they would usually be eaten by the adults. Some of the male rats became cannibals. In some experiments the total infant mortality rose to 96 per cent in the most crowded pens.

The derangement of the males was less directly lethal but was largely responsible for the disturbance of the females. Constant defeats led many of the lower ranking males to 'drop out'; they got up early to feed free of interference, and then remained totally inactive, not reacting even to females in heat. Some became homosexual; rare among rats at a normal density. Some became hyperactive, completely abandoning the normal courtship behaviour of the male rat in ordinary conditions, constantly chasing females even when these were not in heat – and even following them into their burrows to mate with them, which is again entirely unnatural. These forms of behaviour reduced the rate of production of viable young until it only just balanced the adult death rate.

Whether or not this can be regarded as a 'natural' limit is of course open to doubt. Such conditions could occur in nature only very rarely. Nevertheless, it is so often quoted as an indication of what can be expected of heavily overcrowded human beings, that I have felt it worthwhile to include it. It would be wrong to say that there are no lessons for us at all in this experiment. But there is no doubt that its relevance to our own case has often been grossly exaggerated; we are not rats and complete correspondence cannot reasonably be expected. This is of course true also of all of the other forms of limitation of animal populations discussed in this chapter.

The thesis of this book is that we have learnt to defeat all of the natural limitations on numbers which affect our co-lodgers on the planet, and that we have therefore landed ourselves with the responsibility for our own fate. The object of this chapter has been to show the kind of problems which we have had to solve in the past, and in the next chapter I shall discuss the ways in which we have solved them.

Three

The Defeat of Our Natural Limitations

Evolution of Homo Sapiens

The early stages are far from certain. I shall describe what is essentially a theory consistent with the few known facts, rather than an established series of events. The timing in particular is entirely speculative, and I am writing at a dangerous time when I might quite soon be proved wrong. Forty years ago I could have been sure that I would not survive to see my guesses refuted, and twenty years hence the answers may be reliably known—at least in outline.

Ten to twenty million years ago, during the Miocene epoch, our ancestors lived in southern Africa, and were much like medium-sized anthropoid apes. A fossil ape known as *Proconsul* which was found by Leakey in Kenya, and which had a skull capacity differing little from those of the modern chimpanzee or gorilla, was either our direct ancestor or a close collateral. There is then a gap in the records lasting the better part of ten million years. Robert Ardrey, in his book *African Genesis*, has made a very plausible case for our ancestors, at the time the fossil record starts again, having been a more advanced carnivorous ape known as *Australopithecus*. This flourished from perhaps five to less than one million years ago. Remains have been found in some numbers at Taungs and Sterkfontein in the last few decades.

This creature was small; perhaps 120 cm. (4 ft) high, and had lost the big canine teeth of its ancestors, but walked upright and could run well. In spite of the loss of any teeth which could be used as effective weapons, the remains are associated with the bones of considerable numbers of other animals, and make it clear that *Australopithecus* was capable of killing large antelopes and other animals of comparable size. This could hardly have been done with bare hands. Among the remains, there is a large excess of bones from the front legs of medium-sized antelopes, each carrying a knuckle which made it a very effective club. These, together with the many smashed-in skulls of their victims, make it seem extremely likely that the australopithecines armed themselves with the leg bones when they hunted. Not only would this have been consistent with their apparent way of life over a long period, but it would help to explain the disappearance of the long canine teeth which are the main offensive weapons of the other big apes. It is extremely rare that evolving animal species, any more than modern nations, give up important weapons until they have something considerably more effective still. Whether for killing deer, for driving off hyenas or for fighting each other, a stout bone with a good large knuckle at the far end would be more effective than the most useful set of canines. It would still be of very little use for an individual facing a lion or some other big cat. But even if he had had the canines of a leopard, it would not have paid *Australopithecus* to bite a lion.

By two million years ago, *Australopithecus*, or his successor *Homo erectus*, was making chipped flint tools – and went on doing so with hardly any change in technique for nearly a million years.

During the five or ten million year period between *Proconsul* and the earliest known remains of *Australopithecus*, the average population grew only very slowly. Since it was quite sparse, it is unlikely that it was controlled to any great extent by disease or parasites. The most probable basis of this stability is limitation by a combination of food shortage and predators. The very slow rate of reproduction and growth of anthropoid apes, which was much slower than that of the bigger cats which preyed on them, makes it unlikely that the population had the wild oscillations that we saw among the Hudson Bay hares. Nevertheless, we can see how the necessary negative feedback could have kept going a slow oscillation in numbers. When the apes were few, the roots and fruits and animals on which they themselves fed would have become widely abundant, so that the apes had a good choice of

The Defeat of Our Natural Limitations

habitat, and did not have to travel far to feed. This meant that they could choose their breeding places in places difficult for large animals to reach, and could forage at times when the predators normally slept.

As a result of this comfortable state, the big cats would have had to feed on something else, and the apes would have multiplied. Since most predators find it easier to concentrate on particular kinds of prey which are common, and in killing which they can get particularly expert, they might well not have bothered even with the occasional ape which they could have caught. As the apes went on multiplying, they would have had to spread into less satisfactory places, and would have had to forage for longer periods in more dangerous areas. Eventually they would have spread enough to become vulnerable, and to become again an attractive prey for the predators. These would then have redeveloped the taste for ape meat, redeveloped the art of obtaining it, and the ape population would have fallen again.

As in other such predator-prey balances, this situation could have remained stable indefinitely, and indeed must have done so, until some important event occurred to disturb the balance.

This need not have been an external event, but could have been the first and most vital of the occasions in which our ancestors discovered how to overcome a population control which was not to their taste. It would have required the combination of only two new tactics, neither requiring more brain power or physical strength than *Australopithecus* quite certainly possessed.

The first of these was the co-operation of considerable groups of adult males in hunting, or in defence of the troop. This may have been established for a long time before the second tactic appeared. The hunting of antelopes and other fleet herbivores could have been done better by a co-operating group than by a single hunter, and many far less intelligent animals than the australopithecines use this technique. Such a group, armed with leg bones used as clubs, might also be able to defend themselves against leopards, as do troops of modern baboons armed only with teeth, although a single male baboon is no match for a leopard. By itself, this would still be of little use in defence against a lion, since a bone club could hardly do serious damage, and a practised lion could kill a very considerable number of apes if it were attacked by the companions of one which it had caught.

The Defeat of the Predators

The second tactic required was the use of new weapons – not necessarily bows and arrows, or even throwing-spears. Long stout pointed sticks, or even big stones used as missiles, would have been enough. An apeman could not kill a lion by throwing stones at it, any more than by hitting it with the leg bone of an antelope. But he could throw things without coming within reach of the lion's lethal leap. Hence if a lion pounced from ambush on one of a group so armed, and the others threw their stones before running away in different directions, he could hardly expect to catch more than one even if he abandoned his prey to try – which a lion would be unlikely to do.

Of course the lion will still have succeeded in killing his australopithecine without risk of being killed himself, but at a cost, at best, of a nasty set of bruises; at worst, of a broken tooth, a blinded eye, or if he were standing on rock, a smashed paw, which would interfere with his hunting for weeks or even for the rest of his life. Clearly the lion would look in future for some other quarry.

Co-operation of this kind among apemen would not only remove negative feedback, it would actually substitute positive feedback, since the bigger were the groups of apemen, the more effectively would the predators be deterred. Of course, predation will not have been absolutely eliminated; for a long time, and indeed to the present day, there must have been occasional man-eaters, and an occasional child lost to a lion or leopard. But from this time on the balance will have been destroyed, and effective control of our population by predators ended. This was our first and most vital step in the control of our own destiny.

As soon as this situation was established, our numbers would have increased until they came up against a new limit. This must almost certainly have been shortage of food. Man will have

The Defeat of Our Natural Limitations 41

avoided the fate of the Arizona deer by being able to live on a more varied diet, by being less destructive in feeding habits, and by being in general tougher. Adult humans are among the toughest creatures this planet has produced – they can survive appalling hardship and privation – but human young are much less hardy. This will have meant that in bad times the adults will have survived and the young died, with exactly the same advantages to the species as a whole as those of the 'peck-order' system.

We will though have been limited only superficially by shortage of food, but at a much deeper level by competition with each other. We were of course competing for our food with other creatures; with a variety of birds and small mammals for seeds and fruit; with leopards for antelopes; with wild pigs for edible roots; with crows and small predators for birds' eggs and for the insects and other small creatures in our diet and so on. But unless we had an ecological niche of our own; that is to say, unless we were better at exploiting our particular pattern of food and other resources than any other species; we should not have survived at all. The pattern was probably not a simple one: versatility rather than any single expertise, must have been our speciality. In a sense we may have lived entirely on the leavings of other specialist species but, since we could live on a bigger variety of such leavings than could anything else, we were not in serious danger from competition by anything else. We did however need to collect our leavings over a considerable area, and we were in competition with each other.

Learning to Kill Each Other

In a broad sense, in every species the individuals are in competition with each other; that is what natural selection is about. In the territorial species, the competition has been beautifully organized, so as to kill off the minimum numbers in the most painless possible way – for the survivors. We do not know which were the most important factors which made our competition into a more direct and lethal affair than it is for most species. It may be that our territorial pattern had first developed to be like a communal version of that of the red grouse, but that, being uncommon animals, we only rarely had common boundaries across which to fight. Then the drastic reduction of the danger from predators, which resulted from better weapons, led to the establishment of extensive common boundaries more quickly than adaptation of instinctive behaviour could occur. Alternatively, it may be that in our boundary fighting we always had the traditional ruthlessness of the dove, and never developed the merciful inhibitions of the wolf, simply because we were so badly equipped physically for killing each other. A defeated troop could be beaten and bitten into submission and flight without any great number being killed, however murderous the intentions of the victors. When the new weapons appeared which could deter a carnivore, they turned a border dispute into a bloody massacre.

Finally, it is possible that initially we had exactly the same inhibitions against killing each other that are characteristic of other dangerous animals. When our numbers began to increase, these inhibitions, humanly desirable as they are from our present viewpoint, became a liability to the species rather than an asset. Australopithecine territories were not small and easily defined like those of a grouse or a robin. They must have extended over several miles from the clan centre even for a troop of only a hundred or so individuals. Some areas of territory would have been left unvisited for considerable periods; thus some specific regions might be occupied only when particular fruits were ripe, or particular species of migrating antelopes passed through them. In good years when food was plentiful nearer home, the more distant areas might not be visited at all. We have no physical method of marking our territories, unlike dogs, who use urine, or tom-cats, who secrete an odour from special glands. Consequently borders would be poorly defined, and a border region could be confidently regarded by more than one group as its own territory. Then a fight which led to the expulsion but not the death of a weaker group would not be effective. No group could be big enough to guard all of its borders at the same time, and animals much less intelligent than the australopithecines could learn to raid only the unguarded parts of disputed territory for food in bad seasons. Consequently a powerful group which had established wide enough boundaries to keep itself adequately

The Defeat of Our Natural Limitations   43

supplied even in bad years, could still find itself seriously and increasingly short of food at the end of a long dry season.

The first group to lose their inhibitions, and use their new and powerful weapons to kill their opponents in a demarcation dispute, even when these had acknowledged defeat, would gain an enormous advantage. That 'all they that take the sword shall perish by the sword' is true only if the other fellow takes a sword as well. In a mixture of groups, some of which still retained in full force the inhibition against killing others of their species, and some of which did not; and of which all were expanding in numbers without other important limitation, the inhibited characters would rapidly vanish.

It would of course have been important that the inhibition should persist inside each group. A group operating under the new and more serious external threat could not afford to weaken itself by too lethal a brand of internal fighting. The British Tradition that fighting with fists is manly, with knives wicked; and that in external fighting practically anything goes; has doubtless been with us in some form or another since the time of our Pliocene ancestors.

We do not know much about the inheritance of instincts and of patterns of behaviour, but we do know that both of these can be modified quite quickly by selective breeding. During the relatively short period of domestication, the natural aggressiveness of bulls and of many breeds of domestic cocks has been much reduced, while that of fighting cocks has been increased. The selection among our ancestors in favour of willingness to kill outsiders must have been strong over a considerable period, and for hundreds of thousands if not millions of years, the murderous fighting between competing groups must have represented the primary control of our numbers.

The effects were not only on our numbers. Much as it goes against the grain for a humanist influenced by Quaker views, I find it difficult to avoid the belief that it was just this murderous inter-group fighting that changed us from *Australopithecus* – or something very like him – into *Homo erectus* and finally into fully human beings.

I can imagine no other source of the enormous selective pressure needed to cause the explosive rate of growth of human brain capacity in the past million years, unprecedented as it has been for any other species.*

After the development of weapons to the point of deterrence of carnivores, our intelligence was already entirely adequate to cope with the few non-human dangers of our environment. Inside each group, the advantage of increased intelligence would have been less than the advantage of increased size, which would give a much larger advantage in the competition for mates, or for status which would give extra food for oneself and one's family. This is still true for fights between individuals today. Certainly some champion boxers, and possibly even some champion wrestlers, have been intelligent men, but intelligence has not been the main factor leading to their success. Before the heavyweight championship fight of March 1971 between Mohammed Ali and Joe Frazier, over a dozen vital statistics of the combatants were published right down (or up) to the circumference of the open mouth,† but intellectual prowess was not included.

At the time when fighting between troops began to be important, it is likely that the groups concerned were organized much as other primate troops such as baboons are now – that is to say, with a well-defined leadership by one or a few strong and experienced males, and with a rough hierarchy or 'peck-order' below them, which defined the order of access to communal supplies of food. This hierarchy would be established for each generation in turn, by a succession of serious but not murderous fights between the adolescent males. When intertribal fighting for food became the limiting factor in controlling numbers, it became at the same time the chief factor in natural selection. Hence the choice of the best possible leader or leaders became likewise of great selective importance. Since experience in fighting is worth a lot of untrained intelligence, the value of selection of someone who had succeeded in a lot of serious fights increased. The existing pugnacity of young expendable primate males would have been reinforced, and if the exploratory instinct of the young led them into someone else's territory, experience of actual killing could be gained at little loss to their own tribe.

---

* Knowing as we do, nothing of the present or recent rate of growth of the comparably-sized dolphin brain.

† Six inches for Frazier, eleven inches for Ali.

The Defeat of Our Natural Limitations

There has been a slow but steady increase in size during our development which suggests very strongly that there has also been selective value in being good at hand-to-hand combat. This gradual increase of size is extremely common among animals, and may often have led to the extinction of species, as the optimum size for their ecological niche was left behind under pressure of the selection for breeding. Women, free of direct selection for size, are smaller than men, and are presumably closer to what would be the optimum size in the absence of inside group fighting.

If we could avoid hand to hand combat, there are many ways in which it would be an advantage to be smaller. In particular, our strength to weight ratio would be improved; a man of half the present height would weigh eight times less, but each of his muscles, having four times smaller cross-section area, would be only four times weaker. It is an interesting question, whether the well-known greater longevity of women, once they are past the hazards of childbirth, is due in whole or in part simply to the fact that they are smaller, with consequent reduction of strain on heart and lungs. While the Registrar General's returns are given sorted by sex but not by size, we shall probably continue not to know the answer to this.

The Forced Development of Intelligence

Our increase in size since *Australopithecus*, however, has been little if any faster than the increase in size of other species. Our increase in brain capacity and intelligence has been enormously faster. It seems to me inescapable, that this was due to natural selection for effectiveness in lethal tribal fighting.

As we have seen, intelligence is not a determining factor once hand-to-hand combat has begun. Practice, speed of reaction and physical strength are all far more important. But in fighting between organized groups, the intelligence of the leader, or of anyone with influence on group decisions, can be absolutely vital. Even if intelligence has no correlation at all with the strength and speed needed for hand-to-hand fighting, a ruthless group with an extra bright leader will outmanoeuvre and eventually destroy an appreciably larger and equally ruthless but uniformly stupid group. And even if inside the group the extra bright one leaves no more children than the rest, the group must have had at least some genes conducing to brightness among them to produce him. So the group with these will have survived, and the group without will not. For this reason, selection for intelligence could be expected to have been far faster than would selection for other qualities. A numerical example to illustrate this quantitatively is given in Appendix II.

In stressing the military factor in developing our brain power, I do not wish to deny the existence of other factors. As groups increased in size, the children which grew up among more, and more intelligent, adults had the opportunity to learn more to their future advantage, if they had the brainpower to assimilate it. This was doubtless true for other co-operative gregarious animals such as wild dogs or wolves, which have also indeed developed a good level of intelligence – but have lacked the stimulus of being limited chiefly by each other.

The intelligence threshold at which speech became possible must have led to an enormous leap in military effectiveness – to as rapid a growth in the specific ability to learn to talk as in general intelligence itself.

A small saving grace in my somewhat unedifying picture of our development to what we are, is that selection would throughout be so specially effective only for intelligence used to the advantage of the group as a whole. Intelligence used for the advantage of the individual within the group would of course still be selected for, if it led to his or her having more surviving children, but it would be selected on the normal slow scale as for size; not on the special fast scale just explained. Hence co-operation and – up to a point – self-sacrifice would continue to be strengthened.

No special novelties were required of us in this. The ability to co-operate inside the group, and to attack those outside it, is common to practically every gregarious species. The example of the ants is instructive. Several species can defend themselves effectively against other insects, just as our ancestors learned to deter the carnivores, and are limited by the same combination of food shortage and competition as our ancestors. In these species wars between nests occur quite regularly. These wars are

The Defeat of Our Natural Limitations

no mere skirmishes. After a fight between two colonies of wood ants a layer of corpses has been seen two centimetres deep and covering several square metres.

Behind this similarity of reaction to similar limitations, there are important differences between the ants and ourselves. Each ant behaves as if rigidly programmed with a fixed set of responses to outside events. One sub-programme will lead the ant to escape from danger. Another will lead it to attack an apparent danger to the colony. Human beings have similar reactions. But in the ant the sub-programme concerned with defence of the colony invariably overrides that concerned with individual survival. Ours does not; we have to decide whether to fight for our group or whether to run away. This is not because we are less well adapted than are the ants. But if every one of our ancestors had attacked every possible menace to the group, they could not have survived and we should not be here. Equally, if every one had invariably run away we should not be here. Natural selection for the optimum balance between cowardice and courage may well have laid the foundation for the present balance of selfishness and altruism which has determined our history as a race and as individuals ever since.

The Final Step to Homo Sapiens

The limitation of our ancestors by internecine combat must have continued throughout our development of brain and brawn to full human stature, and may perhaps have motivated the emigration to Asia and to Europe during interglacial periods.

In the small, early australopithecine troops every individual, as he or she grew up, would get to know personally and intimately every other member of the group, so there would have been no need of the scent 'labels' carried by all the ants of a particular colony. Anyone not known personally was a stranger and an enemy. But where food was plentiful, tribes would grow in size. Among tribes as among individuals, 'a good big'un would always beat a good little'un', and the smaller ones would be destroyed. As the groups grew, and particularly when a very successful group formed daughter groups, as it would necessarily do when the territory controlled became too large for continuous contact, different methods would be needed. Initially, no doubt, big tribes fragmented into warring factions as soon as they grew too large, but again a cluster of tribelets fighting outsiders as a single unit would always beat the largest single unit capable of maintaining a separate existence, so that any technique for maintaining unity would be strongly selected for. Speech would have been essential for unity of operation, but would not necessarily have been sufficient to maintain social unity of distant groups. Common allegiance to an effective and venerated leader could have been effective. If this were to be carried on after his death, conviction of his continued support could have great value. This may or may not have represented the origin of religious belief. By whatever means this originated, natural selection would certainly have maintained and strengthened it. A common religion between a local cluster of tribes would have preserved cohesion and given a major competitive advantage over the separate units, and one could expect that once local religions, of whatever (non-pacifist) kind, were established, the irreligious – i.e. those with no co-ordinating theory – would soon have been wiped out. To the religious person, this is a minor aspect of a deeper truth, but to the agnostic it offers an understanding of the near-universality of religious belief, together with an explanation of the regularity with which leaders of the most theoretically pacific religions will support extreme forms of violence including war.

This shift from the control of numbers by lethal competition between small groups, to the control by similar competition between groups of groups, would have put a further premium on intelligence and on co-operative capacity, but involved no change in the basic results of the control; much the same average number of people as before could have found food enough in every thousand square kilometres. Discovery of fire, and the further development of chipped stone weapons, will have increased the size and number of species which could be preyed on for food, but the main value of these techniques must have been to increase enormously the variety of climates and habitats in which human beings could live. Global numbers could then gradually increase by an important factor, with little change in population density, and no change at all in the food-and-fighting form of limitation

The Defeat of Our Natural Limitations 49

which had persisted since we overcame the food-and-lions control.

Agriculture and the Spread of Disease

The first important step towards overcoming the food-and-fighting limitation in turn, came with the development of agriculture. This increased the food supply at a stroke – on the leisurely prehistoric scale – by perhaps a hundred times. The important part of the discovery of agriculture as ordinarily conceived, with one exception that I shall mention later, was not the discovery that seeds could be sown and that crops of edible seeds or fruits would follow. This could well have been known for a very long period. They naturally appeared at the same time of year as did their wild ancestors but we were never limited in numbers by shortage of food at the time when the main harvests of wild fruits ripened. The vital technique was that of storing the abundant food of harvest time, to be available at the time of food-minimum; at the end of the dry season in the tropics, and at the end of the cold season further north or south. The idea that grain or other seeds could be stored for long periods, could no doubt have been found only by accident. But it would have required a major advance in combined foresight and self-control to leave enough of the stores intact when food got less easy to find, so that they would still be available when it became impossible to find enough fresh food to keep the children alive. Of course, the full value of storage could not be gained until the total produced was also increased but increases of production without storage would have saved no lives and, seeds being not particularly appetizing, could have been discovered many times without being systematically maintained or serious cultivation developed. Storage of wild grain on the other hand, even without increase of production, could have saved lives from the beginning, and would have been carried on by people far less brilliant than the major innovator who recognized its value for the first time.

At first sight there is no obvious reason why this should have changed the basic form of control of population. An increase of food supply in a competitively limited population merely leads to a new equilibrium at a higher density; either with larger tribes or with more tribes per thousand square kilometres. Indeed, in many areas this was essentially what it did do; with the advantage of somewhat increased stability of supply.

In other areas a fresh factor, previously insignificant, rose suddenly to primary importance. This factor was epidemic disease.

Disease will not become epidemic unless the chance that on the average each case should infect someone else before he dies or recovers, is greater than evens. Generally speaking, for food-gathering populations the odds are against its being transmitted at all before the victim dies (i.e. the growth factor G is well below 1), except for the less virulent diseases which can persist for long periods in their victims, without killing them or even making them too ill to earn their living. In tropical or wet subtropical areas, there are far more diseases available than in a cool climate. These are mostly of the long-persisting debilitating kinds, but many of these, with plenty of people to infect, can readily evolve into lethally virulent kinds. The rich supply of sickness is partly due to the round-the-year presence of biting insects to help spread the responsible organisms, but it may also be partly due to the fact that human beings have been available to be infected for far longer in the tropics. The tropical diseases themselves have therefore had longer to evolve.

In equatorial regions there may be no particular season when food is short, so that agricultural production will have been more, and storage much less, important than in the drier colder areas. The staple foods of equatorial Africa are root crops such as yam and cassava. Roots store themselves in the ground longer and more safely than above it, and the intentional planting of these could have long preceded Middle Eastern agriculture. A multiplication of density by ten or one hundred times in the tropics, however, would have brought G well above 1 for several different diseases. Before any local population multiplied enough to press on the new enlarged food supply, some epidemic or other would thin them out. With plenty of food they would begin to multiply again, until the same or another disease again cut them back. In such areas disease would have replaced food-shortage combined with warfare as the main controller of numbers. At the same time as food became plentiful, therefore, the need to fight for

The Defeat of Our Natural Limitations

survival also vanished, but instincts do not disappear instantaneously when the reason for them has gone. Agriculture began ten thousand years or more ago, but this is a trivial time in evolutionary terms. The inhabitants of the tropics could not at once become pacific, and redevelop their inhibitions against killing.

It is unlikely that the conscious motive for fighting had always, or indeed often, been directly for food, although the need for food made it necessary. As we saw in the last chapter, the vast majority of food-limited birds and mammals struggle for real estate, rather than for food, usually indeed at a period when food is still relatively freely available, and time can therefore be spared for such activities as display and threatenings. Our ancestors were doubtless the same; without territory they would have died of starvation rather than of claustrophobia, but it was the territory and not the food for which they fought. Consequently, when food was abundant, they continued to fight for territory, as unconscious of the reason why it was no longer needful to do so, as they had been at an earlier stage of the reason why it *was* needful to do so. Nevertheless, the real need having gone, the immense pressure to develop new and ever more effective weapons had also relaxed and though murderous border skirmishes doubtless continued, the major wars were rarer than in the colder parts of the world.

As humanity expanded northwards, it came up against ever more difficult conditions; fire was indispensable for survival through the winters, and agriculture was impossible until a more advanced technology was available than had sufficed for its beginning further south. A low density of small hunting communities, controlled by the earlier limits of food-shortage and internecine strife, persisted for a long time after disease had become the major controlling factor in climatically more comfortable regions. It may not be altogether fanciful to suppose that the extra millenia of fighting for their lives contributed importantly to the greater size, aggressiveness and enthusiasm for developing weapons, which have characterized Europeans when compared to Africans or southern Asians.

By the time of the middle ages, however, food technology had improved, and accordingly population density had increased until disease could catch up with fighting, even in Europe, as the main form of population control. It operated in a slightly more complex way than in Africa, where even in villages the population density of a few years' crop of babies was sufficient for killing diseases to operate. In mediaeval Europe there was a consistent natural increase of population in the country districts, while in the towns the death rate from disease was consistently greater than the birthrate. The towns therefore represented a reliable and bottomless sink into which much of the overflow from the country could be absorbed and destroyed without significant fuss.

The Contribution of War

Territorial wars continued and maintained a share, sometimes important, of the mechanism for keeping numbers within the limits of food supply. Unfortunately they were no longer efficient, as they had been in the early history of the race, in holding the population close to the largest number that the area could steadily maintain. Armies often tended to burn and destroy, with a view to damaging the capacity of the other side to strike back rather than with the object of capturing territory on to which their own tribes could expand, and kept the total human population of the continent well below the level which technological skill would have made possible.

Military efficiency remained a vital necessity for independent survival of clans or nations. Whether instinct or social tradition was involved, although the lives of the ruled changed little with the ruler, people were almost as willing to fight for the independence of the largely unknown nation with which they identified themselves, as they had earlier been to fight for their recognized clan-mates and the possibility of living at all. Considering the small proportion of a population involved in the actual fighting of mediaeval times, this was perhaps less stupid, if no more morally admirable, than it now seems.

With no knowledge of how to improve the output from the land, and from the workshops of the craftsmen, there was no way of getting more for each but by taking it from someone else. Although some ruling classes took so much from their peasants that the production of the latter actually dropped, most of them

The Defeat of Our Natural Limitations

were fairly efficient at keeping the peasant's standard of life marginally above the minimum level at which he could do the maximum amount of work for their benefit, and yet reproduce himself. Consequently, to get more still, they had to take it from an outside group. With a less inefficient military organization than the other side, and a reasonable slice of luck, the amount of loot derived from a war could exceed by a large amount the cost – or at least, the cost to those who shared the loot – of fighting for it. Consequently, even those who had no desire to attack anyone else, and no confidence of winning if they did, could not even keep what they had, if they were not prepared to defend it against someone else more wicked or more enterprising than themselves.

At no time in history has it ever been a paying proposition to fight a war and lose it, but whenever there can be a good profit in fighting a war and winning it, there will remain a steady natural selection in favour of those prepared to do so. The effectiveness of this selection process was abundantly demonstrated by the uniformly successful pattern of robbery with violence indulged in by the European nations, when technical improvements in navigation enabled them to make contact with Asian and African races, which had been selected mainly for their ability to survive attacks of tropical diseases rather than of each other.

Although steady improvements in the technique of living allowed a gradual increase of population, the new pattern of control of our numbers by disease, assisted from time to time by war, remained almost unchanged until the early part of last century.

The Defeat of Disease

Up to this time, the effect of medical treatment had been marginal, and by no means always positive. With no knowledge of micro-organisms, hospitals were focuses of infection. Prospects for the patient were perhaps better in 1800 than in mediaeval times – when a useful improvement in survival rate from knife wounds is said to have been achieved by treating the weapon, rather than the patient himself, with the disgusting mixtures which the therapy of the time required. But his prospects were not much better.

During the nineteenth century the situation was transformed. By far the most important part of the transformation was nothing to do with either medical understanding of disease, or with treatment, but was due to the building of effective drainage systems in cities. In mediaeval cities a large part of the faeces and urine of the inhabitants were thrown into the streets. Night soil carts existed but were only partially effective. As late as 1840 'gardelou'* bells were rung in Edinburgh at 10 a.m. every morning, warning people to keep off the streets, so that all chamber pots could be emptied out of the windows together, enabling foot passengers to walk safely along the sidewalks for the rest of the day. Street cleaning services existed, again somewhat inadequately, but much of the excreta remained to support an immense population of insect larvae. The insects, unfortunately, often flew on to exposed foods, and the immunity of the surviving adult population was bought at the cost of an infantile mortality of several hundred per thousand from fly-borne disease.

The establishment of water closets, a piped sewage system and a general improvement of hygiene, reduced the infantile death rates in the cities by several times, and though the country remained healthier than the towns, the latter began to grow by their own natural increase, as well as from the immigration from the rural countryside.

Although less important than drains, the discovery of smallpox vaccination by Jenner published in 1789, and the establishment of antiseptic surgery by Lister in the mid-nineteenth century, following Pasteur's discovery that diseases could be caused by germs, all helped to lower the death rate. None of these advances, it will be noted, had anything at all to do with curing diseases once they had been caught. They merely reduced the chance of catching them. In each case this meant that the probability G of passing on an infection by each victim to somebody else was reduced to less than 1, and hence, though diseases might arise, they could rarely lead to epidemics. The sewage system did this directly, by removing excreted germs of intestinal diseases rapidly,

* from *gardez l'eau*.

before they could be passed on to anyone else, and so also did the use of antiseptics, which killed the germs after they had been passed on, but before the wound on which they might have fallen could become infected.

Vaccination against smallpox worked indirectly as well as directly. Not only were vaccinated individuals themselves protected from the disease, but if large enough numbers were treated, the density of the remaining susceptible part of the population would be much reduced. Accordingly, the growth factor G of the disease could be reduced to less than 1 among this unvaccinated part as well.

The new techniques of disease prevention spread through Europe and the rest of the world and new ones were discovered and developed. Chlorination of water supplies, which was first introduced in Italy in 1896, practically eliminated a further set of waterborne diseases such as typhoid and cholera. This last had killed 53,000 people in England and Wales in a single year in 1849, and had occurred frequently in smaller epidemics, which killed between them many tens of thousands more.

With these discoveries death rates dropped and populations rose. No doubt, if our way of life and our medical knowledge had frozen at this point, we should in due course have run up against a limit set either by other diseases such as tuberculosis, or by food supply. But medical knowledge achieved further successes in developing effective methods of inoculation against diphtheria, tuberculosis, infantile paralysis and a number of other less lethal complaints, and at the end of the 1930s a genuinely novel advance took place. This consisted in the development of the first really successful methods of treatment and cure of diseases after they had been contracted, with the discovery first of the sulpha-drugs and penicillin, and later of the huge and expanding range of modern antibiotics.

We have so far specialized in the diseases of the rich, that is, those which affect the Europeans, and the Americans, and the Russians and the Japanese – the inhabitants of the industrialized countries which can afford a qualified doctor for every two or three thousand people, so that a useful proportion of them have time for research. Naturally, the diseases on which the doctors do their research can only be those which occur in their own countries. In about 150 years, therefore, we have learnt to defend ourselves against all of the diseases which used to exert any significant control of population growth in the industrialized countries of the temperate zone. We have not made much impression on the death rate from malignant diseases such as cancer or leukaemia.* We have learnt almost nothing about the degenerative diseases of old age, but these have no effect whatever on the rate of reproduction and therefore have only transient effects on population size.

Very much remains to be done in the tropical countries, but enough has been done, even with the tiny resources which have been applied so far, to produce enormous rises in the rate of population growth. In several countries, after a long period of near equilibrium, the time required to double the population has dropped to twenty-five years or less, as the result of getting rid of the Anopheles mosquitoes which carry malaria, even though many serious diseases still remain. When the inhabitants of the countries concerned have the money or the industrialised countries have the will, the rest of these diseases *could* be eliminated.

Technical, Economic, and Political Limits

Inability to cope with various serious diseases (which significantly affect size of populations and quality of lives) can be technical, economic, or political. There are of course many diseases we are so far technically incapable of eradicating, but others are still rife for other reasons. Bilharzia, for instance, could be eradicated – but this would require adequate sewerage (plus appropriate education) for large areas of the underdeveloped world, and it is not in these areas that the necessary know-how and economic resources exist. Venereal diseases, which are now spreading almost out of control in many countries including Britain and the United States, could equally be brought under control, except that this

* These, surprisingly, kill between them more children than anything else bar accidents; this is due mainly to our outstanding success in eliminating practically everything else which kills children. The proportion of people killed by malignant disease before the normal reproductive age is past, is too small to have a significant effect on population growth. (See Appendix II.)

The Defeat of Our Natural Limitations

would require compulsory testing for whole populations, and many would consider that an infringement of their human rights.

Many writers are convinced that large-scale starvation is genuinely inevitable during the next few decades. They are probably right, but for economic and political reasons; not for technical ones. There are no insurmountable material problems involved in feeding the whole world even if numbers continue to increase for generations. But many have accepted the proposition that hunger cannot be cured, as a technical statement. This reduces the political possibility a great deal. Most of us would much rather not spend a lot of money on other people a long way off. We prefer not to admit this, but find it easy to claim that we *ought* not to spend the money because it could not possibly do any good.

Can We be Fed?

The rapid and sustained rise of population, following the last 150 years of applied medicine, effectively confirms my thesis both that disease has been the major factor controlling our numbers in the last few centuries, and that we have learnt how to deal with this limit and have broken free of its control. Other factors have had local importance, but have clearly not recently been the main limitation. They, too, are at least temporarily pushed back.

There is no doubt that a large part of the world already lives on a great deal less food, and poorer food, than is needed for maximum health, and is worse off in this respect than it was a few decades ago. This is not in the short term preventing a very rapid increase of population, which is surviving in spite of it. Furthermore, the situation is slowly improving, the food output per head having gone up slightly but significantly in most of the years since 1957 as is shown in Table 1. The later rise is due mainly to the establishment of the new high-yield strains of rice and wheat, produced by the use of radiation-induced mutations.

This food increase should, with luck, continue for some years. The very large scale culture of only one or two variations of crop, however, drastically increases the risk of a catastrophic spread of

TABLE 1

Year	Food production	Population	Food per head
1957	100	100	100
1958	106	102	104
1959	108	104	105
1960	111	106	105
1961	113	108	105
1962	117	110	106
1963	119	112	106
1964	123	115	107
1965	125	117	106
1966	128	119	107
1967	132	122	108
1968	137	124	110
1969	138	127	108
1970	139	129	108

Variation of world food output, world population, and food output per head, averaged over the world between 1957 (taken as 100) and 1970. Figures are taken from Food and Agriculture Organization Reports and UN Monthly Bulletin of Statistics. It is uncertain that the total annual food production has been based throughout on equally reliable data, but it seems certain that there has been a gradual improvement in food per head over the period. While this illustrates an increasing *capacity* to feed ourselves, it must be remembered that these averages conceal a serious drop in food per head over the same period in a number of important areas.

rusts or other plant diseases. It is thus of major importance that we should develop a series of further strains, of comparable yield but different genetic background, so that all should not be susceptible to the same infections. These and the existing varieties could then be sown in alternating patches of moderate size so as to break up the present huge areas of monoculture, and thus establish a built-in safeguard against the simultaneous destruction of entire crops. Meanwhile, the staffs of skilled men, and the stocks of fungicides or other chemicals needed to handle a major outbreak, should be established and kept on the alert.

Even if we are neither lucky nor prepared, it must be remembered that the richer part of the world is actually limiting its output of food for economic reasons, and could easily increase it rapidly if it were decided to do so. Adequate stocks to cover a major crop failure could quite easily (technically) be built up. It is more likely than not that there will be a major famine, but this will be the result of our economic or political inability; not

The Defeat of Our Natural Limitations

because of scientific or technical incompetence.

In the absence of major disasters, it is apparent that we have coped for the time being with food shortage, well before it could become a serious limitation. If we fail to cope in the immediate future it will be our own fault. The further future will be discussed in later chapters.

The remaining population control is war. This can arguably be presented either as a natural or as an artificial control. As we have seen, it was of some importance up to and somewhat past mediaeval times. Its importance in the last few decades is often pointed out, but is usually exaggerated. The total killed in fighting during the 1914-18 war was under ten million, and was considerably less than the number of deaths in the influenza epidemic a year or so later – though it could fairly be argued that many of these deaths occurred because of malnutrition in Germany and Central Europe, due to the British blockade following the end of the war. A 'baby boom' following the war, however, largely cancelled out the effects of war plus influenza together. The increase of British population between 1911 and 1921 was 3.9 per cent and between 1921 and 1931 was 4.3 per cent. The reduction in rate of growth, produced by what was numerically many times the most disastrous war in our history, was hardly greater than the uncertainty of measurement.

The growth of British population during the decade 1939-49, including the last war, was actually a lot greater than the growth in the decade before. Over the world as a whole the estimated seven million German, twenty million Russian and a few million other dead did have a perceptible effect – over the five years it may have reduced the average *growth* of the world population by a quarter. Most, and perhaps all, of this was made up in the next five years.

Clearly, we are now in a position to make war a far more efficient controller of population if we so choose, but equally clearly it has not played an important role in this connection in the present century. Whether its small effect in recent times can be regarded as evidence that we have learnt how to avoid it, its importance as a controller of population is, like its naturalness, arguable.

Technically we have eliminated the incentive to war described above, in that it is no longer effective in getting a larger total product for our own group or even for the majority of the ruling classes of our own group. A vital achievement of applied science in the last fifty years is that it has made factory production of practically everything so cheap, and armies so expensive, that it no longer pays to fight a war for any material gains, even if you know you will win. Anything you could win is obtainable more cheaply by other means. Not all (historically educated) politicians have yet grasped the importance of this change, but it means that whereas in mediaeval times you had to fear attack from the clever knave, who could see a profit to himself, now you need fear only the stupid knave who cannot see the loss to himself. While the stupid knaves may be dangerous for another generation, they should soon be ousted by the clever ones, even if there are no clever men of honest good will available. Natural selection at least is on the side of peace, and if we give it time it will win. Whether we shall give it time, of course, I don't know, but technically we now have free choice and I shall therefore take it that, as a *natural* limit, we have eliminated war like the rest of our erstwhile physical controls.

I shall not discuss here possible psychological limits of the kind shown by Calhoun's rats. They are not controlling our numbers at present, and indeed the most appallingly overcrowded slums are among the ones which are multiplying fastest. I shall return to this point later. As far as natural factors go, however, we have learnt to destroy or reduce to impotence every one of the natural controls which have limited our numbers so far, and are therefore expanding without natural limit. This is unprecedented in the history of living things. In the next three chapters I shall consider the results to be expected if we choose to employ none of the many artificial controls now available, then what *new* natural limits might arise, and what, if anything, could be done about them. These chapters do not represent a prophecy and I do not expect for an instant that we shall follow the route I describe, any more than a manufacturer of steel girders, who publishes tables of breaking strains for his products, is prophesying that they will all be broken. The object of such tables, in fact, is to ensure that as few are broken as possible.

It is my object, in exploring some of the ultimate and undefeatable breaking strains of the human race, to help ensure that as few as possible of us are broken.

Four

Britain as it Could be in Eighty Years' Time

I want to begin with the fairly small step of considering what might happen in the lifetime of a good proportion of babies born this year (1972) if present trends continue.

Although the vital statistics for Britain are among the best-recorded anywhere, it is absolutely impossible to make a meaningful estimate of the population in eighty years' time. This is no longer limited or driven by any technically uncontrollable factor whatsoever. It depends entirely on human choices – and in particular, it depends on the choices to be made by a generation of young women whose mothers are not yet born. Naturally, recent and present trends give us a guide to what these choices may be. But which trends? Do we consider the trends represented by the fantastic change since 1945 in the public attitude to contraception and abortion, and in the rate of publication of books like Professor Ehrlich's, or like mine? If so, the population of Britain in eighty years' time could well be less than it is now.

Do we consider political trends? If there were a united Ireland in ten years' time, presumably Irish immigration would come under the same rules as that from the rest of the Commonwealth, and by far the biggest source of new people with the tradition of having large families would dry up.

Do we consider that the trend towards more extreme attitudes will continue, and that we have achieved all of the conversions to the idea of birth limitation that we are likely to get?

In this case, the part of the population that has persisted so far with its tradition of having large families will grow extensively, more than off-setting the slight fall in the part which has now accepted the desirability of birth limitation; and the population in eighty years' time will be much larger, and also increasing much more rapidly, than it is now.

With a view to increasing the probability of the first proposition, that a sensible degree of family limitation will become part of our way of life, I want to consider the situation that might be expected if instead, for whatever reason, the population should continue to increase, at a rate which is itself slowly increasing. On this basis, it is entirely possible that in eighty years we should reach some 120 millions. To house these at present standards we should need two more Greater Londons in Kent and Surrey, plus five more each of Birmingham, Manchester with Salford, and Glasgow, plus sixty more Brightons to give a continuous city along the south coast from Dover to Land's End. This would still leave enough to double the population of every other city, town or hamlet south of Oxford.

If none of the extra population wanted to live in high-rise flats, and if every family wanted a car, they would need more space still. Judging from what has happened over the last two decades, it is rather unlikely that we would either build anew until we had two-and-a-half times as many big towns as we have now, or that we would make all our existing towns two-and-a-half times as big. Our present pattern of behaviour shows the north of the country actually shrinking in human population, while the south, and especially the south-east, grows far faster than the average. Then by the year 2052 a large part of the entire population would be concentrated in an even greater London and in a few other big towns in the Midlands and the South.

Before discussing this in detail, or even in general, I must give some reason to suppose that there will be any of us here to discuss in eighty years' time. Professor Ehrlich has made the quite positive prediction that Britain has only an even chance of surviving for one more generation; until the year 2000. The dangers, which he doubts our ability to survive, include direct poisoning by industrial wastes, destruction of the oceanic plankton and other vitally important wild life by global pollutants such as DDT, and the loss of food imports as the increasing populations of the food-exporting countries begin to eat all their own produce.

All of these dangers are real, and potentially catastrophic, but there is little reason to suppose that they are irresistible. In fact, if they are not resisted, it is entirely our own fault.

Pollution

I will take first the problem of industrial pollution. This is undeniably disgraceful in many areas, but it is by no means obvious that it is even getting worse, let alone becoming a mortal danger. The air and rivers of Britain, dirty as they are, are actually cleaner than they have been for generations. Fish have recently been caught in reaches of the Thames where they have not been seen for 150 years. Central London, which has lain beneath a pall of smoke for four hundred years, has now the same annual sunshine as the country towns of twenty miles away. There is plenty to be said on the other side, but few of us are likely to die by direct poisoning in the next eighty years.

Destruction of the plankton is much less under our own (British) control, but the USA, which so far has been the main source of global pollution, is now taking the matter seriously, and has much reduced the indiscriminate spreading of DDT and some other insecticides. It is well known that flies, mosquitos and most other common insects develop resistance after a few years, and it is difficult to believe that this will not also be true of the far more numerous plankton organisms. The total ecological effect may well be less than that of the utterly inexcusable hunting down of the great whales.

I am not saying that no irremediable damage will be done. Already many of the less common species in the plankton and elsewhere must have been exterminated, not having the evolutionary resistance which vast numbers can provide. But I am saying that it is unlikely that we ourselves will die as a result. If even five million people, less than a month's world production, were proven to have died as the result of pollution, we should do something about it – at once.

A more comprehensive worry is rather widespread in a rather narrow circle – if that is not geometrically impossible. This is that, by using up oxygen and releasing carbon dioxide, we are so changing the atmosphere that animal life on this planet will become impossible. Some go so far as to give a date to the catastrophe; currently the most imminent I have heard is 1979. The belief that the end of the world is at hand, has of course been around for a very respectable period; doubtless long antedating the mediaeval thousands who confidently expected it at the first millennium AD. Naturally it tends to attach itself to important topical events. During the Christian eras of implicit faith in the Bible, complex arithmetical calculations from data presented therein, especially in the Book of Revelation, were used to produce dates far enough ahead to be advertised, and close enough to be interesting. Later, the dimensions of the Great Pyramid were very popular. Now it is pollution. This is better, because while calculations based on the number of letters in the Authorized Version of the Bible are difficult to refute, concern about the air can be settled by doing the sums.

At the present moment, the atmosphere contains close to 300,000 tons of oxygen for every living human being. Burning the whole of the known, recoverable fossil fuels in the world would reduce it by 0.7 per cent, so that we should have left only about 298,000 tons each. At our present rate of fuel-burning we are using this up in Britain at about fifteen tons a year each. If, quite improbably, we produce a new and unlimited supply of fossil fuels so that we could keep the present world average rate of use, which is around eight tons each per year, and assuming *no* oxygen to be replaced, we should have used up ten per cent of it, leading to some discomfort for the inhabitants of Tibet, in about 3,500 years. If the increased carbon dioxide leads to increased plant growth, as is not unlikely, there may be no difference at all. Even if we soon manage to destroy the world's wild life, including all the plants, the problem is not exactly urgent.

A more sophisticated group backs the proposition that the steady increase of the insulating carbon dioxide will reduce the radiation cooling of the earth, and that the temperature will increase to a level at which all life is destroyed. A similar group, however, concludes that the increased carbon dioxide will cause an increased evaporation from the oceans, and hence more clouds and more snow at the Poles, leading to a new ice age. If either of these somewhat contradictory fates ever seems to be imminent, we should be wise to switch over to nuclear power, and plant some more trees.

Carbon dioxide is increasing at about 0.8 parts per million per year, so if we do not do this, and if no compensating biological absorption takes place, and if the increase in cloud cover does not reflect away enough sunlight to compensate; the *maximum* rate of rise of the earth's surface temperature has been calculated in the Williamstown Study of Critical Environmental Problems to be about 1.5°C per century – less than the random variations, which seem to occur in much shorter periods, quite independently of carbon dioxide. Some authorities consider that the present level of carbon dioxide already makes the atmosphere opaque to the relevant parts of the infra-red radiation, and, since the atmosphere cannot be more opaque than opaque, that no thermal effects whatever are to be expected. Whichever view is right, no heat catastrophe need be feared in the next eighty years.

Food Supplies

At present we import about 40 per cent of our needs, but the prospect of even keeping this constant is extremely poor. The growth of population in the present food-exporting countries in the next eighty years will probably lead to a complete cessation of imports of bulk foods. It would certainly be prudent to prepare for the possibility that this may happen, and that our entire food supply may have to depend on our own unaided efforts.

Doubtless we could grow a good deal more than we do now in Britain, but it is difficult to see how conventional agriculture could give a good and varied diet for 120 million people, when at present we are providing for little more than thirty million. Some useful kinds of fish-farming should be established by then, but by far the most reliable source will be the production of food by unconventional and increasingly synthetic means.

The main bulk of our food consists of carbohydrates such as starches and sugars. These require nothing but carbon – perhaps in the form of carbon dioxide – and water as raw material. They can already be made by direct chemical synthesis, but at present they can much more cheaply be produced naturally by agricultural methods. If the demand became too great to be met by agriculture, however, large scale factory production could readily be organized. This would probably not, at least at first, be entirely or even mainly chemical in nature.

Small floating green plants such as algae (for example, *Chlorella*) will grow on exceedingly simple and cheap chemical raw materials: carbon dioxide and water, with small amounts of ammonium sulphate, phosphates and salts. On the other hand they require their energy supply in the form of light, within a certain range of wavelength. While this light energy may be used with an efficiency of 30 per cent or more, light of appropriate wavelengths is itself difficult to produce with high efficiency, and the overall efficiency may be less than 1 per cent from the primary source of power to the finished product. More complex processes, using both micro-organisms and chemistry, should do better than this in the long run; the algae are mentioned here, mainly because they have already been used on a sufficient scale to show that really large-scale production is possible, without the major research effort that will undoubtedly be needed for the more sophisticated methods.

Very recently it has been shown that the tiny floating duckweed *Wolffia arrhiza* can also be cultivated in bulk in a similar way. This has already been grown in ponds in south-east Asia for a long time.

Both the algae and the duckweed produce fats and proteins, the other two main constituents of our food, as well as carbohydrates. There are many practical problems to be solved before either plant could be economically produced on a really large scale, but if we should find a real shortage of food approaching, the final feasibility is not in doubt.

Currently the essential food in shortest supply on the world scale is protein, essential for the growth and maintenance of the body. Accordingly, it is this on which most work is being done.

Production of a first-grade protein is being developed by Ranks Hovis McDougall, using a strain of the mould *Penicillium notatum*. This is grown on cheap carbohydrate, which could be derived from any of the bulk basic foods such as potatoes, cassava, yams etc. which are often plentiful where protein is short. Flour waste is now being used, and a pilot plant producing first class protein suitable for direct human consumption came into operation in 1971. Factories capable of producing hundreds of tons a week should be built within the next two or three years.

During 1971 a fermentation plant for the production of protein from an even cheaper raw material, the unwanted waxes in diesel oil, came into full production at Grangemouth in Scotland. This plant was built by British Petroleum (now ShellMex-BP) and is using a yeast (*Candida lipolytica*), to produce 4,000 tons of proteins per year under the trade name of Toprina. A second plant at Laverna near Marseilles is scheduled to start production in 1972, with an initial production of 16,000 tons. Smaller plants in Japan and China are already operating, and many other countries are planning to set up their own. Plants for 100,000 tons a year are already envisaged, each of which could meet the protein needs of four million people, and the cost is less than a fifth of that of the cheapest cuts of beef or mutton.

At present Toprina is being sold as feed for pigs and poultry, rather than for direct human consumption, since it contains more nucleic acid than we can easily metabolize. A technique for removing the excess has been developed, but while there is no real shortage of protein for human consumption in Britain, it is economically advantageous to use it to replace fishmeal for livestock. Many generations of hens and pigs have now been fed from pilot plants, with complete success.

The supply of paraffins, the important constituent, is not unlimited, and is likely to be seriously restricted in eighty years' time. Simple compounds such as hydrocarbons are, however, relatively easy to synthesize by direct chemical methods. Petrol has been derived from hydrogenation of coal, at Billingham in Britain, for nearly forty years. Coal too will eventually run out, but, rather more expensively, the necessary carbon as carbon dioxide can be obtained from limestone or chalk. As we have seen, carbon dioxide is now thrown away in such enormous quantities that concern has been expressed about the effects of its addition to the atmosphere. We are throwing away about three thousand million tons a year. Even without mining for extra chalk or limestone, that should keep us supplied with carbon for quite a while.

The only other element required for the production of hydrocarbons is hydrogen, and since two-thirds of the atoms in the oceans of the world are hydrogen, this too should have no risk of running out. In the production of protein a few other elements are needed: nitrogen from the air; sulphur and phosphorus from mineral deposits, and salts of a few common metals. All of the chemical syntheses of the simple compounds of these required can already be done and there can be no question that, as the need gets greater, better and better methods will be developed.

Proteins certainly, and those other bulk foods probably, will soon be considerably cheaper for industrialized societies if they are produced in a factory, rather than on a field. This is useful, but even if they cost twice as much as natural foods it would matter little. The human race has lived for most of its existence on the basis of using 80 per cent or more of its effort to keep itself fed. Recently, in the USA, food production has occupied only some 5 per cent of the labour force. This number has a large supporting technical industry, the size of which would be difficult to determine accurately. We should not go too far wrong, however, if we assume the 'loading factor' of about 2.5 by which an industrial firm multiplies his salary in estimating the real cost to the firm of one of its employees. This would give us an overall figure of 12.5 per cent of the total human effort in USA devoted to food production. An increase of even four times in the proportion of production effort, and hence cost, of food would be accepted in preference to starvation, even if it was not popular, and would not reduce the people accepting it to a level as close to mere subsistence as most people have in fact lived hitherto. Indeed, if in Britain we had to achieve this change in eighty years, it would require less than 2.5 per cent per year increase in our gross national product, and could be combined with a small actual increase in our general standard of life.

Far more important than the fact that the factory foods will actually be cheaper in effort than 'natural' foods are now, is the fact that their production will take less space than currently conventional methods. There would be no problem whatever in producing food for ten times our present population, if we could find twenty times the area of good agricultural land which is now in use. The problem arises only because this doesn't exist.

To produce one ton of beef a year from our own land, we

should need two to three hectares of grassland under very intensive management. There is one ton of protein in five tons of beef, so that to match the 16,000 tons of protein to be produced each year at Laverna would need over 400,000 half-ton oxen, grazing some 200,000 hectares or 800 square miles. (We use a much smaller area than this at present, because much cattle food is imported. This may be impossible in eighty years' time.) The 16,000 tons of oil-based protein will come from a factory covering only about seventy hectares, less than a quarter of a square mile, and much of this will be covered by administration and other ancillary buildings, so that still larger factories will use proportionally less. Furthermore, such factories can be built on flattened, stabilized slag heaps, or on land which has been used for open cast mining, just as easily as on agricultural land. In an important sense, therefore, there might well be more room for 120 million people in Britain in eighty years' time than there is for fifty-six million now.

The objection is often made that even if artificial food could be produced, people would refuse to eat it. Doubtless some would indeed do so. Some people now refuse to eat white bread, or vegetables grown with artificial fertilizers. But experiment has shown that most people do not mind in the least.

Suppose that you were required to sell, for human consumption, a fluid consisting of a dilute solution of a highly corrosive mineral acid, made from fossil seagull excreta, sweetened with an artificial organic chemical formed by the combination of two poisons with a mild anaesthetic, and the whole saturated under pressure with a gas capable of killing a healthy adult in less than five minutes. If you were required to put this accurate technical description on the bottle, the market might indeed be pretty quiet. By *not* putting this accurate technical description on the bottle and calling it lemonade or 'pop' the British soft drinks industry has in fact found it possible to sell over a thousand million bottles a year. It is of course quite harmless. Correspondingly, factory-made protein would sell well if described on the tin as 'selected first class protein balanced for growing children'.

And, if it were cheap, tasty and nutritious (in that order), who would object?

Another objection is that artificial foods would prove deficient in some vital constituent. Doubtless they would, every one of them. So are all of our present 'natural' foods. But, like our present foods, different brands will be deficient in different things. Apart from human milk – and even this, so far as I know, has never been tried as a complete diet for adults – there is not a single thing we eat which would prove satisfactory if we consumed it, and water, and nothing else whatever. Cows' or goats' milk or unpolished rice come close, but in each case we would have to adapt our interiors to handling a very large excess to get enough of everything.

We deal with the natural deficiencies empirically, by choosing as varied a diet as we can afford, and hoping that no important constituent will be lacking in every part of this diet. We should do just the same, if most of our foods were artificial.

Sugars and fats produced by purely chemical methods would probably, like existing natural but refined sugars and fats, be deficient in minerals and vitamins. Factory-produced protein, made by any process involving yeasts, might well have a larger content of the vitamin B complex than do our existing animal products. Some vitamins and some minerals, however, might be short in every one of the bulk products, as these came off the production line. But this is true of our bulk foods in Britain *now*. The practical fact, now, is not that we are having to supplement artificial foods with natural ones to keep in health, but that we are having to supplement *natural* foods with *artificial* ones to keep in health.

There is little doubt that many people take a great many vitamin pills which are entirely unnecessary. Children have suffered from hypervitaminosis D (an unpleasant condition produced by an excess of vitamin D) as a result of having over-anxious parents, who have supplemented the recommended doses of codliver oil, with ultraviolet treatment and with large doses of the much more concentrated halibut liver oil. Nevertheless, before we compelled by law the supplementing of bread by calcium and vitamin B, of our margarine by vitamin D and of our table salt by iodine, we were most of us deficient in one or several of these vital constituents. Our bodies are well adapted to getting rid of moderate excesses of all of them, but are entirely unable to make any of them for ourselves except for vitamin D, and that only with the help of sunshine on the bare skin.

Another, perhaps even more striking example of supplementing an inadequate natural diet with the help of artificial chemicals, is the addition of lysine to rice diets in South East Asia. Rice provides considerably more protein than do most cereals, but in common with most vegetable proteins, it has a very different distribution of its essential amino acids from our own body proteins. In particular, it contains only about one-third of the lysine which is needed for the same weight of animal or human protein (which itself contains only about 7.5 per cent by weight of lysine). Consequently, to get enough of this single minor component, the consumers must eat some 3.5 times as much rice as they would otherwise need; the extra 200 per cent being wasted, in a protein-starved world. Addition of a few per cent of artificial lysine makes almost the whole of the natural protein available, and enables the same amount of rice to supply nearly twice as many people with an adequate protein diet.

To return to the problems facing Britain in the next few generations, it is not unlikely that new and unexpected deficiencies might appear if we switched suddenly from our present diet to an entirely factory-produced one. Of course we shall do nothing of the sort. Little by little, as field-grown foods get scarcer or more expensive, they will be replaced by factory-made ones; sometimes deficient in fewer trace requirements, sometimes deficient in more. Identical effects may happen, following changes in our intake of natural foods. For example, the extensive switch from fluorine-rich tea to low-fluorine coffee in Britain since the war, may result in a whole new group of elderly people needing to supplement their fluoride intake, to reduce mineral loss from their skeletons, besides the non-tea-drinking children who here, as in other countries, need it for the proper development of their teeth. Changing food habits of any kind need a constant watch, but there is no reason to suppose that the problems arising in the future will be more difficult than those of the past, and there is every reason to suppose that we shall get steadily better and better at solving them.

I do not wish to suggest for a moment that in as little as eighty years we shall have abandoned agriculture entirely in Britain.

It is likely that much, or even most, of our present agricultural land will still be in production. It is easy to believe, though, that the growing of tulips will increase more than will the growing of wheat or sugar beet, and it seems exceedingly likely that meat production, even in the cheapest broiler house form, will be actually reduced by the competition of the far cheaper factory protein. This will never be tough; will be presented in a vast number of flavours, textures and colours, and will be sold in a great many ready-made combinations with fats and other foods. Fresh fruit, and perhaps milk and cream, could easily be the only really profitable products, the land unwanted by these being turned over to the production of the maximum weight of organic material per year, as a useful intermediate raw material for the factories making food carbohydrates. The direct edibility of the plants used would be immaterial, and they could be selected at least in part for their amenity value. Forests of horse chestnut, or flowering cherry, may be less productive of cellulose than are fir trees, and fields of buttercups far less so than grass, but they look much nicer in spring, and, in case anyone feels that I am hopelessly idealistic to think that this could possibly have any effect whatever on British national policy, would attract a great many more money-spending tourists than would the efficient but humdrum alternatives.

Water Supplies

After food, our next major concern should perhaps be water. As with food, there is not the slightest technical reason why we should run short in our eighty year span, though, again as with foods, our forms of production and utilization will doubtless change. In considering the probable direction of change, we have a great many choices.

As in all fields of endeavour, the first choice of the majority would be simply to go on doing what we are now, only more so. We are now using about a quarter of a ton of water per head per day. If this continues to increase at 3 per cent per year, it will double in a generation. At the same time, we are using up some of our 'capital' of underground supplies. The first choice, therefore, of going on as we are, is probably not open to us for more than another twenty to forty years, and then only at the expense of major increases in cost. More and more protests would also be made as we built new reservoirs in areas which have escaped, so far, only because other areas have been available involving fewer protesting voters.

The two main choices after this are either to use water 3 per cent more efficiently each year, instead of using 3 per cent more of it, or to develop fresh sources. Either of these is perfectly possible, and cost is likely to be minimized by combining the two. The cost of increasing efficiency lies in the capital cost of cooling or cleaning once-used water, and then recirculating it. Sometimes, as in the establishment of efficient sewage plants, the cost would be very high, but the value of the direct by-products such as fertilizer or methane gas, and the indirect ones such as unpolluted rivers, on which pleasure boats or angling permits could be sold, may largely or even entirely compensate for this.

The re-using of industrial waste water may sometimes be easy; for example when water is used only for cooling, the partial re-circulation of it through a cooling reservoir may be sufficient to save 90 per cent of the water used, except on a few hot days each year. Sometimes it may be very difficult, as when liquid wastes containing large amounts of undesirable chemicals are being disposed of.

Here there is a marked distinction between established traditional industries and newly developed ones, to the great disadvantage of the latter. For example, the law controlling the addition of undesirable effluents to streams and rivers is, for new industries, adequate. That is to say, if it were obeyed by all firms, our streams and rivers would all return to a healthy condition, both in temperature and chemical constitution. Game fish could live in them, children could bathe in them, and with no more than the standard precautions, they could be used for drinking water by the towns along their path. Industries already established by 1937, however, which would find a similar cooling and cleaning of their traditional effluent a serious or crippling expense, have not been required to operate within the same limits.

Detection and conviction of the firm responsible for the occasional release of a particular contaminant, which infringes even the more permissive legislation, is often difficult and expensive, and finally local authorities may be very unwilling to interfere with a large firm in such a way as to risk substantial unemployment.

If the maximum penalties for pollution are applied, they are probably adequate. A civil action for nuisance or negligence may result in an Injunction – an order to desist. The penalty for disobedience may be, as for contempt of court, imprisonment until consent to obey is given.

Under the 1951 and 1961 legislation it is a criminal offence to discharge a noxious substance. A first offence may lead to a fine of £100 to £200, which is probably negligible compared with the cost of amendment, but a second offence can lead to a fine of £50 per day, or six months' imprisonment or both.

Breaking a local authority bye-law concerning standards, even after a second conviction, is only £5 for each day this offence is continued, which is probably a great deal cheaper for any large firm than to clean up its effluent.

I have found no record of anyone ever having actually been imprisoned, and progress is slow.

As a result, although there has been much improvement in the last thirty years, some 6 per cent (2,000 km or 1,300 miles) of our once productive and beautiful rivers are dangerous, stinking and dead, and an uncertain but much greater length is seriously affected.

This distinction between what is allowed to the new, and what is allowed to the old, can have some odd effects. Some years ago, the Atomic Energy Authority wished to set up a new 'facility'; i.e. a small experimental reactor, close to Harwell. This was to run at a level involving no radioactive output at all, but requiring a fair quantity of water for cooling. This could conveniently be taken from the Thames. The water would have come in no contact with the reactor core whatever, as it would have been passed through a stainless steel heat exchanger, where it cooled the water in a totally isolated primary cooling unit. The general safety controls proposed were acceptable to the local authority, and, although the Thames water would be returned with a few degrees' rise in temperature, nothing whatever would have been added. The scheme had to be abandoned, because the level of contamination of the Thames, by established enterprises above the point concerned, was such that the whole river was already more contaminated than was permissible for new additions. In fact, it was illegal to extract water from the river in a clean bucket and throw it back in again, unless one could establish that it was essential to one's business and that one had been doing so regularly since 1937. It is much to be hoped that this irrational situation will improve. A more efficient use of the water supplies we have could make a large or even major contribution to the supplies we should like to use in eighty years' time. This by itself, however, would not be sufficient, and fresh supplies will certainly be wanted.

Neglecting such untested procedures as importing fresh water by fitting million-kilowatt nuclear-powered outboard motors on to large Arctic icebergs, there seem to be two practical procedures, both of which may be used. One of these is to site more and more of our water-using industries and power plants round the coast, where they can use salt water for cooling. There would be considerable expense in building corrosion-resistant equipment, but this may be less serious in eighty years' time, when non-brittle ceramic structures should have taken over many of the duties for which metals are now required.

If this were done also on the other side of the Channel, it would lead to a measurable rise of a few degrees in the temperature of the North Sea. It is difficult for anyone who has been wrecked in the North Sea in winter, or indeed who has bathed in it in summer, to feel that this would be an unmitigated disaster, but it might have significant side effects such as a fall (or rise) in the fish population. It would almost certainly increase the extent, duration and number of fogs. This would not be important, except to those who wanted to see the white cliffs of Dover (assuming that these would not yet have been made into cement). With the increase of shipping corresponding to the increase of population envisaged, all vessels would certainly be radar-guided and computer-controlled.

The second practical method is to produce new supplies of fresh water by desalination. Desalination plants of adequate scale have already been designed, and will, only a little more expensively than traditional sources, be able to make up any shortfall after economy and salt water have been exploited to the full. The plants would be large ones, run by purpose-built nuclear power stations of the order of a thousand times as big as those which we are now using, but much cheaper in proportion. The principles of a design study were published in December 1962* for a desalination plant based on a hundred-thousand-megawatt nuclear reactor, to produce fresh water for irrigation in California. It could deliver four million tons a day at a cost of only about six pence a ton. A more recent design assumes dual purpose plants, producing electric power as well as water, which would be more efficient since the desalination plant could use heat which would be wasted by the power plant. These could provide water at 4p per ton. Ten such stations in Britain, supplying the major southeastern conurbation, would make up the fresh water that we should need, without destroying the way of life of whole farming communities in Wales, or causing further ecological tragedies such as that of Teesdale.

If we had used the time and money we have spent on TSR2 and Concorde to do so, we could already be well on the way to having such a desalination plant built, with the confidence that it would be worth its cost, and with at least as big a chance of selling others abroad at a profit as the most optimistic can believe we have for Concorde.

Finally, of course, there may be entirely novel technical developments, that could solve the water problem in some now unforeseeable way. I am not attempting to prophesy what we will do. I am concerned only to show some of the things that we *could* do, if we choose to multiply our numbers in the future as we have in the recent past.

Power

There is one other vital requirement, besides water and basic chemicals, which will be needed for the production of food, and which must be considered before we can be sure of being able to maintain ourselves artificially if the need should arise. This requirement is power. Chemical factories need a lot of power to

* *Nucleonics*, 20, 45, 1962.

produce the high-energy compounds needed for human food. Micro-organisms may not appear to need power, and indeed it may be needful to cool the vats in which they live and work. This is because they are capable of oxidizing part of their petroleum or other food supply to produce the power they need; not because they do not need energy at all. Part of their food supply, therefore, can be considered as equivalent to the fuel used to run a purely chemical plant. The efficiency of micro-organisms is usually higher, but on the other hand they may be more liable to unwanted changes than is a chemical factory.

We must now go further and estimate just how much power we shall need. Even if we suppose that by the time the artificial production of food becomes extensive, the 1 per cent overall efficiency that we can already attain will be increased to 5 per cent, the energy needed would be substantial: 40 kilowatt-hrs per person per day. This would be needed, however, only if we start from the simple basic chemicals already described. If a significant part of the raw material could be in the form of the complex organic compounds found in wood, or leaves, or sewage, the energy used could be cut considerably. If the full 40 kilowatt-hrs is needed, however, it does not add a serious cost. All other raw material needs are far cheaper than any of our present foods and may come to only a few pence per person per day. Even if the total should add up to 80p per person per day, this would doubtless be found if it were the price of life.

With 120 million people in Britain, the total power continuously required, for feeding them alone, could thus be 200 million kilowatts. This is about five times our present electrical output, but at the present rate of increase this would be reached in twenty-five years, and would be only a few per cent of our output in eighty years' time.

Whether or not we still have useful amounts of natural gas, nuclear energy has developed far enough for it to be clearly capable of supplying us safely with power on a very much larger scale than anything mentioned so far, with only moderate advances beyond existing techniques. The supplies of fuel for the nuclear power stations will be fully adequate for a great deal longer than eighty years as will be shown in detail in Chapter Seven.

To summarize, we are now reaching, and shall soon have passed, a critical point in human history. So far, with all our technology, our societies have been, dietetically-speaking, animals; that is to say they have been absolutely dependent on plants, directly or through other animals, for their life and growth. Advanced societies have now the capacity to become, dietetically speaking again, plants; requiring for their life and growth only a few simple chemicals and a source of energy. They will, however, have the advantage over plants of being able to produce at will the energy and raw materials that they need, without having to wait for whatever the sun and their surroundings happen to provide.

Raw Materials

Having considered the three indispensables: food, water and power, there is no need to be very much concerned with the availability of other special materials. Ever since I was at school in the twenties, a number of items, stated to be vital to our civilization, have been scheduled to run out within a lifetime. The dates fixed for disaster have not come any nearer in the past forty years, because new supplies of practically everything have been found, faster than we have been using up the previously known supplies. As a result the feeling of urgency has been lost, but the process clearly cannot go on for ever, and we must suppose that a lot of raw materials which are now of vital importance, will either have gone in the next eighty years or will have become so expensive as to preclude their large-scale use. Bad management could easily let this lead to serious trouble, but it is difficult to think of any loss which could produce real hardship.

Mineral petroleum is often cited as an absolutely vital commodity. This will almost certainly, it is true, have become far too rare and expensive to be considered for use as a fuel in private motor cars, central heating or anything else. But in any case it is likely that electric transport only will be permitted in or near cities for the sake of cleaner air. Alcohol for industry and for long-distance transport could however be produced, given plenty of nuclear power, in much the same way as food carbohydrates—from miscellaneous bulk vegetable matter if this were available, but from chalk and water if it were not.

Several metals such as lead, mercury, copper or zinc may have reached a similar state. We shall not give up the processes in which they are used, but shall use something else instead. As was, I think, first pointed out by Dr Wolfers, it is obvious that gold and platinum are the only satisfactory metals for a great many electrical components. But we do not give up using electricity because gold and platinum are too expensive. We use unsuitable material, such as copper or brass, and put up with the fact that they have to be cleaned after short periods in corrosive atmospheres, and have to be scrapped and replaced after very few years of use.

When copper and zinc are gone, we shall do the same jobs, with a little more cost and trouble, using aluminium or titanium. The abundance of titanium in the earth's surface layer is around sixty times, and the abundance of aluminium is more than 1,000 times, that of copper, and their more recent development is due only to the greater technological skill required to extract and handle them.

Most structural metals will be replaced by ceramics or the intermediate materials known as cermets. The shape of things to come is clearly illustrated by the way in which a very moderate increase in the price of lead has caused its almost complete replacement by plastic in its bulk uses for pipes or cable shielding. Often this has given an actual improvement in performance, and has certainly caused no sign of faltering, let alone collapse, in the industries which used to find lead indispensable.

It will be a very great pity if copper, which is the base of many very beautiful, as well as useful, alloys, is wastefully used to the point of real scarcity, but its loss would not destroy our civilization as some writers have appeared to believe.

In Grimes's Graves, near Brandon in Suffolk, there still survive the pits dug about 5,000 years ago by Neolithic man, in his search for flints of tool-making quality. These workings date from a time when technical advances in how to live in cold climates had led to a rapid increase of the British population. If the flint miners could have done the arithmetic, and had calculated the growth of population at the same rate of increase over the next few thousand years, they would confidently have foretold that civilization would collapse when the flints ran out – around the time of the Norman Conquest.*

In concluding this stage of the discussion, I do not claim to have *disproved* Professor Ehrlich's gloomy prediction that Britain has no assured future beyond our present century. I have shown that we can have a future in the twenty-first century *if we try*.

An interesting question, but more difficult to guess even than our numbers, is how most of us would live at the population size supposed in eighty years' time. As stated at the beginning of this chapter, I am going simply to extrapolate selected present trends, and will try to show a self-consistent set of answers to the new problems arising.

Future Ways of Life

The controlling factor in changing our way of life at the moment, is unquestionably the private car. The current doubling time for numbers of cars on the road in this country, is perhaps ten years. In eighty years' time a constant growth rate would give us about 3,000 million, or twenty-five cars for every man, woman and child in the population. Even the motor manufacturers might doubt the value of this. Evidently the rate of growth of car numbers must decrease very markedly and quite soon. A car each for every adult able to drive, making a total of perhaps sixty million cars for 120 million people, might be practicable in a bigger country than Britain. Since we cannot expand the country, life would be exceedingly uncomfortable for us if we had even two or three times the eleven million private cars which we now possess.

It is clear from experiment that many people are now ready, if not willing, to spend an hour each way sitting in a car in

* Professor Shotton has pointed out to me that the Geological Survey of the time would have predicted the discovery of many new sources of flint, but that this would not have affected the arithmetic, because nobody would have listened.

going to and from work. At two hours each way – though this would help a lot to solve the problem of what to do with our leisure as working hours get shorter – some might falter. At three hours or more there might be real changes of attitude. From this point on, the motor car may not be the controlling factor in the design of our way of living.

If this is accepted, the advantage of condensation of the population to very high densities becomes very great. At present the mean speed of cars or buses in the rush hour, bringing people from their homes to the centres of the big cities, is less than twice a normal walking speed. If the city shrank to half its radius, while giving the same population the same living accommodation by building four times as high, cars could not be used at all; but people could get to their work more quickly than before by, in fact, walking. At this four-times-greater population density, fast underground systems would become fully economic in many cities where they are only marginally so today. Halve the radius again and raise the height to sixteen times the original, and people could walk to work in half the time they now take to drive. In practice, of course, we should not attempt to give the same accommodation, or build to anywhere near sixteen times the original height. The tendency to smaller and smaller rooms, with more and more compact equipment, will continue and an average of thirty storeys could well suffice.

The bottom floors would be occupied by light and medium industry, with heavy or noisy equipment directly on the ground. The next few floors, thermally and acoustically insulated from the activities below, would consist of the associated stores and offices. Only above these, with further effective soundproofing, would come the residential and smaller commercial units.

With the number of people per unit area who could live in this way, it would become economic to roof in the city, and install artificial ventilation so that the walkers would no longer have to protect themselves from cold and wet. Furthermore again, the cost of continuous moving ways would become tolerable. It is a most striking fact that such moving ways were forecast for the year 2100 AD over seventy years ago (1898) by H. G. Wells in *When the Sleeper Wakes*. With two or three stages leading up to a high-speed strip at 20 kph, the freedom of choice of destination would be as good as, and travel would be much faster than, it is now by car. Overhead hand-straps would ease movement from one strip to the next. By the use of quasi-elastic strips which could broaden out and slow down at intervals, to enable people more easily to step from one to another, a fast strip moving at 30 kph could be obtained; a speed which has not been achieved in cities since they became unsafe for bicycles.

There would be a complete absence of either queues, which afflict the traveller by bus, or the uncertainty of travel time, combined with frequent delays in unhealthy, malodorous traffic jams, which afflict the car owner. If buildings had a uniform minimum height of twenty or thirty storeys, systems of roadways could be constructed at more than one level, with a different pattern of fast-moving ways at each level, and with escalators or continuously moving paternoster-type lifts giving frequent interconnections.

Such a design of city would reduce enormously the need for heating in winter, owing to the inhabitants' body heat, and better insulation. Permanent artificial lighting, indoors and out, might well be cheaper than the maintenance of switchgear to turn it on and off. Money saved in the winter might, of course, be lost in the summer in the cost of air-conditioning, and it could well be that the optimum height of the city would be so designed that the power required for heating in the winter was equal to that required for cooling in the summer. The latter could be minimized by aluminizing the entire city roof, to reflect all the heat of the sun. If this were impracticable, because of the appalling dazzle for aircraft, white paint would be nearly as good.

Most goods transport could be done through a computer-controlled automatic system, with standardized containers, operating on a level to which pedestrians normally had no access.

Social life might easily be better than it is now in big cities or their suburbs and there would be no need for the terrible isolation of our present high-rise blocks of flats.

Complete artificial ventilation and lighting, with multiple independent supplies in case of power failures, would make it possible for each floor of a single building to house a population comparable with that of an average village. Each floor could have a number of small play areas with sand, water, plastic bricks and push-around toys, suitable for the under-fours, each one surrounded and overlooked by the kitchen-living rooms of perhaps a dozen housing units. Toddlers could trot in and out to recharge themselves with confidence by contact with their mums, and still have an amount of space, and equipment, and companionship in their play, that is available to very few nowadays.

Open style, rather than open air, cafés for the adults would be possible; catering for tea and gossip, coffee and conversation or beer and talk.

Each floor could have its kindergarten, and every fourth or fifth floor its primary school, so that children going to and fro would be passing along routes with few strangers and no powered traffic. Each floor could have its general store, run rather on the lines of a travelling shop today, with only a few standard commodities always in stock, but with a much larger list of things which could be produced for the next visit, and a number of viewing booths from which 3D colour tape-recordings of dresses or furniture or steam yachts could be dialled.

Gymnasium-type playrooms in which older children could attempt physical achievements of increasing difficulty, swimming pools and skating rinks, could be constructed only on one or perhaps two floors. Equipment for larger-scale and more vigorous activities for teenagers, might need a separate building, communicating space from several buildings, or an adequately supervised part of the road system. Provision of a satisfactory environment for adolescents might indeed be the most difficult task for really dense communal living.

In eighty years' time we should know very well the extent to which vandalism, gang-fights and other unprofitable teenage activities, can usefully be controlled by early upbringing, and to what extent by effective discipline and by providing alternative outlets. The simple liberal view, that good early conditions are all that is necessary, is still not quite untenable, but the current rapid, simultaneous improvement in the conditions of early childhood, and worsening of general teenage troubles, cannot be regarded as strong experimental evidence in its favour.

There was in the distant past strong selective advantage to a primitive group in favourable conditions, if it had a number of expendable youths, not yet with family responsibilities, who were anxious to explore beyond the normal home territory, and willing to fight beyond it, even at considerable risk to themselves. Such characteristics, valuable though they can be to primitive societies in hostile environments, are a definite nuisance to stable societies in friendly environments.

At present, we try to find the answer to the problem by the classical method. This consists in discussion, without systematic experiment, of the relative credibility of persuasive and popular theorists. All ideas which would cost a lot of money to implement are ruled out.

If, instead of using the classical system, we should in the next eighty years spend real money on practical tests, we should know several effective ways of containing the nuisance. Fairly successful methods in the past have included: intense, and compulsory, involvement in vigorous team games, as in British public schools; painful and difficult initiation ceremonies, requiring long and uncomfortable preparation, as in many African and North American Indian communities; firm, effective and immediate physical discipline by adults within adult territory, combined with an uncontrolled hinterland of woods and commons, containing moderate risks, into which to escape, as in traditional English villages; and many others.

Many, possibly most, communities have believed in the past that a young man cannot develop fully without meeting and facing a risk to his life. This does not seem likely to us nowadays, but I know of no evidence that it is altogether untrue – though it is experimentally clear, that for many young men the risk does not have to be very large. Getting into gang-fights and dodging the police, driving too fast, taking dangerous drugs, or going for long mountain walks without adequate food or clothing, may be quite sufficient. It is possible that appropriate conditioning as children (or a good upbringing, or brainwashing; they all mean much the same thing) may eliminate the internal need to take risks, without spoiling the resulting adult. It is possible that entirely imaginary risks can be adequate, if made sufficiently spectacular. It is possible that the emotional need to accept risk cannot be eliminated, but can be sublimated by providing risks of painful and temporary disablement, without having to have any risk at all of death or permanent damage. Without knowing which if any of these is in fact possible, I cannot say what will be the occupations provided for teenagers, but we can perhaps have fair confidence that we *shall* know. We can then see to it that whatever facilities are provided, they will not involve simultaneous danger to children who have not yet reached the risk-requiring age, to men who have already passed it, or to girls whose desire for adventure usually requires less physical violence. Today, when the main opportunity is provided by high-performance cars and motor cycles or by various levels of gang misbehaviour, everyone is involved.

Very important, and with luck making more violent activities unnecessary, would be provision of the greatest possible variety of constructive occupations; not only for teenagers but for many adults who still desired active occupation after their short working week. Small theatres for dramatic societies, making their own dresses and scenery; local teams for everything from chess and .22 rifle shooting to breeding racing snails; model-building, painting or constructing operational cars or hovercraft; all could be provided for. It would not be necessary that these should all be within easy reach of everyone. Sometimes young people rather prefer the occupations which require them to go a long way from home into unfamiliar territory.

For adults, it would be of enormous importance to re-establish the idea of leisure to loaf and gossip as of value in itself, and its possession as a status symbol more important than material possessions. This view was normal in Europe in the eighteenth century, and is common in many parts of the world today. (This would even be useful now; if unions struck for more time off, instead of more pay, unemployment would rapidly vanish.)

A big potential advantage of the village-per-floor pattern of living which I have proposed, is that the inhabitants, and particularly the children, have a ready-made group with which to identify themselves; large enough for social variety, and small enough for every individual in it to know personally every other individual in it. We must surely have evolved our basic attitudes in just this situation for important periods. We are better than most animals at adapting ourselves to life in widely different conditions, but it seems likely that we could adapt more easily to the necessary novelties of condensed living, if we did not require ourselves to adopt to unneccessary ones.

Crime, always a good indicator of the number of people unadapted to the established forms of society, is well known from long experience to be rare in such 'village' conditions.

The high density of living described, will have made possible the overall concentration of the activities of something like eight million people, into a region of which any point could be reached from the centre within fifteen minutes. This means that as many jobs as can now be found in London, Birmingham, Glasgow and Manchester with Salford together, would be within a quarter of an hour's 'walk' from home. Very few would need to change their homes simply to change their jobs, so that there would be none of the external pressures to migrate which are now destroying the stability of our remaining village communities.

Remembering that during the next eighty years, if we continue to multiply as we are now doing, there will be about 100 times as many scientists in the world as have lived in the entire history of the planet up to the outbreak of the war in 1939, it would be unwise to discuss the kinds of jobs that we should be doing. It seems a safe bet that the proportion of office and design work would increase very greatly, as against direct factory production work, and that better communications would make more decentralization of large organizations possible. Indeed, it is not altogether clear that there will be so many large organizations. If we look at biological systems, we find that the enormous reliability of animal muscles and chemical units is obtained by using a large number of small and moderately reliable units in parallel, rather than by using a small number of very efficient units which never break down. As crude total output gets less important, and reliability gets more so, we may well go the same way.

At present we are building power stations, factories and almost everything else for the maximum possible efficiency. This leads to the construction of larger and larger units, and furthermore leads to the requirement that these should run as closely as possible to their maximum rated output, for the largest possible number of hours each year. Accordingly, if unexpected demands are made on them, or accidents reduce their efficiency, they have little capacity in reserve. Thus, as in the New York blackout, they break down, with catastrophic results.

Most biological systems are, in economic terms, very heavily over-capitalized, and run in routine conditions with a safety factor approaching ten. In routine conditions this is extremely wasteful but enormous unexpected overloads can be handled without trouble or fuss.

As the complexity of our social structure approaches that of a living organism, it would be profitable to follow the same pattern. We in the seventies pride ourselves on the (purely relative) cheapening of electricity consequent upon the replacement of vast numbers of little generating companies by a national grid. We should be horrified at the cost of bringing back again a lot of little units – by little I mean about the size of Calder Hall – and not even bringing back only the minimum number, but bringing back enough to have every house and every street supplied from two or more independent power stations. But it would not cost us more in fuel, and 'blackout' would become an archaic piece of jargon.

What We Shall Be Doing

It does not seem to me very likely that men – or women – will be replaced on any scale by computers. Rather, most jobs now done by people may be done by people – plus – computers. If we are aiming at reliability rather than efficiency, there will be plenty to do.

I have made it clear that a doubling of the population is incompatible with a continuing increase of dependence on private cars, and that the particular future I have described is entirely independent of such cars for its working life. If for their holidays, people liked to visit a different environment, they could still do this more conveniently and independently by private car than by any other means, but since extensive leisure would make the pressure high on all areas favoured for holidays, visits to these would certainly have to be controlled by price or permit. Most townspeople would therefore be likely to hire a car for the occasion, as part of a package deal, as so many do now when going abroad, rather than to keep one of their own outside the city.

Britain as it Could be in Eighty Years' Time

The condensation of much of the population into highly mechanized cities, manufacturing much of their own food, would not necessarily reduce the pressure on the countryside. Increased efficiency of living and of production would leave more leisure, longer holidays, and more money to spend on them. Although the year-round population of the sea-coast towns and country villages would fall, the summer population might increase. Even if the actual coast-line were firmly protected, a wide continuous belt of bungalows and caravan camps could be expected around the entire island just inside the coast. A network of motorways could bring tens of thousands of people to within ten miles of anywhere in the country. Their crowded workaday lives would leave the great majority quite uninterested in wild life, and happy to see easy motor access to every lake and mountain.

It would make no difference if a few people regretted the proliferation of car parks, and wished to have an occasional area left to walk in undisturbed by noise and crowds. Probably there would be such a tiny few that they would have no influence whatever on the great and little District Councils who wanted the income that the crowds would bring. But even if there were a few millions who wished to preserve the dwindling open spaces, and whose votes might have a marginal political value, their own rambling multitudes would destroy the solitudes they sought to save.

Some dwellers in the Lake District feel that the beauty of Lake Windermere has already been tarnished by commercial development. If we continue to multiply, we can expect that it will be transformed into a state compared with which a sunny August Sunday afternoon of 1972 would seem deserted. Giant carbon-whisker-reinforced spans could support a plastic roof over the entire lake, so that even Lake District rain could never interfere with the holiday makers. Artificial lighting, including longer wave ultraviolet which would tan without burning, could be operated round the clock, and half the hotels could be equipped with full black-out facilities, so that a night-shift could enable twice as many visitors to enjoy their country holiday.

Internal combustion engines would have to be forbidden, to prevent the build-up of fumes on the roofed-in lake, but the cheerful noise of outboard motors would need not be replaced by dispiriting silence. It would be easy to equip the thousands of electric motor boats with recordings of well known racing jets, and powerful speakers, so that the traditional happy holiday atmosphere could be maintained. Durable plastic kingcups, water lilies or flowering rushes could be changed according to the season. The lake could be warmed to a comfortable bathing temperature all year round by the nuclear power station required to supply the holiday town, the scenic railways round the slopes of Loughrigg Fell and Wansfell Pike, and the hotels and strip-tease clubs of the Lyth Valley.

The picture does not appeal to me, but people do not regret what they have never known. The main discontent to be expected would be raised by Highland Scots, outraged by the usual unfair discrimination which had grudged them the capital to provide as rich a transformation to Loch Tummel and Loch Rannoch, and forgetting the hundreds of millions sunk in underwater safaris to shoot the artificial monsters of Loch Ness.

These details may be, and probably are, entirely wrong, but the general effect cannot fail to be right. With 120 million prosperous inhabitants, there could be no part of these islands free of direct and major human interference. The interference might consist in total destruction of our present country scenes, or might take the form of their transformation into parks staffed with wardens to keep the public off the grass. In either case, I should not like it. But the 120 million would be warm, and well fed, in familiar company, and perfectly contented.

Five

Armageddon?

Some people may feel that I have been quite improperly optimistic in supposing that there will still be a Britain in eighty years' time, and that in any case we shall have been wiped out by a nuclear holocaust, long before our numbers call for any drastic changes in our way of life. I do not know how widely this view is actually held, and how widely it is merely stated as a convenient and all-embracing excuse for avoiding thought or action for the future. But since the idea comes up pretty frequently in discussion, I shall take it as a serious proposition, and digress somewhat from my main theme to discuss it. Readers who think it improbable, or who dislike arithmetic, should skip to Chapter 6.

The holocaust theory comes in three models; the exclusive, the popular and the large economy size. The first merely supposes that civilization will be wiped out, and that the human race will go back to a new savagery, peopled by monsters as described in Aldous Huxley's *Ape and Essence*. The second supposes that the whole of humanity will be wiped out, and hopes that the rats or the ants or the amoebas will start again and do better. The third supposes that all life on the planet will be wiped out, and that we start clean as from 3,000 million years ago. One or other of the models is so widely and so dogmatically stated, that it is worth while to explain in some detail why none of them is likely to be true. Like so many errors made by the intelligent and well-read innumerate, the ideas have nothing qualitatively wrong with them; the demonstration of their falsity depends upon doing some arithmetic, based on the known characteristics of nuclear weapons.

Fire and Blast

We start with the accepted fact that a single H-bomb, of the one-megaton size standard in American ICBMs, could easily kill five million people if let off at a suitable height a few kilometres above one of the world's big conurbations. The larger Soviet model, believed to be around five megatons, would kill rather less than twice as many, not because of lower efficiency, but because of the absence of sufficiently large and densely populated targets. It can however still kill the first five million, even when it is less accurately aimed. If, then, the whole population of the world were gathered into compact cities of five million each, of which there would now be about 750, the three thousand odd H-bombs now operationally available at short notice, would be more than adequate to dispatch them all. In fact people are not so concentrated. It would be technically easy to kill the 450 million people in towns over 100,000 inhabitants, but most of the bombs available would be needed for this, and after that it would get difficult. If we take the average of the Russian and American bombs, severe damage to reinforced concrete buildings would be expected to an average radius of about six kilometres, assuming the explosion to be at the best height to do long-range damage. In clear weather, exposed persons would suffer second-degree burns on unprotected skin up to a distance of twenty-five kilometres. People who happened to be behind trees or buildings would not be hurt by the flash.

Not everyone would be killed at the distances at which severe damage is done to reinforced concrete buildings, but on the other hand quite a lot would be killed at greater distances still. If, therefore, bombs were dropped simultaneously twelve kilometres apart, most people not below ground would be killed by the bursts. Each side is supposed at the moment to have 1,500-3,000 H-bomb rockets available, perhaps a quarter of which are deployed as ICBMs for immediate delivery, in addition to numbers of bombs for aircraft to deliver. If we suppose that on the outbreak of war each would have 5,000, but neglect the few hundreds in Britain, France and China, and suppose that every bomb bursts at the correct height and time on the intended target,

Armageddon?

we shall not underestimate the effect. The total area devastated would then be about 1.2 million square kilometres. The world's free land surface is about 100 million square kilometres. Even with a pact between Russian and American General Staffs not to interfere with each other's pattern bombing, therefore, direct blast could not even kill all the civilized humans in the world, let alone all life.

We must, of course, consider other ways of killing than blast. Heat flash must be expected to set alight everything inflammable within sight of the burst, to at least twice the distance of the severe blast effects, if the atmosphere is clear and free of low clouds. Anyone in a town of any size within such a distance, and not killed by the blast, therefore, would be likely to be burnt or suffocated in the ensuing fire storm. Very much larger bombs, exploded fifty kilometres up, could set things alight more efficiently still, and destroy vegetation over enormous areas, but would deliver no blast and no radiation to speak of, so although on a clear winter night they could be catastrophically effective, they would have no effect on regions covered by cloud, and would usually leave large areas untouched.

Direct radiation from H-bombs set off at the height to give maximum blast effect is, oddly enough, much less important than it was for the relatively tiny bombs used at Hiroshima and Nagasaki. Practically all of both neutrons and gamma rays will be absorbed by less than four kilometres of air, so that nobody surviving the blasts and fires would get any significant radiation dose directly from the explosion.

Long-Term Radiation

The radioactive isotopes produced must be taken more seriously. A bomb which burst high up would deliver essentially the whole of its radioactive yield into the upper atmosphere, via the 'familiar' mushroom cloud. An immediate rainstorm, derived from the warm wet air taken up with it, would bring some activity down at once but very locally; the greater part would drift downwards gradually over many years, until it reached the lower part of the atmosphere, when it would be washed to the ground with the rain. The greater part will therefore have had plenty of time to be distributed very uniformly over the globe, and the amount reaching the ground at any point will be closely dependent on the local rainfall.

As a result of the bomb tests over the last two decades, we have a direct experimental measure of the rate and amount of deposition from the 410 megatons of H-bombs exploded in the atmosphere up to the middle of the sixties. Over most of the world, the total resulting dose received by the population since the tests has added only about 20 per cent to the amount that it received in the same time from natural causes. In a few cases, particularly among rice-eaters in south-east Asia, the dose was up to ten times higher, owing to heavy rainfall during the growth of the rice.

The 10,000 bombs we have considered would liberate some 30,000 megatons of energy, or eighty times as much as has been liberated in the tests. These would therefore give most people some fifteen to twenty times the natural dose for a decade. This, however, is still little more than the dose legally permitted for the general public, from X-rays, effluent from nuclear power stations, and so on. The rather unexpected result is then that, although a number of people in south-east Asia might be made ill, almost nobody would be killed directly by the long-term fall-out.

Delayed deaths, due to leukaemia and similar conditions might amount to one person in 5,000. The number of undesirable recessive mutant genes that we carry already would be increased, and in a population of thousands of millions, would eventually result in tens of millions of extra deaths, or disastrous hereditary impairments. The increase in undesirable recessive genes would, however, be only 1.5 per cent of our present total load because, though radiation is the best known cause of mutations, it has caused only a small fraction, perhaps 5 per cent, of the total mutant genes we carry. Most of these mutant genes are for recessive characters, which are bred out by natural selection only very slowly. Nevertheless they do not accumulate forever, and the number which we carry has been shown by Haldane to be equivalent to the number which have affected our ancestors, over a period of the order of 3,000 years. To double the number of mutant genes we carry – which would multiply by four the

Armageddon?

number of children born with something disastrous the matter with them – would therefore require the sudden addition of perhaps twenty times the radiation dose that we have received from natural sources in the last 3,000 years. This would represent the long-term fall-out from something like a million bombs. The radiation effects from ten thousand would clearly be far less than would the effects of the blast. The relative mildness, however, is largely due to the fact that nearly all the most dangerous short-lived radioactive atoms would have decayed to harmlessness in the upper atmosphere, before they reached the ground.

Short-Term Radiation

If bombs burst directly on or even in the ground, or under water near shore, the blast and fire effects would be much less, but radiation would be much more serious. In this case the radio-active elements produced would be mixed with a million tons or so of soil or water, and, though thrown high into the air, would fall back to the ground again over a considerable area within a few hours of the burst, when the level of radioactivity was still fantastically high. The shape of the area affected would depend on the strength of the wind, and might represent anything from a circle round the burst, to a long narrow ellipse extending over 200 kilometres or more. From detailed measurements on the distribution and amounts of fall-out, from the Bikini test explosion in 1954, we know that within an area of some 5,000-10,000 square kilometres the total radiation dose in the first four days from a Russian-sized bomb, might reach the short-term median lethal dose for unprotected persons. (The median lethal dose is that dose which will kill half of the people who receive it, assuming them to be untreated. It is usually taken as 400 rem.) Treatment has only a very limited effect and twice this dose would kill essentially everyone. A short-term dose is merely one which is received within a few hours; much larger total doses can be taken without being killed, if they are spread over weeks or months. We do not know how much larger, the median lethal dose would be if spread over four days, since for obvious reasons no human beings have been kept in such highly radioactive regions for anything like this time. Some rat experiments suggest that we might be able to stand four times as much. We shall not, however, make any allowance for this, since the proper factor is unknown.

In a well-built house, and especially in the basement of a big building, people would receive ten or more times less than in the open, and the lethal dose would be attained over an area of unpredictable shape, but not much greater than the area destroyed by blast from a bomb bursting at the optimum height. A small degree of extra protection can be given by various chemical substances, of which the best known, though not the most effective, is alcohol. A small gain in life expectancy might therefore be added to the other obvious advantages of remaining dead drunk for the first four days of a nuclear war.

The total area coverable by the possible number of bombs with a radioactive dose lethal to people (or most animals) in the open would then, allowing for the effects of overlap, be 100-350 million square kilometres, equal to or more than the habitable land area of the world. It would destroy many of the world's forest trees, some of which can stand less radiation even than we can, but, even in the most heavily irradiated areas, not all vegetation. Some plants are much more resistant than human beings; for example, the common groundsel can survive several thousands of rem. per day, for weeks on end. The damage to plant life would not be permanent, as seeds will stand a great deal more than adult plants, and would generally survive – although with a proportion of mutations, mostly nonviable. Most of the unprotected birds and mammals would be killed as easily as we would, but few insects, which are much more resistant, would be affected at all. A large proportion of species would, however, be exterminated by destruction of their habitats or of their food supply.

There is one real remaining long-term hazard to be considered, and one popular but imaginary one. I will deal with the imaginary one first; this is the cobalt bomb. There are indeed plenty of cobalt bombs in existence; they are the pieces of radiocobalt in bomb-shaped lumps of lead which are used by hospitals to treat cancer. They do not explode. If an H-bomb were sheathed in a ton of cobalt, this would certainly be made radioactive, but the ton of uranium, which is at present used in the current 'dirty' bomb, is made about a hundred times more radioactive still, in the first critical four weeks after the explosion, and can contribute up to ten megatons equivalent to the blast, while the cobalt contributes nothing. We can take it that no military force will be so humane as to use cobalt where uranium would do.

The real hazard would be carbon-14. I suggested that mutations would be unimportant, in discussing long-term fallout, with the bombs likely soon to be available. With ten times this number, the accumulated dose from the shorter-lived materials – most of them bone seekers and not attracted to the genital system – would still not be disastrous. But for several decades the carbon-14 content of the biosphere would be over 200 times its present level, and carbon-14 would be incorporated in the DNA molecules that form the basis of heredity. Then diseases like haemophilia, genes for which now arise perhaps once in 50,000 babies, might occur once in 4,000, if we suppose that the 5 per cent of our mutations which are now radiation-induced are all due to carbon-14, and we might find for some generations that 5-20 per cent of children had something disastrous the matter with them.

We can now consider which of the prospective types of holocaust, favoured by the various schools of thought, is most likely to occur.

Survival of Plant and Animal Life

First then, the suggestion that all life on the planet might cease is certainly untrue. The vegetable and insect world would continue, superficially almost unchanged, though probably with a burst of evolutionary change resulting more from changing habitats, due to the loss of many species of birds and mammals and a few species of plants, rather than to the sudden accession of 10,000-50,000 normal years' worth of extra mutations in a few months. Fifty thousand years of normal evolution produces few striking changes, and even in these conditions the numbers without significant mutations would be far larger than the numbers with. For every species, the survivors from a radiation dose killing

50 per cent show a large majority apparently normal and certainly viable.

Survival of Human Life

The destruction of the whole human race is less obviously impossible, since, as we have seen, the habitable land area of the globe could in principle be rendered lethal for unprotected people, with the number of bombs which may be available now or in a very few years, and which it would be quite possible (technically; not necessarily economically, and one hopes not politically), to multiply by ten in another fifty years.

The greatest imponderable is the possible inefficiency of delivery systems, and the precise amount of confusion among the higher commands as to what exactly had already been achieved, and what yet remained to be done.

Since even a rather improbable means of destroying the whole human race is a matter of concern, we will assume that the planning and delivery systems are alike perfect, and that no defensive systems have any effect whatsoever. This is exactly equivalent to supposing that the computer operators on each side, seeing the enormous and needless inefficiency of lobbing their bombs half across the world into inadequately known conditions, sensibly make a pact each to organize the destruction of its own side. Each country would be given its appropriate quota of H-bombs and its own computer would determine exactly where, and at what height or depth, they should be let off for the greatest possible effect. All undestroyed gaps left in the pattern by aircraft getting lost, rockets failing to work, or explosions taking place at the wrong height, would thus be eliminated. With the number of bombs that I have assumed, I do not see how even this could possibly kill everybody – unless every last individual on the planet willingly co-operated in getting killed. In this case a free issue of cyanide tablets would be just as effective, and much less trouble.

In no place can the distribution of wind currents be exactly known, and if they were, they would be seriously disturbed by the bombs themselves, so that some of the fall-out patterns would overlap more than necessary, and others not enough. Even if the fall-out distribution was exactly as planned, hardly anyone would be out in the open after the first flash. There would be from some minutes to an hour or so to get under cover after the flash before the fallout began to come down, and over most of the area the dose inside a solidly built house might not be more than a tenth of the lethal dose. In a good cellar it would be less still, and in a nice deep cave it would be negligible.

We can take it, therefore, that all the bombs likely to be available in the next few years, perfectly placed, would leave a large number of people alive, although quite a few would not be well, and hardly any would be happy. There would be no animal competition except from dogs and cats, but doubtless plenty of rats and mice, if not rabbits, would be available to eke out an adequate, if uninspiring, protein diet of worms, snails and insects.

Ten times the number of bombs now available would be more serious, but even here, I do not see how the most perfect computer placing could kill everyone. As has been stated, there will be an hour or more in many places between seeing the flash and the arrival of the main fall-out, leaving time for a lot of people to get into caves, and down mines, with a few weeks' food supply, and since after only a week it would be quite safe for unprotected individuals to take turns, every day or so, to spend an hour or two on the surface collecting supplies – and tinned goods or bottled drinks would be perfectly safe and untainted – it is certain that many would come through. People in ships at sea would suffer little from radiation, so long as they wore complete overalls while washing down the decks from land-based dust. Activity falling in the sea could eventually kill a lot of fish but the smaller organisms would be little affected.

The effects of carbon-14 would plague the survivors for a long time. A well-organized technical civilization would not be bothered. It could use tank-grown algae, fed with carbon dioxide derived from uncontaminated limestone, as the basic food for man and beast. Survivors from nuclear war would probably be unable to do this, and, following the use of 100,000 bombs, many would lose up to 20 per cent of their children from disastrous mutations. The human race has, however, frequently survived periods when only two or three children in ten could expect to live.

So long as people did not fuss about minor changes, such as unusual numbers of fingers or unconventional distributions of hair, neither of which would have the faintest correlation with the basic human qualities of intelligence and compassion, we could expect to survive again.

We can see, therefore, that there is no chance of the whole human race being killed off in a nuclear war for some decades, or even in a less probable future war with ten times the number of bombs which are available in the seventies.

Some people seem to be much disappointed by this conclusion. I can perhaps console them by pointing out that there will surely come a time, if our technical skill continues to increase, when we *could* kill off the whole human race. Of course our technical skill in preventing or escaping the universal death may also improve, and it is not at all obvious that we shall ever be able to do so without a great deal of consumer carelessness, if not consumer co-operation.

Survival of Civilization?

From the above discussion it must be clear that, though a lot of people would survive the worst that we know how to do, they would hardly be in a position to maintain a civilization even remotely resembling our own. They would be unlikely to build nuclear weapons, but in the highly probable absence of any large predators, they might well rebuild civilization by intertribal competition as did *Australopithecus* and *Homo erectus*, and could be awfully handy with clubs and spears. (It may be remembered that Einstein was once asked what weapons would actually be used in a third world war. He said he didn't know, but he knew what would be used in the fourth world war: clubs.) Starting at a more intelligent level than *Australopithecus*, we should probably get back to civilization a good deal more quickly, although we should be hampered by our already having used up the easily available ores of most metals. Our average intelligence would presumably improve further in the process, though

Armageddon?

whether this would save us from repeating a nuclear holocaust, or whether we should merely reach it sooner, I do not know.

I would reiterate that this represents the worst possible case; when we consider what is even faintly probable, rather than what is technically possible, it seems to me highly unlikely that our technically based civilization would be altogether destroyed. The only important numbers of weapons are, and are likely to stay, in the hands of USA, the Soviet Union and China. The few that Britain and France possess, and the few that the third-round countries may yet possess, are less in total than the uncertainty that the Russians must have about American stocks or that the Americans have about the Russian stocks. They will not therefore affect materially the calculations of the major powers, and the minor powers are rather unlikely to start anything important, to anyone but themselves, on their own. Now in real life, most of the Russian and American H-bomb rockets are not intended for a pest-spraying operation to kill as many people as possible, but are aimed at the other side's air and rocket bases, usually in more or less deserted areas. Presumably, some at least would succeed in this preventive operation, and therefore some areas scheduled for destruction, on each side, would not in fact get destroyed. Satellites would doubtless report this, but would be most unreliably listened to by their highly stressed owners. Again, the anti-ballistic-missile system, though designed to protect rocket bases rather than people, would in practice sometimes destroy the wrong weapons, and protect occasional towns by mistake.

Many rockets and planes would go astray, and waste their bombs in evaporating a lot of people who were already very convincingly dead, and, while any follow-up weapons remained on either side, they would be likely to be directed at points on the other side which were suspected still to have some such operational weapons. It is really very difficult to believe that, while the US was still firing H-weapons, the Russians would waste ammunition on, say, India or Borneo or even New Zealand – apart from a few ports which might be suspected of acting as supply bases for nuclear submarines. Similarly, the USA would be likely to use its weapons against China and Russia, and Russian-occupied Eastern Europe, while either Russia or China was still shooting, and would be unlikely to destroy the Congo or Tanzania, or even all of Europe.

So though civilizations in the northern hemisphere would probably be disrupted to the point of destruction, it seems to me almost incredibly unlikely that all of the towns of the southern hemisphere would be even seriously injured, let alone destroyed. Much knowledge would be lost, but there is a vital and specific characteristic that differentiates our civilization from all preceding ones that have ever existed. We have learnt how to find out what we don't know. The knowledge only that something has once been known, ensures that with money and time it can be known again. The distraught and demoralized survivors in Europe and North America, and Asia north of the Himalayas, might well, even if numerous, be unable to do much. At first, they would probably try to reconstruct, since after all previous wars it has been possible, within the lives of the generation that wreaked the destruction, to reconstruct far more than was lost. After an H-bomb war, it would soon be quite obvious that this was impossible, and they would build something else instead, with no necessary connection with what had gone before – except that in China and Russia it would not be called Communism, and in the USA it would not be called capitalism or democracy. However, if they gave up and relapsed into savagery, as is entirely possible, they would no doubt be recivilized again in a few generations, by expeditions from Ceylon or Patagonia.

I know that I am again much blamed by many for presenting this optimistic picture, but it appears to be a great deal more realistic than the expectation that the whole of civilization would be destroyed, technically conceivable though this may be.

The possibility that chemical or bacteriological warfare could be used instead can be quickly dismissed. There are *no* chemicals so poisonous as the short-lived radioactives produced in atomic explosions, and as we have seen, these are defeated by the problems of distribution.

Biological weapons cannot be tested in operational conditions except in war itself, and almost nothing tried on a large scale works as expected first time. Nobody will be very keen to try, with the risk of failing and stimulating the other side to try, and perhaps to succeed. Secondly, bacteria and viruses are horribly dangerous to the side using them. Doubtless, before use, the side

Armageddon?

using them will have inoculated with a reliable vaccine all of its population likely to be important to the war effort, but as we have seen, micro-organisms mutate. In killing a million of the enemy vast numbers of mutations will occur, against some of which the vaccines may be ineffective, and these may return to attack their distributors. Diseases will never do a really thorough job, because as the population attacked becomes rare, the milder strains will be selected for as we saw in Chapter Two. Finally, we have in fifty years defeated all the diseases, that we have thought worth defeating, that Nature has invented in the last ten or a hundred thousand years. It is likely, therefore, that we should defeat any new ones that we have invented ourselves. Again, this situation may not last for ever, but for the foreseeable future neither the destruction of humanity, nor the destruction of civilization, is going to happen, and any problems to which such destruction might represent a permanent or temporary solution will have to be resolved in other ways.

I have spent a lot of time discussing the possible effects of a nuclear war that I think is rather unlikely to happen at all, but it is always very difficult really to concentrate on the solution of an awkward problem, when there is even a slight chance that the problem won't exist. Our rising population presents such a problem, and while this might be modified by war, it would be postponed rather than removed. Furthermore, if there is to be a major war, it matters very little what we do while we wait for it. For the rest of this book, I shall concentrate on the risk that there will *not* be a major war, and discuss what we can do about that.

Six

Providing for the Multitudes

I expect myself that in eighty years' time the world's population will reach a peak, and that after that it will fall for some time with a consequent easing of pressures of many kinds. If this does happen, however, it will certainly not do so because we have run into a new and unforeseen natural limit, but will be the result of conscious choices and action on an international scale.

It may be that this is optimistic, and that no intentional choice or organized action will occur. Other things being equal, one must expect that religious or other groups, which oppose effective artificial methods of limiting births, will leave more offspring than the groups which approve such limitation. Certainly, if children regularly follow their parents in this respect, and conversions do not occur, the birth-limiting part of the population would have become an insignificant pool in the ocean of the others in a few generations. Again, I think myself that conversions will occur on an adequate scale, but I might be wrong.

In a previous chapter I discussed a possible course which might be taken by Britain, if present family patterns persist, with a steady decrease of those who are reproducing at a rate below the present average, and a steady increase of those who are reproducing at a rate above the average.

If we make the same assumption about the rest of the world, most of which is multiplying faster than we are, in eighty years' time Britain will no longer be far ahead in population density, but will be close to the world average. From this point on, therefore, I shall consider the world as a whole. This has the advantage that movements of people from one country to another do not need to be considered. The total world population in eighty years' time would have reached about 20,000 millions, and its

Providing for the Multitudes

average rate of multiplication might itself have increased considerably. It is difficult, however, to estimate by how much this rate would have increased, so we shall work on the assumption that the rate of increase remains at its present rate of 2 per cent per year, giving a doubling time of thirty-five years. An increased rate would change the situations described below only by making them happen a little sooner, which is of slight importance.

The Limits of Agriculture

I shall suppose that the new techniques of food-production, mentioned in Chapter Four, would have spread throughout the world. Wishing to be conservative in my assumptions, I shall suppose that the production of carbohydrates and fats from plants grown in the open will remain cheaper than their chemical synthesis from carbon dioxide and water. Carbohydrates and fats form the main bulk of our food and are the most suitable bulk raw materials for factory protein production. Intensive agriculture, using only very moderate improvements on current practice, would still be able to supply the necessary carbohydrates, but there would be serious competition for land between cities and roads on the one hand and agriculture on the other. Concentration of the people into giant multistorey cities would free a lot of land, and expenditure of money on the scale now reserved for armaments could bring into use a great deal of land in tropical areas, which is so poor in nutrients and so unstable in structure as to be unusable today. Another doubling of population might be possible, and perhaps even two doublings, giving a world population of 80,000 million, if useful amounts of supplementary carbohydrates could be obtained from the sea. The denser areas would however have either to limit very seriously the number and width of roads, and hence the number of people allowed to use them, or would have to put all the roads underground to leave the surface for plants.

Liberty and the Prevention of Crime

Limitation of travel would be a rather minor part of the interference with individual freedom that would be needful. Some kinds of freedom would have increased; one could expect a hundred television channels for every one we have now, and the range of materials for the plastic arts, or of instruments for the musicians, would have increased at least as much. Someone from our era visiting the period, however, would be more liable to notice the limitations.

Orwell in his *1984*, and many less able writers of science fiction, have visualized a world coming more and more under the domination of dictatorships. This is possible but not very likely. Dictatorships, whether of Hitlers, or of white minorities, or of the proletariat, are born of scarcity or fear of scarcity, and a minority's desire for a larger share of limited resources than they could get without rigid political discrimination in their own favour. When technology is rich enough to give everyone a house, and a car, and a boat to be seasick in, and holidays abroad, it is difficult to see how anyone could achieve the initial mass support to gain for himself and his associates more of the same things platinum-plated. But if people are crowded close enough together, the number of things they can do without getting in each others' way will inevitably get less. The most equalitarian democracy is as certain as any dictator to stop children riding along crowded streets on bicycles, or to forbid people to have pets in flats, or to cross the street when they want to, or to connect up their own gas cookers.

A point which does not seem to have been noted by anyone, is the increase in non-political crimes that would be likely to occur, if adequate means of prevention were not set up. A criminal is essentially someone who has been unable to adapt to the society in which he or she is brought up. Our evolution has left us well adapted to co-operation with a small in-group which is individually known to us, and ill adapted to living entirely alone. The worst criminals usually have at least a girlfriend, or a small gang, with whom they can feel safe. But the adaptation to a much larger group has had far too short a time to establish the desirable behaviour instinctively, and the social conditioning of childhood does not always 'take'.

Men form a very large majority of serious criminals at present, being on the whole less adaptable than women, and having evolved to compete for status and to display discontent more aggressively. As suggested in Chapter Four, a change in ways of living might reduce the proportion ill adapted to society, but as people become ever more crowded, the misfits might again increase and be less easy to cure. As the permitted forms of behaviour become necessarily more and more closely defined, the attraction of forbidden actions would, for such misfits, increase. The objectives of thieves might be licences to travel or to go to football matches, rather than cash, and fiddling computers to deliver leisure-permits might be commoner than burglary, but almost any society must give some rewards to be earned by effort, that somebody would like to get without making the effort. The important, and I think novel, point which I want to stress, however, is that as the number of potential victims of confidence tricks or violence increases, it will produce a *greater* increase in number of criminals. If we stop looking at the individual criminal, and consider instead the role of criminals as a group in society, we can see a very close analogy between them and parasites of other kinds on animal hosts. We saw in Chapter Two that for any particular host-parasite relation there was a possible situation in which the numbers of each remained constant, but that a succession of major oscillations was more likely. A rise in the number of the hosts would at first leave the number of parasites behind, but the numbers of the latter, with a richer supply of victims, would then increase by a much larger factor than had the hosts.

We have direct experimental evidence for the relevance of this. In the table below is shown the variation in the numbers of

TABLE 2

Increase in crime rate with increase in size of town.
Urban crime rates per 100,000 population, 1968.

Type of crime	Size of cities		
	Over 250,000	50,000-100,000	Under 10,000
Total violent crime	779	224	113
Murder	20	8	4
Forcible rape	32	12	6
Robbery	433	88	18
Aggravated assault	294	116	85

From *Statistical Abstracts of the United States*, 1970.

serious crimes per hundred thousand persons in towns of various sizes in the United States.

It was said some time ago that there was a mug born every minute. With 80,000 million people in the world, there would be a sucker born every second. Even to avoid increasing our present proportion of parasites, it would be essential to have a considerably more effective procedure than we have now for catching and dissuading them. Deterrence would be better still, but is already very difficult. In the past it has been run on the same statistical basis as a lottery, in which there is only a small chance of getting a prize at all, but if you do get a prize you get a big one. Successful lotteries can also be run on the opposite lines, as at children's parties; the prizes are very small, but nearly everybody gets one.

In deterrent terms, in the good old days, you almost always got away with your crime if you had any skill at all, but if you *did* happen to be caught, you were flayed alive in public to discourage others. In 1972 we catch a higher proportion of people, so we do not need to flay them in public; most people are adequately deterred by a moderate chance of spending a year in jail or by a large chance of having to pay quite a small fine. This has a lot of advantages, whether under a democracy or a dictatorship, but to extend the process further, even if highly desirable, would get more and more difficult as the population grew. Our evolutionary background would make it easy to develop intermediate misfits, who behaved well in their own villages, but who regarded distant strangers as fair game. A city with fast moving ways, and fifty million people, would represent a totally impossible environment for a police organized only as they now are, and with their present information services. Any well organized villains prepared to wreck local lighting units, or the moving ways themselves, or to throw something painful and disabling in the way of gas bombs, could do almost anything they wished. They could mix themselves back into the crowds ten storeys up and a hundred blocks away within minutes, and would need no recognizable car confined to a few busy streets. The only answer I can see, is to maintain far closer checks on every single individual than would be either possible or tolerated today.

By 150 years from now, every big city would take for granted

Providing for the Multitudes

the need for computer control of all the city services, and these would certainly have to include the security services and the police.

Forty years ago, computers did not exist. Now we can already build computers capable of storing, and producing within seconds on demand, a small dossier giving the health record of every single individual in the United States. Such computer-controlled dossiers have not in fact been set up, because of the fear that they would infringe personal freedom. The exact personal freedoms which they would infringe are not usually specified, although some of those which are in mind are fairly easy to guess. A general distrust of Government, and a fear that it might extend the dossier to facts unconcerned with health, probably has much influence, and it is unlikely that such computers will be installed for some time.

Freedom however is a relative thing; people are prepared to accept quite a bit of inconvenience to be free of widespread crime, and there must certainly exist a critical level of illegal violence, above which control by computers would seem a lesser evil.

In 150 years' time there should be no technical problem in having a computer system capable not merely of storing dossiers, but of keeping a continuous and exact record of the whereabouts of every single individual from the cradle to the grave. After any crime therefore, a 'playback' of everyone who had been close to the scene, over any desired period, could be obtained, and a check made of their current positions and possessions. The very reliable apprehension of criminals by this system would mean that penalties would not have to be large. They might well consist of depriving the culprits of equipment or opportunity to commit the same crime again, with as little interference as possible with their normal permissible activities.

Whether everyone had his or her own characteristic pattern of metal strips permanently grafted under the skin to be registered by wired circuits in the houses and roads; whether some kind of personal transmitter was involved, or whether some more subtle recognition system was used, there would be no technical difficulty, once the idea was politically acceptable.

An important feature is that there would not be one enormous computer in the basement doing the whole job, and vulnerable to carefully planned attack. In line with my expectations that service industries are likely to be set up from large numbers of smaller ones working in parallel, to avoid risk of failure, I would similarly expect the task of supervising people to be carried out by very large numbers of 'small' computers. These would have extensively overlapping 'nervous systems' for data collection and intercommunication, and would be of the type already existing in simple form, which can learn within a pre-determined range without detailed specific programming. If each were also able to control the mechanical extension of its own detection networks, and its units for communicating with other computers, all the information about every citizen could be stored in a large number of independent 'memories' and there would be no human being, or even computer, which could tell just which of these memories had the records of any particular person. Such a system would be invulnerable even to a major bombing attack by saboteurs, just as our memories and mental functions are insignificantly damaged by the surgical removal of any one cubic millimetre of tissue from the relevant region of our brains.

Production and distribution of food and power would also come under the control of the computer complex, so that the vast majority of people would be unconcerned with the practical business of living, just as were the aristocracy or the rich of last century, with their big houses and armies of servants. What people *would* be doing, I can guess even less than I could for Britain eighty years ahead, but history suggests that failing anything more active, the least functional of human beings quickly adapt themselves without difficulty, and manage to spend their whole time in growing their fingernails, arranging their hair, just gossiping or in other equally non-productive activities; together with as much sexual activity as social customs or physical stamina permit, without serious neurotic disorders.

It is likely that the switch from dependence on plants grown in the open to factory-produced bulk foods will take place long before it is essential, simply because it will become cheaper. It is, however, interesting that we can give a rather well defined answer to the question 'At what population level *will* it be essential to do so?'

Food from Oceanic Algae

Different plant species differ a great deal in their efficiency in producing material edible by us. Evergreen conifers are quite good at using sunlight efficiently, but hardly any of their yield of organic material can be processed by human digestive systems. Unicellular plants of the marine plankton (the drifting plants and small animals of the open sea) are better, in that they do not waste effort in growing wood or roots, or in producing inedible oils to protect themselves from freezing, but at present we eat only food derived from them very indirectly, after a series of steps up a complex food chain. The primary plants (typical examples are algae such as diatoms) use the energy of sunshine to produce food compounds, from carbon dioxide and water and a few mineral salts. Before reaching us, these will usually be 'eaten' by minute herbivores; these in turn are eaten by rather larger plankton carnivores, including the larvae of a great many fish and crustaceans, and these are eaten by adult squids or fish. There may easily be a further stage of larger fish still before they are large enough to be caught and eaten by us. It is well known that in general the efficiency of each successive stage is only about 10 per cent; i.e. a ton of algae will be needed to produce 100 kilogrammes of herbivores which produce ten kilogrammes of small plankton carnivores, a kilogramme of larger ones, and these finally provide 100 grammes or less of fish.

If we wanted to get the maximum yield of edible material from the ocean, and were prepared – as we already are – to supplement our diet with factory-produced protein, we could certainly not tolerate this enormous loss. The maximum yield for human beings could be obtained only by wiping out the whole complex of wild life, excepting only the primary plants, and harvesting these direct. The same principles apply to land-based plants. The inedible woody or other parts of these could be used for the protein factories – with a small diversion to goats for the luxury market. A goat keeps a very effective orchestra of micro-organisms inside itself, to help it make goat out of the most improbable raw materials. Even if goat meat were not still to be regarded as a luxury, it might well remain a status symbol, when essentially all other edible vertebrates had gone.

In such a simplified world, we can calculate quite closely the limiting amount of food substances which can be made, if the whole of the sunlight falling on the entire planet were utilized for this purpose. Photosynthetic organisms – i.e. plants – use only certain ranges of wavelength of visible light and it has been shown by A. A. Niciporovic that the maximum possible efficiency of any such organisms using sunlight is about 8 per cent. A minimum daily diet for adult human beings is said to require eight million joules (or 2,000 'calories'). Hence one human being will need to use all the food produced by plants from 100 million joules of solar radiation. The sun provides about 1.4 kilowatts per square metre at the top of atmosphere when directly overhead. A lot of this is absorbed in the atmosphere and reflected by clouds, and the sun is exactly overhead only at one point on the earth's surface at a time, so that to provide 100 million joules per day will on the average require about ten square metres of earth's surface. Much of the light will necessarily be lost by absorption or otherwise outside the plants, and harvesting, processing, and distribution to consumers will all involve losses.

Some of the plant material will also be needed as raw material for plastics, special fuels and so forth, so that the actual area needed to support one person would be nearer 100 square metres. This would mean that the world could feed some five million million people, on a level rather above the minimum, since we have calculated quantities on the basis of a population composed entirely of adults, and the smaller children will need a good deal less. At the present rate of multiplication this number would be reached in the year 2335, 363 years from now.

To achieve this maximum yield would involve a lot of co-operation, and some major changes in way of life. It would be necessary for nearly the entire unfrozen surface of the planet to be available for photosynthesis, and for every one of the two million species of plant and animal which now share the planet with us to be destroyed,* apart from the few heavily modified unicellular plants and other micro-organisms which would have

---

* Of course a reserve of specimens of potentially useful species could be kept, possibly as frozen germ plasm, or in a dormant state so that no food was required.

Providing for the Multitudes

replaced domestic animals and grain as our staple source of food. It would also be essential that the unicellular plants should have the optimum conditions for growth, both in temperature and in the supply of nutrients such as carbonates, nitrates, and mineral salts.

There is no risk that we should run out of these, or any other vital element, before we reached this point. It would not matter in what chemical form the necessary elements were found. The chemical compounds which plants require are all simple, and even now we could make any of them from the necessary elements, in whatever form these were presented. We can indeed, now make the elements themselves in a nuclear reactor, but the process is exceedingly expensive in energy. Fortunately this would not be necessary with a very much greater population than five million million.

For this number, more than enough of everything except phosphorus is available in the oceans and the atmosphere. Phosphate rock is now available in large quantities, but whether the several thousands of millions of tons required would still be available in the form of rich ores in 363 years' time, or whether we shall have used it up, I cannot of course say. If the phosphate from excreta were used for the algae, and that from cremation of bodies were used – perhaps indirectly – in the synthesis of soft drinks, the additional material required each year from mineral sources would be under a thousand million tons. If the concentrated ores have been used up, this is the amount to be found dispersed in the top millimetre of the rocks of the earth's crust. So some pretty superficial mining and some rather good chemistry is all that would be required.

Ways of Life

We can now turn our attention to the ways in which living conditions could be established in which human beings could survive to eat the food provided. The average density of the world population would still be lower than that within the big cities mentioned in Chapter Four, and so conditions for living and working in multistorey structures would not have needed to change too much over the intervening 280 years. Whether our actual occupations would be even remotely similar I have no way of telling, or whether they would include anything at all that could possibly be described as 'work'. All I can say is that changes, if changes there were, would not have been dictated by the environment. By this time the psychological disorientation produced by rapid change should surely have been recognized, and we should certainly be rich enough in all material things to keep changes as slow as we wished. It is quite possible, therefore, that the change in social organization would actually be less in the 280 years which are supposed to have gone by since Chapter Four than it would have been in the eighty years separating Chapter Four from the present day.

One occupation likely still to be flourishing would be the writing of books – or their equivalent – on population. The sums which I have done approximately here would have been done with great accuracy, and the fact that we should have to change our way of life considerably within a further generation due to shortage of sunlight would be likely to form a rather major theme. Naturally the prophets of doom would be having a field day, and would be foretelling the imminent destruction of the human race with more emphasis and confidence than they had ever shown before. They would not be listened to of course; partly because they would still be wrong, but mostly because there would have been similar forecasts every year or so for over 400 years and the people hearing them would be immune. If they were susceptible to any such warnings, the highly improbable situation described could never have arisen. If it does arise, the world will be peopled only by those who have evolved a religion or code of behaviour over the 400 years, which allows or requires them to continue present patterns of reproduction regardless of warnings. The boy who cried 'Wolf! Wolf!' did not have to go on doing so for 400 years to stop people listening to him.

A notable novelty would be the elimination of any serious travelling for the enormous majority of the population. An area as large as Britain would contain about twice the present population of the world. With no surface travel permitted, it would be difficult to move a million a day (which would be required

Providing for the Multitudes

to give everyone a trip once in twenty years) even across the Channel and back. Furthermore, the uniformity of big cities everywhere, determined by the environmental requirements, would much reduce the interest in travelling.

A number of aircraft comparable with or even more than our present numbers would be acceptable (so long as they did not produce contrails which would reduce the sunlight reaching the ground). They could not have surface airfields, but if they took off from holes or under-surface ramps, terminating in big archways pointing towards the poles, they would not need to reduce the sunlit area of surface at all except in the tropics, which could afford the relatively small loss of area when the nearly vertical sun was shining a little way down the ramp. Such aircraft, however, would be carrying specialized equipment and engineers, rather than business men or people attending conferences. Communication would certainly have improved to the point of making unlimited conferences possible between people whose bodies stayed in their homes or offices. There would doubtless also be a large absolute number of holidaymakers, but these would be very highly privileged and a tiny proportion of the whole.

Cities Under the Sea

Some interest in travel could be restored, and a number of other problems solved, if we abandon the assumption that most people would live on land. In particular, we could solve the major logistical problem of getting to the consumers the 3,000 million tons of food produced each day in the surface waters of the Atlantic and Pacific oceans, and of returning and distributing the sewage and other nutrients required by these vast areas. Big multistorey towns spread over the oceans of the world could bring the consumers to the food instead of the food to the consumers. These towns would not, of course, float on the surface, since this would all be required for growing algae on which the cities fed; they would float with their 'roofs' some fifteen metres down. Assuming only fifteen inhabited storeys to avoid excessive external pressure differences, the 'groundfloor' of the living space would be about sixty metres below the ocean surface. Power would be derived from nuclear power stations hanging below the city. An extensive cooling network, rather than a heating system, would be needed inside the city, since the total heat produced by people and equipment would be more than would be required to balance loss from the surfaces, and to maintain acceptable living temperatures. The underwater cities would be large enough and heavy enough to be as stable as dry land, and could be joined by vast flexible tubes to the surrounding cities for transport of goods and people. For larger distances, electric or nuclear-powered submarines could operate below the city zone, and, using inertial guidance, could carry a much larger number of people than aircraft do at present. Although slower than aircraft, they could be of unlimited size, and with multiple automatic pilots using echolocating equipment, could safely pass far more closely to each other than can aeroplanes now. Submarines have the same advantage as airships, in that they can stop without falling down, and there could be a very large number of docking points all round each city.

Each city, of perhaps twenty kilometres diameter and containing twenty to forty million people, would have room 'indoors' for plenty of open space for sports, and could afford to permit skindivers to disport themselves freely both above and below the city so long as they did not spend too much time on the surface, interrupting the sunlight, during the brighter parts of the day. Severe agoraphobia, resulting from the sight of unlimited space in any direction, would probably prevent anyone from even wanting to spend any time on the surface, apart from a few of the hardy masochistic types who now spend their time rock climbing. Floodlit artificial scenery below the city, however, could be made attractive to everyone for every degree of adventurousness displayed by the citizens – probably, on our scale, the entire range from very slight to none at all. Artificial fish could be built and programmed for any speed, capacity for evasiveness, or even aggressiveness, and could be used, remotely controlled, for an interesting variety of war games or even for three dimensional team games of the general nature of polo.

Private cars or aircraft could obviously no longer exist on land, but the extra dimension in the sea would make the use of electrically driven private submarines, capable of reaching the

Providing for the Multitudes

bottom of most oceans, entirely possible. Collisions could be practically eliminated by a few simple rules, rigidly kept. These would be no more than a systematic extension of the present rules for aircraft, which lay down well defined flight paths on main routes, together with controlled approach lanes and stacking heights near airports. In the city zone or in the zones for commercial traffic, all vessels would be controlled by autopilots or echolocation, and in all but the bottom zones where the topography would make it impracticable, the depth – easily measured by a pressure gauge – would determine the direction of motion. With a continuous variation, one degree of change of direction corresponding to one metre increase of depth, vessels moving in opposite directions would then be 180 metres apart in depth. A turn to the right would involve a helical downward turn, one degree per metre of fall, and 'landing' would require a similar rising turn to the left to reach the uppermost travel zone in the correct direction, before peeling off into the slow automatically controlled rising-to-dock zone below each city.

The main structure and the inner bracing of the city would have to be pretty massive to stand the pressure outside, but this would be unimportant – it would have to be massive in any case to float in equilibrium with no tendency either to rise to the surface or sink to the bottom. There would be no real need for cities to be anchored at all, since pumps could continually maintain the buoyancy and hence the depth, while inertial guidance equipment could ensure that they remained over the same spot. Alternatively, they could be made capable of migration, to follow the sun away from the poles in winter and towards them in summer. It would, however, save a lot of more sophisticated equipment to make them normally too buoyant by a very small fraction – say ten million tons excess displacement – and to use correspondingly heavy anchors to maintain their positions, perhaps with pressure-controlled winches to allow them to rise and fall with the tides.

An entire city would live very much as an oyster or barnacle does now, filtering micro-organisms from the sea for food, and discharging waste products back in return. Like the oyster, it would have machinery for keeping a steady flow of water past the filter inlets, perhaps discharging nutrients round the edge, and sucking in seawater near the centre, at a rate which would give the algae on which it fed time to make full use of the nutrients by the time they were sucked in. As in all other vital structures, everything would be done by a very large number of entirely separate units, all working well below their maximum capacity, so that a proportion would always be out of service for repair or replacement. This would be a lot less efficient than having one immense processing plant, but in such a system absolute reliability would be far more important than efficiency.

It is likely that, rather than returning a fraction of each crop of algae direct to continue multiplication, the fresh ones required would be grown under controlled and sterile conditions in 'seed beds'. This would prevent the risk of spread of undesirable mutants, producing a less well balanced chemical content, but multiplying faster, and hence by natural selection replacing the more desirable.

The nutrients supplied could consist mainly of suitably processed sewage. Whatever supplementary minerals were required could be chemically extracted from the deeper ocean, or dredged from the bottom, whichever proved cheaper. Unlike the oyster, it is improbable that the city would find it convenient to draw its oxygen supply also from the sea; it would almost certainly be more convenient to suck in the few million tons of fresh air it needed each day direct from the atmosphere. If the exhaled air were bubbled out round the edge, much of the carbon dioxide which it had acquired from the inhabitants could be added directly to the sea with the other nutrients. A lot of power would be required to compress it to the pressure prevailing at the depth of release, but the air jets would give excellent mixing, and might be worth while for this purpose even if the algae could get carbon dioxide enough for optimal growth direct from the atmosphere. The fresh water supply would present no problems; nuclear powered desalination plants would be as easy to run under the sea as round the edge, and should have reached a level of thermal efficiency to contribute an unimportant amount to the heat economy. Industrial cooling would undoubtedly be done with seawater much more easily than at present, and water for agriculture would not be needed, so that much less fresh water per head would be needed than is needed now.

Providing for the Multitudes

Having dealt with the feeding economy of a single city, we must check to see whether any disastrous global effects would occur, as a result of the interaction of all the cities with the ocean or the atmosphere. As far as the atmosphere is concerned, two factors alone seem likely to be significant; the carbon dioxide turnover, and the total output of heat by human activity.

The first certainly needs consideration, since the turnover of carbon dioxide feeding the unicellular plants for five million million people would be in the region of 1.4 million million tons per year. This is twenty times the rate of turnover of carbon dioxide by all the present living creatures of the world, which is roughly 70,000 million tons of carbon dioxide each year. This gives, incidentally, a nice reminder that the weight of human beings would be around ten times the living mass of all the million or more animal species now on the planet (not twenty times since much of the world's present animal population is cold blooded, with a much smaller oxygen-carbon dioxide turnover rate than we have). This suggests that since we should be breathing out only 98 per cent of the carbon dioxide needed each year, to feed the plants that our 2 per cent bigger population would need next year, some supplementation might be needed. I am not sure of this, however; the present world growth of plants is not generally limited by carbon dioxide concentration. In the whole atmosphere there is about 1.5 million million tons at present, but dissolved in the oceans is another ninety million million tons or so. The total amount is steadily if slowly increasing at the moment as a result of the large rate of burning of fossil fuels and of the production of lime from chalk. There will certainly be no fossil fuels (oil and natural gas) left to burn in 360 years' time, if we have multiplied at the rate described, and the lime-burning would be reduced. The carbon dioxide content of the atmosphere may not, therefore, be very much greater than at present. A mobilization into the top few metres of the ocean, and into the land plants, of some 1.5 per cent each year of the oceanic carbon dioxide would still suffice to do the job. Nevertheless, it might be worthwhile to avoid the dispersion of all our exhaled carbon dioxide from the undersea cities to the general atmosphere, and to see that it remained in the thin growing layer of the sea; leaving the general atmospheric supply for the land areas.

The second global problem which we have mentioned is the atmospheric heat balance. This could be of some importance; not because we should care what the outside temperature was, when anyway nobody was allowed on the surface either of land or water for any appreciable time, but because the proportion of cloud cover would be of vital concern, and would depend very greatly on the heat transfer between sea and air.

We are supposing that, averaged over the world's surface, we should have reached a density of around one per person per 100 square metres. Since little individual heating would be needed, and most mechanical and electrical devices would be running at very high efficiency, two kilowatts per person round the twenty-four hours should be a reasonable allowance. The total used by everyone in the world would be only about 6 per cent of the amount reaching the world from the sun, but being derived from nuclear power, and therefore being directly added to the solar contribution, it could represent an important change. If it were passed into the sea as we have supposed, it would cause a rise in temperature; although this would be small, as it would soon be balanced by the increased evaporation. The overall effect of this is difficult to determine. Precipitation of rain would clearly be 6 per cent or so greater, but where it would occur, and whether it would involve a major increase in cloud cover in otherwise sunlit regions, is not known. If this were troublesome, it might be possible to transfer the heat from the ocean cities, as well as the land ones, directly to the atmosphere, when the oceans could stay at roughly their present temperature. While I do not know what would be the optimum arrangement, both composition and temperature of the atmosphere would be largely under control, and it is reasonable to suppose that some possible changes could be organized to lead to an actual decrease in the shielding of the surface by clouds.

Enough has been said to show that the underwater cities would not only be possible, but would have advantages over land based ones of the type I have already described. It might be felt that they would be vulnerable to damage, but the energy required to cause such damage would be rather large. To balance the buoy-

Providing for the Multitudes

ancy of the forty-five metres depth of air-filled living space, and perhaps twenty metres more of factory-space at higher air pressure, the equivalent of forty metres of concrete could be shared between the roof and the floor. With a layered construction, this could be made immune to the impact of a very large vessel or a major bomb. It would easily be destroyed by an H-bomb, but so would any other city of the same size on land. It could be hit by a large meteorite, but would anyway have automatic waterproof doors to handle accidents at the submarine docking airlocks; and the damage would not be widespread. Any of the big dams of the world could be hit by a large meteorite, and kill as many people, but this does not cause anyone serious concern.

The last comment I will make on this type of living accommodation, is to discuss briefly the rate of building required. A population of five million million increasing at 2 per cent per year will be adding new people at the useful rate of a hundred thousand million a year. If a standard city when full took forty million people, this would mean a production rate of 2,500 per year, or a complete city every three-and-a-half hours. Since one can hardly expect such a city to be built in less than a year, using even the techniques of the year 2335, this means that 2,500 must be under construction at once – with plans being made for twice as large a rate of production in thirty-five years' time.

It would be inconvenient to build them small, and to increase their size when in position and operating. It is much more likely that we should build them on the same principle as present day ships; in docks twenty-five kilometres diameter and 100 metres below sea level, which could later be flooded to allow the new city to be floated out to sea. A skeleton crew of 100,000 families or so could then get all the life-support systems operating, and connect it up to the existing city network. City-yards could be built anywhere along the edges of existing continents, preferably close to the edge of the continental shelf, and close to an ocean current which would allow their products to drift part of the way to their final position with little help. The necessary labour force would rather obviously be available; in effect each person on the earth would have on the average to build the equivalent of his own accommodation once every thirty-five years. We are having to do this now, and to improve standards as well. We make a fair amount of fuss about it, but we do not find it difficult.

It will be remembered that the state we should now have reached is that in which the population is the largest which could be fed with the most efficient possible use of the whole of the solar energy reaching the earth. No unsurmountable technical difficulties seem to have arisen. It is more likely that we should already be producing much of our bulk food by purely chemical means, but if this were still much more expensive than growing algae in sunlight, the engineers would not yet be at the end of their tether.

Let There be More Light

During the last decade we have put some thousand or so tons of satellites of various kinds into orbit round the earth, mostly near to the minimum distance which will keep them clear of the atmosphere. In 365 years' time there should be no difficulty in increasing this by a factor much larger than the 1500 times increase in population.

This would make it possible to put large satellite reflectors into orbit on the side of the earth away from the sun, to reflect light back on to the dark side, and eliminate the waste of time every night. To double our radiation income, we should need a total area of reflectors at least as great as the projected area of the earth itself – about 130 million square kilometres. Made of aluminium foil a tenth of a micrometre thick (a micrometre is a thousandth of a millimetre) this would weigh about thirty-five million tons. With plenty of time and people this should not be difficult by the time it would be required. The project would of course be carried out from the moon, not from the earth, making it possible to use single-stage oxygen-hydrogen rockets. Aluminium is already known to be a major constituent of lunar rock, as it is of terrestrial rocks. Very little hydrogen for the rocket fuel is found in the near-equatorial rocks, but it is expected that considerable quantities of ice will be found below the surface near the permanently deep-frozen lunar poles. Oxygen in combination forms nearly half by weight of the entire moon. Large amounts of power would be needed, but could readily be provided by nuclear reactors set up for the purpose. The project is made easier by the fact that a stable orbit exists for the mirror, around 1.5 million kilometres (four-and-a-half times as far as the moon) from the earth on the side away from the sun, in which the mirror can rotate once about its own diameter and revolve once round the earth in exactly the time that the earth takes to go once round the sun. Once set up, therefore, it would remain always facing the earth on the side of the earth away from the sun, and would always be at the zenith over the equator at midnight. The construction of a single mirror of this size, and of the correct curvature, would tax the abilities of the engineers even in 365 years' time. Besides this, its centre would be almost totally eclipsed by the earth, and the rest of it partially eclipsed. A single circular mirror with a hole in the middle big enough to take the earth's shadow would be better but even more difficult to make, and in practice a large number of much smaller mirrors, near to, but not exactly at, the optimum point, crossing and re-crossing the plane of the earth's orbit in a complex prearranged pattern, would be far easier to build. Each would have movable reflecting 'sails' which would use the pressure of sunlight to control any small deviations from the optimum orbit, and could be operated by small motors, powered by solar cells, for the slow speed required, and controlled automatically.

The resulting doubling of the radiation received on earth would give the effect of two noons every twenty-four hours at the equator, with one sun rising just as the other set. This would give us another thirty-five years. Another set of mirrors in rather more complex orbits could be used to double our received radiation again, bringing the radiation received at the poles and over the dawn and dusk regions up to the same level as equatorial midday. The quadrupling of the total heat received by the earth would lead to melting of the polar ice – which would require the cities on land near sea level to be suitably encased and prepared to change to underwater operation. It might, however, lead to a lot of difficulty with clouds and might therefore fail to give us the expected one more doubling time of thirty-five years.

A better arrangement would be to use the fact that plants employ only a part of the solar spectrum, and that the rest is providing only unwanted heat. A suitable filtering film set up in the other stable orbit which exists, between the earth and the sun, and between the outer mirrors and either sun or earth could cut the heat input by 60 per cent. The second set of mirrors could then be used with impunity, and indeed increased a little in area, to give us a two-and-a-half times multiplication of population in forty-five years. We should thus have reached twenty-five million million people in the year 2415 AD, 443 years from now, and I can see no further chance of extending cheap photosynthesis by cost-free sunlight – this must be regarded as a dead end.

This does not even yet, however, mean that the Malthusians would at last have been vindicated, and that the prophets of doom crying 'Wolf! Wolf!' would at last have seen a real wolf. It would mean only that we should have, from here on, to turn more and more to complete factory production of our basic food supplies, even if this were more expensive. In fact, of course, so determinedly reproducing a population as I have described would have changed over long since, without messing about with mirrors. I have included these basically to illustrate the power of a technological civilization to find a workable solution to a novel problem – and even if inessential, it might be used temporarily if it were cheap enough.

The most obvious form of factory production would be still to grow algae for the main bulk of our food, followed by yeasts and moulds to produce extra proteins and vitamins, but to use light derived from local nuclear-powered sources. The overall efficiency from heat source to photosynthetic product, using techniques available in 1972, would be less than that using sunlight; but this would almost certainly not be so in 450 years' time, and in any case it would make it possible to allow the ocean temperature to increase substantially without disadvantage. In fact, if, as is probable, the thermal efficiency of food production from local sources of light was greater than that from sunlight, it would be an actual advantage to have a large part of the latter reflected away by a continuous cloud cover.

If then we suppose that the artificial efficiency was as good as that of the best 40 per cent of sunlight, we should be able to support well over twenty-five million million people, with a total

Providing for the Multitudes

energy expenditure of about 700 watts per square metre, round the clock.

This would be all right for the time, but the world's surface would soon begin to warm up at an important rate. The mean temperature of the oceans at 700 watts per square metre would rise at about 1.5°C per year. One more period of thirty-five years, taking the population up to fifty million million, would take the oceans well on the way to boiling, making refrigeration on a major scale essential. Melting of the arctic and antarctic ice would give only another year or so, and boiling of the oceans would be unacceptable for a number of reasons, the most definite of which is that, when boiled entirely into steam, the pressure at the bottom of the atmosphere would be equal to that now at the bottom of the ocean. Multistorey buildings could certainly not be built to support this weight, even in 450 years' time. This therefore would be a dead end. We have reached a new controlling limit for our species, which is entirely novel for vertebrates. The only creatures for which their own heat output forms an effective limit are the thermophilic organisms, which produce the hot compost heaps on which cucumbers and marrows do so well. When these organisms are growing in too large and well-insulated a mass of suitable material, such as a haystack, they may raise the temperature to near the boiling point of water, and if chemical oxidation then takes over as the material dries out, may even cause it to be set on fire to their own utter destruction.

Even at this point, however, *Homo sapiens* would not be beaten; we are not bacteria any more than we are rats, and the engineers would have one last technically feasible plan which could give the sociologists a full 300 more years to learn how to change the reproductive habits of the population.

I shall deal with this in the next chapter.

Seven

The Blazing Limit

The impending danger of being cooked by our own power output would have been clear before we had reached the point at which the sun and the sea could no longer give us our daily (alga) bread.

At every point in our history so far, we should have been able to eliminate or circumvent each natural limit as we came to it. Here we have the simplest kind of limit of our entire existence; one which the engineers would already understand completely, without the need for any new scientific or psychological knowledge. They could see clearly that the interplanetary mirror approach would be shortsighted, since, although it supplied food cheaply, this could be done in other ways, and that in producing the extra food it accentuated the coming problem of heat. They would therefore abandon the previous piecemeal approach and attempt the design of an Ultimate System which would represent the absolute best that the planet could support.

Getting Rid of the Heat

Taking first things first, they would begin by seeing how to handle the heat menace as effectively as possible, and then see whether the ideal solution for this was compatible with other requirements, or whether it would need to be modified.

The heat problem could be tackled from two directions; first to work out how to get rid of heat as efficiently as possible, and secondly to see how far we could reduce the heat output required to keep everyone alive, and happy enough at least to avoid troublesome protests.

The Blazing Limit

It has already been shown that it would be useless to try to use the arctic ice or even the oceans to absorb the waste heat; this would quickly lead to disaster. The only other solution would be to radiate the unwanted heat into space.

The prospects for this would be good. At present the earth receives about 1.4 kilowatts of radiation per square metre when the sun is overhead, and therefore receives an average over the whole globe, and round the whole twenty-four hours, of a quarter of this; 0.35 kilowatts per square metre.* Since the surface temperature has altered little in thousands of years, the average rate of radiation loss by reflection or re-radiation by the earth must be the same; also an average of 0.35 kilowatts per square metre round the clock.

Now it is well known that the heat radiated by any object goes up very fast with the temperature of the object. While we were using the surface for growing living plants, even microscopic ones, we could not take advantage of this by letting the surface rise in temperature so as to radiate more heat away into space. Even when we turned to artificial power sources, and abandoned the surfaces of the sea and land, we could not afford to let the ocean boil, and so the sea surface at least could never be allowed to go much above 100°C. Well below this level, the increase in cloud cover would reduce the efficiency of radiation of heat, just as it would reduce the efficiency of absorption of heat from the sun, and this would more than nullify the advantage of the warmer radiating surface. The answer to this would be to radiate the heat from a roof, above the clouds, and insulated from the oceans and from the living quarters on land. The living regions would then be kept at a comfortable temperature by large scale refrigerators or air-conditioners. A refrigerator, of course, does not destroy heat. This would be contrary to the first law of thermodynamics, the principle of conservation of energy. What it does do is to take heat from a place in which it is not wanted, such as a freezing compartment or a living room, and put it somewhere where it doesn't matter. Since the refrigerator itself needs an outside source of energy to keep it going, and since this energy must not be left in the freezing compartment or the

* (The total surface area of the globe is $4\pi r^2$, while the projected area on which the sunlight falls is only πr^2.)

living room, the quantity of heat delivered to the outside is greater than that removed from the region to be cooled. Now in most of the systems used at present, the heat removed is simply passed into the atmosphere, and allowed to look after its own disposal from there on. Trouble has occurred only on those rare occasions, as in New York in summer, when the airconditioning refrigerator of each building is sucking in air warmed by the heat put out by the airconditioning refrigerators of other buildings. As a result, it has to work harder, and rejects an extra lot of heat into the atmosphere. As a result of this all the surrounding air conditioners have to work harder, and reject more heat still. On still, hot, humid days, this process has led to a steadily increasing power load until the power stations have been unable to bear it, and have had to shut down – with exceedingly uncomfortable results for the inhabitants of the buildings.

In the situation facing our engineers of 400 years in the future, it would be obvious that simply rejecting the heat to the atmosphere would be useless; it would have to be led systematically to a solid upper surface 'roof' from which it could be radiated directly into space. Outer Space is one part of our environment that we can say, without any risk of contradiction, will *never* be in short supply.

The engineering problem would then consist straightforwardly of setting up radiating surfaces at the highest practicable temperature, so as to radiate as much heat as possible into space. They would have to be well insulated from below so that they would not re-radiate any heat back to the ground. Calculation of the best area of the radiating surface is easy; it is the entire surface of the globe. The right material to make it of, is that which can be used at the highest temperature without evaporating. Among the metals, this means tungsten, which could be run for long periods at nearly half the temperature of the surface of the sun, without evaporating at a serious rate. A few compounds have comparable properties, and some might be a trifle better, but the difference is too small to be of importance, and we shall therefore take tungsten as the material of choice. Different materials radiate with different efficiencies at the same temperature, but the maximum theoretically possible efficiency has been known since 1884, and roughened and highly corrugated tungsten sheet

The Blazing Limit

can be brought very close to it indeed.

At 2400°C, such a surface could get rid of heat at the rate of 2700 kilowatts per square metre, or some 10,000 times as fast as the earth as a whole does now.

This looks to be a pretty effective answer to the heat limitation which we reached at the end of the last chapter, conclusive as that seemed to be. It is indeed good, but not quite so good as it looks. The heat which can be radiated at 2,400°C is impressive, but the living space below must still be kept at around our present comfortable room temperatures. The refrigerating heat pumps for transferring our waste heat at 25°C up to the surface at 2,400°C would require a vast amount of power, and would inevitably themselves produce a large fraction of the heat which finally arrived there. Furthermore, the heat pumps would have to do better than push the heat out at 2,400°C. The top skin would need to be thick enough for reasonable strength, and heat would need to be conducted through it from the final hot stage of the compressed fluid refrigerant. The thickness between fluid and radiating surface could hardly be less than three millimetres, and with 2700 kilowatts per square metre, this would require a temperature of at least 3000°C on the inside of the skin. Again, even if we had got used to an indoor temperature of 30°C (86°F), which is quite comfortable if the air is dry and you do not have to do very much, the cooling units which would form the inputs to the refrigerating systems would have to run at a lower temperature, which I shall assume to be 7°C. Even so, fans would be needed to circulate the air and to bring it to the cooling units.

The power required to run an absolutely perfect refrigerator or heat pump, between any two temperatures, can be calculated from the laws of thermodynamics, and, since all this power has finally to be radiated together with the heat abstracted from the living quarters, the total power radiated for each kilowatt removed from below can also be calculated. It works out that to remove one kilowatt from the living space, the perfect refrigerators would require eleven kilowatts to drive them, and hence twelve kilowatts would have to be radiated from the top. We shall not in fact do so well as this. At the bottom of the system, very high rates of transfer of heat can be obtained with small temperature drops by using condensing liquids, but several stages of these will be needed, and there will be a wasteful loss between each pair of stages. There are other types of refrigerating systems based on semi-conductors, but it does not seem likely that these will work with high efficiency at white heat.

All in all, it is difficult to believe that the complete refrigeration system from end to end could possibly run at more than about half of the theoretical maximum efficiency, even though good commercial refrigerators working over the comparatively tiny range of $-15°C +30°C$ can reach 80 per cent of their theoretical maximum.

Finally, then, as a result of radiating 2700 kilowatts per square metre from our 'roof', we should be drawing the much smaller figure of 110 kilowatts per square metre from the part of the building we decided to keep at a suitable temperature for living in. This is, however, so much better than the kilowatt or so per square metre which could be radiated from the earth's unprotected surface, that it would represent a major gain in the battle against the heat limit.

Before it could be achieved in practice there is one further big – though not very difficult – step which would have to be taken. Tungsten will stand an exceedingly high temperature without evaporating at a serious rate, but it can do this only in vacuum, or in one of the non-reactive 'noble' gases such as argon, with which electric lamps are usually filled. Consequently, for the tungsten surface to operate as planned, it would have to be placed outside the earth's atmosphere. It would be difficult, even in 400 years' time, to put a white hot surface round the earth at a height of 100 kilometres or so, but though it would be difficult to put the tungsten roof above the atmosphere, there is no serious problem in fetching the atmosphere down below the tungsten roof. It would have to be compressed of course, so as not to take too much room, but it would not be necessary to construct vast numbers of huge pressure-vessels. At the bottom of the deeper oceans, air at ordinary temperatures is compressed to a density close to that of seawater. Hence if it were pumped to the bottom of the Tuscarora Deep or the Mindanao Trench, extended a bit to take the necessary volume, all of the air not wanted in the living space at the top could be formed into a pool which would

The Blazing Limit

have little tendency to float, and which could be prevented from dissolving in the sea and diffusing back to the surface – if this were rapid enough to matter – by covering it with a weighted sheet of polythene or some similar airproof substance. Even better, it could simply be pumped down below the buildings, where it would form a layer 50-100 metres thick at high pressure on which the building would float as on an air cushion. This would make a superb shock absorber for disturbances due to earthquakes at the bottom of the ocean. The pipes used to pump it down could be left in position, and used to tap it as required for supplies of oxygen or nitrogen to supplement the food supplies.

The argon of the atmosphere, which at present forms about 1 per cent, could be separated and left outside. This would not corrode the hot tungsten, and would, in fact, reduce somewhat its rate of evaporation, as it does in a gas-filled electric lamp with a tungsten filament. The low-pressure atmosphere it would provide would be useful, too, in that it would form a perfectly effective stopper for micrometeorites. Although these are too small to do serious damage, they would gradually erode away the tungsten surface.

Feeding the People

Having worked out this end of the plan, the engineers would have to think of the other end: just how many people could be kept fed and clothed and able to reproduce at their usual morally untouchable rate in these conditions.

At this stage, the planners would certainly not consider perpetuating further the built-in inefficiencies of using living organisms for food or anything else, since much of their energy-turnover is concerned with unnecessary (to us) structural complications, to enable them to reproduce themselves, rather than being concentrated entirely on the chemical assembly of digestible molecules.

I have no idea what chemical techniques for food synthesis there may be in 450 years' time, but, as with the refrigerators, the established science of thermodynamics can give us the limits within which we have to work; that is to say, if we know the thermodynamic limit, there is an indefinite number of ways of being less efficient, but no possible way of being more efficient.

We know quite well the power required to run one human being. The total energy output of our basal metabolism is around sixty watts, but this increases with eating and with every other physical activity, so that an average of 100 watts per person round the twenty-four hours gives us a good working estimate. This energy, in whatever form it is first used, eventually appears as heat, and must be added to the heat produced from all of the industrial and other sources, to be removed by the refrigerators. Now this body heat is all derived from the combination of our food with the oxygen we breathe to produce carbon dioxide and water, with a great many more complicated compounds, which are finally rejected in urine and faeces.

Now, I have naturally no knowledge of the chemical processes which will be used for producing our food. But we do know for certain that energy will be required for doing it. The main source of raw material would inevitably be the carbon dioxide and water and other excreta which we ourselves produce. Each one of us, in the course of a seventy-year life, will produce some fifteen tons (dry weight) of faeces and sixteen tons of carbon dioxide, and if this were not used it would be very much more expensive to replace the vital elements it contains from virgin raw materials.

Furthermore, much of the excreta consist of compounds already built up a long way from the simple materials which we would otherwise have to use, and hence would use less power to be turned back into food.

The invaluable principle of conservation of energy then tells us exactly what is the absolute minimum of power required to do the job. If one person produces 100 watts round the clock by turning food and oxygen into excreta and carbon dioxide, then *at least* 100 watts round the clock will be required to turn excreta and carbon dioxide back into the same amounts of food and oxygen. To do this in practice would require exactly 100 per cent efficiency, in every single stage, from the power source to the finished product delivered to the consumer. This is obviously not possible. The source of power may be either fission of uranium or fusion of deuterium or hydrogen. Driving turbines to produce

The Blazing Limit

electricity might still be limited in efficiency to 60-70 per cent, but more direct methods of transforming nuclear to electric power should be available, and it would not be too unreasonable to assume that 90 per cent could be achieved. The efficiency of the long series of complex chemical reactions, required for food production, is not easy to estimate. At present we could hardly expect more than 1-2 per cent, but it may be fair to suppose that we should have reached 50 per cent in a few hundred years' time. Then about 200 watts per person would be needed for producing the food, 100 watts of which would appear as heat in the machinery, and the other 100 watts would appear from the body heat of the consumer. The 90 per cent efficient power supply would be wasting twenty watts, so that to keep each individual alive at all, before he did anything in particular, would mean 220 watts to be removed by the refrigerators.

Lighting, transport, works and maintenance services, television and communications; non-essential physical activity for entertainment purposes, and so forth, are again difficult to estimate. In the better off countries we now take for granted that we can dispose of a couple of kilowatts each. The engineers planning the Ultimate System would certainly not consider this for an instant. Provisionally we will suppose that they might allocate 280 watts, making 500 watts per person, all of which would eventually appear as heat in the factory or living spaces, and have to be removed by the refrigerators.

Since, as we saw, these could be expected to remove 110 kilowatts per square metre, the designers of 450 years' time could feel that they had done a good piece of work; as far as the heat output was concerned, they could cater for 220 people per square metre. This would mean a hundred thousand million million (10^{17}) people over the whole world. This would be so good compared with the density of a mere one person per ten square metres achieved so far by biological food production on an open planet, that the planners could well feel that they had pushed the heat limit so far away that something else must turn up before it again began to matter.

Indeed, at first sight a population of 220 people per square metre looks so impractical, that the current criers of wolf would be foretelling the collapse of civilization and the death of humanity within 150 years or less, when we should reach standing room only over the entire globe.

The Ultimate Building Construction

Again, the fears of the pessimists who expected this would be premature. As yet our twenty-fifth century engineers would have looked at the two ends of the power economy alone, with no firm plans for the middle, but plans could also be put in hand to look after this.

So far nothing has been discussed between the white hot roof, and the ground or ocean surface. With the prospects of a *really* dense population, the provision of living space would have to be taken extremely seriously. It is obviously impossible to put 220 people per square metre straight on the ground, but if they were spread out between the floors of a 220-storey building, there would be only one per square metre, and with 2,200 storeys there would be one per ten square metres, and so on. Hence the next problem to be solved is that of determining how high buildings could practically be built, and whether these would be tall enough to house the numbers that could be kept cool.

The usual limitation on heights of buildings is that, as the structure is made higher, the walls or supporting columns must get thicker, and the limit occurs when the thickness of the columns at the bottom is so great as to leave no useful space. If we use present-day good quality concrete, a wall 2,000 metres high is just stable; that is to say, it is just not heavy enough to crush its own bottom layer, but could not support any extra weight beyond its own. If we make it thinner towards the top, we can build it higher, or keep it the same height and make it support something. To be useful, the walls have to support the roof and a series of floors, each capable of carrying appropriate weight. 'Appropriate weight' depends on what one proposes to put on it, but in the living quarters must at least carry without collapsing as many people as might be able to stand on it – say a ton per square metre (200 lbs per square foot). The floors themselves, in some light alloy, would weigh very little if the span were not too great; perhaps ten kilogrammes per square metre.

The Blazing Limit

The hot roof itself, with a series of baffles below it to prevent heat from returning downwards, and the very extensive refrigeration plant, would certainly weigh at least a couple of tons per square metre. It might be a great many times this, but since we have no idea at present whether, or how, such refrigerators could possibly be made, we might as well assume that they could be made quite light – no laws of physics can now be proved to be infringed thereby, and anything that is not against these laws some engineer will sooner or later make.

Since a solid concrete wall could not support even its own weight for a height accommodating 1,000 storeys, it would obviously be very difficult to support a great many floors, people, refrigerators, pipes and miscellaneous bits of machinery for even so much. Steels with forty times the crushing strength of concrete are known, but their density is nearly three times greater and a great deal of space and vast amounts of material would be taken by them for 1,000 storeys or more.

The engineers could get round this by making the floors 'float' on air, in the same way that a lorry is supported by the compressed air in its tyres. Every square metre of air at sea level is now (1972) carrying ten tons of air above it, so that the entire weight of the roof, and of the thin argon atmosphere above it, could be carried by an air pressure five times lower than the ordinary atmospheric pressure in which we live. This is the normal pressure of air twelve kilometres (about 40,000 ft) above sea level, where the supersonic planes usually fly. This would be too low a pressure for human beings to live, unless the air were almost entirely oxygen, which would be dangerous. It will be remembered that one of the American Apollo crews was killed by a fire in their cabin, while this was filled with pure oxygen at reduced pressure, because fires burn far faster and more fiercely if there is no inert, diluting, nitrogen to be swept out of the way as the fire proceeds. It has been stated that flesh itself can catch fire if ignited in pure oxygen. If the pressure were raised by addition of a safety-percentage of nitrogen, the roof might have to be held down, not up. This would be inefficient. It might, however, be quite useful to have a few storeys just below the roof filled with helium, at the low pressure required for support, as a 'service area', free of oxygen, for the maintenance workshops for the refrigeration plants. Engineers in this region would wear light diving suits with their own oxygen supplies. The weight of these workshops, with their floors, supplies and robot staff, would be carried by a slightly higher pressure in the air below them, and by the time the pressure had reached three tons per square metre, or 30 per cent of sea-level normal, it would be quite practicable for people to live in it, with oxygen enrichment much less than 100 per cent.

We should now come to a series of inhabited floors, of the lightest possible construction. Then if provisionally we allocate 4.5 square metres of floor to each person, suppose that he is permitted to have his own weight in toys, feeding and working equipment and communication sets including television, and that his share of the weight of floors, partition walls etc. represents his own weight again, we should have an average weight of fifty kilogrammes per square metre of floor. It might be convenient to hold perhaps ten floors together at the same air pressure, to facilitate movement between them, and then to have a sudden jump in air pressure by 500 kilogrammes per square metre, to carry the weight of the whole lot. The weight of the roof and service floors, at three tons per square metre, would of course still have to be carried by the pressure below, so that we should have gone down a further 140 inhabited floors at fifty kilogrammes per square metre each, before the air pressure had increased to ten tons per square metre, the normal pressure at which we are now living. Each further 200 floors inhabited to the same density would add a further ten tons per square metre.

The weight of the air itself must also be taken into account. If helium were available to provide a helium-oxygen mixture, the weight would be unimportant but present estimates of the total world supply of helium suggests that there is not enough. If oxygen-nitrogen mixtures were used as in our present atmosphere, the pressure at the bottom of 1,000 storeys would be increased by about ten tons per square metre, making sixty in all. So long as the proportion of oxygen was appropriately reduced as the pressure increased, it has already been shown by experiments with divers, people could live at a pressure of sixty tons per square metre, although invalids and elderly people might find it advisable not to occupy the lowest regions.

The Blazing Limit

We have now got 940 inhabited floors. This could readily be extended to 1,000 inhabited floors, if 6 per cent of the weight were taken by conventional metal or ceramic walls. This would be quite convenient, as a strong and rigid compartmental structure would in any case be needed for many reasons, as we shall see below.

With a thousand storeys, and three square metres per person on each storey, we should have altogether 222 people per square metre – just the maximum that the refrigeration system could handle. Although one could expect a lot of space to be taken up by walls, pipes, radiators and services, the remaining operating space for each person would still be some two to three square metres, which is more than most people have had in their houses for most of history up to now. As far as space is concerned, therefore, a lot more people could be handled – though with smaller amounts of permissible equipment as well as of room to move – and the heat problem, good as its solution looked, remains the final limit.

There are, however, several other possible limitations, which we have been able to dismiss at lower population densities, which need to be reconsidered.

Raw Materials and Power

The first of these is the availability of the elements of which the people themselves and their food supplies are made. I shall suppose that the weight of material in the food-supply chain would be equal to the weight of the people themselves. One normally eats one's own weight in two to three months, and the recycling time could easily be made very much less than this, so that this should give a good safety factor. At the maximum number permitted by the heat limit, this means that the total amount of each element required for each square metre of the world's surface would be that contained in the bodies of 440 average people. I shall put in an extra small safety factor (that sounds well, but of course I'm really doing it to save arithmetic) by counting every man, woman and child as a 'standard man' of total body weight seventy kilogrammes, as used in most medical calculations.

The chemical constitution of a 'standard man' is as shown in Columns 1 and 2 of Table 3, while Column 3 gives the weight of each element in 440 standard men.

TABLE 3

eat weight in 2-3 mths

Element	Weight in one standard man (kilogrammes)	Weight in 440 men (kilogrammes)	Weight per square metre in kilogrammes		
			in whole atmosphere	in whole ocean	in 1 kilometre of earth's crust
Oxygen	45.5	20,000	2,000	2,200,000	1,400,000
Carbon	12.6	5,600	1.5	81	2,400
Hydrogen	7.0	3,100	—	280,000	—
Nitrogen	2.1	900	8,000	—	3,000
Calcium	1.1	460	—	1,100	90,000
Phosphorus	0.7	310	—	—	3,000
Sulphur	0.18	77	—	2,400	1,500
Potassium	0.14	62	—	1,000	65,000
Sodium	0.11	46	—	30,000	70,000
Chlorine	0.11	46	—	50,000	2,000
Magnesium	0.04	15	—	35,000	50,000
Iron	0.004	1.8	—	—	125,000
Copper	0.0001	0.5	—	—	270
Iodine	0.00003	0.013	—	0.13	0.15
Manganese	0.00002	0.01	—	—	2,500

The elements essential to human life and their availability in the air, the sea, and the surface rocks of the land. Figures from *Documenta Geigy Scientific Tables* and *Chambers' Encyclopaedia*.

The next three columns give the amount of each element in the present atmosphere, the amount in the ocean, and the amount in one kilometre depth of the earth's crust. In each case the average amount above or below one square metre of the world surface is given, so that it is directly comparable with the amount required in Column 3. The comparison is somewhat surprising. It can be seen that every element of which more than ten kilogrammes per square metre would be needed is available from the ocean or the atmosphere with a comfortable margin, of a factor of ten or more, except for carbon and phosphorus. Most of the rest of the atmosphere's nitrogen would be usefully employed – with half the oxygen – in forming the support for the main living

The Blazing Limit

quarters of the planet. After supplying this and the bodies, there would be little left, in fact, for the gas layer below the buildings.

At the level considered in the last chapter, up to the ultimate limit of sun-powered 'agriculture', the only single element not adequately supplied by sea or air would have been phosphorus, for which mining operations would have been required. On our new level, mining will of course still be needed for phosphorus, on a more extensive scale, but a thorough extraction of the element from just over 100 metres depth would suffice. For carbon, however, which previously did not require mining at all, we should have to dig out and process the whole of the crustal rocks down to a depth of over two *kilometres*. If the heat limit had permitted a further doubling of population, a further two kilometres would have had to be processed in the next thirty-five years, or sixty metres a year. There is no difficulty about this: it is little over a metre of depth per week, perhaps three tons of rock from each square metre, with a couple of hundred people available over the top of it to supervise the digging and extracting machinery. There is also no reason to suppose that the mean power needed by this leisurely progress would contribute anything significant to the load borne by the refrigerators.

It is likely that there is a very adequate reserve of carbon in the inner regions of the earth; particularly in the metallic nickel iron core, with which it would be expected to associate itself chemically. Even in 800 years' time, however, it may prove preferable to take a lot of chemical trouble with a thousand tons of rock within a few kilometres of the surface, than to do very little chemistry with a few tons fished up from 4,000 kilometres down.

As far as the basic elements for life are concerned, therefore, there will be no serious trouble, while we can keep ourselves cool enough to take trouble of any kind.

Materials are required, however, for many purposes other than making human bodies. Apart from the tungsten at the top, for which there is no tolerable substitute – the next best material might well cut the maximum sustainable population by a factor of four or more – there should be an enormous choice of material, for both building construction and machinery. As far as the living quarters go, with a total structural weight of some thirty tons per square metre, there would be several times more than enough of aluminium, iron, magnesium or titanium, in the two kilometres of crust which had been processed for carbon, for any one of these elements to be used for the entire structure by itself. In practice, silicates and titanates would be likely to play a much larger part than would pure metals.

The final supply requirement would be the material basis for the source of power. To maintain the System at the limit, the output into space has been shown to be 2,700 kilowatts per square metre. Since no energy can be allowed to accumulate anywhere in the System without causing overheating, this 2,700 kilowatts represents the total of power produced per square metre, wherever it is produced and whatever it may be used for. There are two and only two kinds of power which could be adequate, both based on nuclear reactions. The first is the production of power by fission of uranium and thorium, and of elements made artificially from these. All of the world's present nuclear stations are based on the fission of uranium-235, which forms only 0.7 per cent of ordinary uranium, but we know in principle how to produce efficiently fissionable plutonium-239 from the remaining 99.3 per cent of the uranium, and how to obtain another fissionable material, uranium-233, from thorium. The amounts of these materials are adequate for the periods so far considered. There is very little of either in the sea – of the order of two or three grammes per square metre in the entire depth of the ocean. There is however much more in the earth's crust; perhaps three kilogrammes of uranium and twelve kilogrammes of thorium per kilometre of depth under each square metre. Two thousand seven hundred kilowatts would be produced by the complete fission of about a kilogramme per year of either. If the power output has increased at just the same rate as the population, doubling every thirty-five years, we can calculate just how much will have been used up by the time we reached the heat limit in 800 years' time. It works out at about twenty kilogrammes per square metre, or the content of 1,300 metres' depth of the earth's crust, over the whole surface of the planet. This would be easily provided as a by-product of the mining for carbon, and supplies would in fact be available for two or three more doublings, if we had not been too hot to survive them.

The second possible source is nuclear fusion, either of deuterium, the rare heavy isotope of hydrogen, or of hydrogen itself. This second may be difficult, but power should be obtainable from deuterium well before 1990. Whether it will soon, or even ever, be as cheap to produce power this way, is an open question. Deuterium forms only one part in 6,000 of hydrogen, so that there are only about thirty-five grammes of it in a ton of seawater. This is richer than the concentration of the fissionable elements, and the sea is easier to handle than rock; but on the other hand, it requires an isotope separation rather than a purely chemical one. Again, the operating plasmas of the fusion process will have to run at over 100,000,000°C, while the fission reactors can operate at 1,000°C with very fair efficiency. It will be a long time before it is as cheap to set up a reactor at 100,000,000°C as to set one up at 1,000°C.

Since one can obtain three times as much energy per kilogramme from the fusion of deuterium, as one can from a kilogramme of uranium or thorium, the deuterium in the oceans would be worth as much as the amount of these in nearly twenty kilometres of the earth's crust. Doubtless, therefore, in 800 years' time we shall have a choice, and would choose the one giving best overall efficiency. I have no idea which choice would be made, but either would leave plenty of energy still available after we had finished with it. The deuterium fusion plants could be arranged to give only a small yield of long-lived radioactive elements, while the fission plants would give rise to several hundred million curies a year per square metre, which could not conveniently either be kept on the premises or dispersed in the oceans. Although these latter could no longer be used for recreation by any large proportion of people, it might be needful to maintain some submarine traffic of VIPs – or rather, VVVIPs since mere VIPs would be too numerous to allow to travel – and of specialized machinery, vaccines etc.

There would be no difficulty about this however. The mining operations already described could well go a bit deeper in recorded places, and sink to the bottom at such places all the radioactive materials which could not usefully be concentrated and used as an additional power source. A kilometre or so of waste rock put down on top after extraction of the useful elements would keep it satisfactorily out of the way.

The Ultimate Building Services and Living Conditions

So far we have considered only the global situation, to check that no known chemical or physical limitations exist that might prevent us from reaching the heat-limit density of 220 people per square metre. Having shown that there would be enough power, and enough of everything else, however, it is necessary to consider how the essentials of life would be handled and deployed. For example, it would seem reasonable to suppose that a great deal of machinery and chemical plant would be involved in the synthesis and distribution of food, the production of new equipment, the salvaging and reprocessing of old machines, and so forth. Apart from the three tons per square metre of refrigeration plant, just below the roof, no weight allowance has been made for this. This was intentional and not an oversight. The need for a large number of storeys of living accommodation made it essential to have the lightest possible floors and other structures, and hence the establishment of heavy units within the living shell would be highly undesirable. The whole of the major machinery would be placed in a series of further storeys, below the living space. Right at the bottom, directly supported by the ocean, would be the nuclear power plants, whose heavy biological shields for radiation would thus be largely supplied by the ocean itself, although, as we have seen, this could not be used for any needful cooling. This has not been forgotten; the excess heat to be removed has already been allowed for, in saying that the power supplies could not be 100 per cent efficient, and that the waste heat would form part of the load to be taken up to the refrigerators in the attic.

The advantages of building over the ocean rather than the land, both for communication and for transport of raw materials from the mines at the bottom, would be very great. It is likely, therefore, that the first part of the Ultimate Building which I am describing would be built over the sea rather than the land, and that the continental ores would be those first used in mining. Then the spoil from the mining could be deposited at the bottom of the oceans, instead of being returned. The lowering of continental areas, and the rise in sea-level resulting from this process, would allow the area of sea surface for the building to increase at least as fast as the increasing population made necessary – the ice caps at the poles would of course have gone long since – so that finally the entire planet could be surrounded with a kilometre or so of water below the Building, by the time the latter was complete.

Apart from the weight-saving, there would be another quite major advantage of separating the machinery from the people. The air-support of the living space alone would have used up the greater part of the world's nitrogen not required for making people, and if no unprotected people were involved, it would be unnecessary to have a breathable atmosphere for the machines. In fact, nearly all machine design would be much easier, if it were known that there would be no free oxygen in the environment. Unlimited amounts of hydrogen could be obtained by electrolysis of seawater. The associated oxygen would be added to the gas cushion below the building. Using compressed hydrogen as a support, we could allow an average floor-loading of a ton per square metre for the machine floors, and still have another thousand storeys of them, with the gas pressure at the bottom little over a hundred times that of the air in which we now live. It is difficult to see what a thousand storeys full of heavy apparatus could be wanted for, but a very large redundancy to avoid the risk of breakdown would be desirable, and human beings generally manage to feel a little short of equipment however much they have.

A hydrogen atmosphere is much kinder to hot metals than is an oxygen-containing one, and all except the chemical plant could run pretty hot and thus, paradoxically, reduce the work to be done by the refrigerators. It is much easier to remove heat from a hot region than to remove exactly the same amount from a cool one.

The building of the structure I have described, over the whole planet, would clearly take hundreds of years, even with the embarrassingly copious labour supply and the sophisticated machinery which would be available. The most efficient method would be to start right at the beginning with structures of the full height, but running at much lower power, over a small area, and then to extend the area rather than the height. It would however be possible to build the top hundred or so storeys first over the whole planet, and then to build on further storeys and larger power plants below them as time went on.

At whatever stage the atmosphere – apart from the low pressure of argon outside – was pumped away, any remaining open water would need to be covered in to prevent evaporation. This might however have already been done at an earlier stage, as the ultimate means of weather control by eliminating weather.

With unlimited computing capacity, there would be no difficulty in running everything automatically and by remote control, without the slightest contribution from the people on top.

In the last chapter, we saw that there would be a choice as to whether suitably processed human excreta, including carbon dioxide, would be returned to the general supply in the ocean or the atmosphere, or whether it would be systematically fed to the micro-organisms forming our food supply. In the System now described there would be no choice in the matter at all. We could not possibly afford the long delay involved in natural biological breakdown in the vast dark ocean under the buildings. The excreta from each floor would have to be piped down directly to the processing plant, and returned quickly as food. Transport requirements would make it necessary for all the food to be kept in liquid form until the time of its delivery, but various textures, and unlimited numbers of artificial flavours and odours, could then be supplied to give a far greater range of foods than we can obtain today.

Since the dry weight of the excreta produced in seventy to eighty years of a man's life is hundreds of times greater than the dry weight of his body at death, efficiency would be reduced by less than 1 per cent if it should be decided not to pass the dead bodies to the food factories. Nevertheless, disposal otherwise would be a problem, and the loss of carbon and phosphorus would not be negligible. If there were any prejudice, therefore, it would be likely that the bodies would be given a kind of chemical cremation, and the resulting solution passed along below the building to the food factories a kilometre or so away, to ensure that the departed was not served up at once to his sorrowing friends and relatives.

As numbers built up towards the final limit, life would become

The Blazing Limit

less and less mobile. Any kind of individual vehicle would of course be out of the question, but continuously running paternoster-type lifts, in each group of ten storeys at constant air-pressure, would allow a lot of movement between floors without taking up too much space. Every tenth floor, there would have to be an airlock, with a pressure drop of half a ton per square metre – no more than the difference of pressure which we notice at present in rising from a valley to the top of a hill 500 metres high. If the lock did not work too fast, the change might not seem much worse than that experienced as a tube train enters a tunnel.

Horizontal travel could similarly be provided by a moving belt system, but no doubt one could be allowed to walk, at a gentle pace which would not cause overheating, for a hundred metres or so. Although this does not sound very far, it would enable one, with a hundred storeys of vertical movement also permitted, to visit any of a million people within four or five minutes, and few people actually need a larger number than this from which to choose their friends and mates and enemies.

The Building would be divided physically and administratively into units, which could if necessary be completely isolated by vacuum-tight and heat-insulated bulkheads. Units comprising a million people in hexagonal regions around 200 metres diameter and 100 storeys high, would seem to be suitable.

There would be a lot of advantages in this, in enabling easy control by the System of antisocial behaviour. An isolated unit, with the refrigeration or food shut off, would soon settle down again from quite serious disturbances. The most important reason, however, would be the control of disease. All known diseases would certainly have been eliminated long since, but novel pathogenic organisms could conceivably arise, by mutation from micro-organisms used to extract carbon from fresh-mined rock, or perhaps from virus-like mutated sub-cellular components from our own bodies, which had got out of control. If any such organisms should prove infective, the growth factor G could be very much larger than 1, and if once established they might multiply faster than any defences could follow. Action would therefore be taken at the onset of any unexplained symptoms, such as a change of pulse rate, of temperature, or of behaviour, which the supervisory computers would recognize as inconsistent with the preceding diet and social activity of the individual affected. The whole unit, and the twenty units around it, could at once be hermetically sealed off until the condition was diagnosed and cured. If necessary a large number of more distant units could be put to sleep to prevent movement. Each unit would have its own medical research team, assisted by video telephone from outside, and if on rare occasions those in an affected unit failed to solve the problem, the whole unit could be sterilized at red heat. After cleaning, at the density of population finally prevailing, the incinerated million could be replaced in one-seventieth of a second.

Life Under the System

In ordinary conditions, visiting would be permitted between any one unit and the eight units with a common face, but the need to maintain conditions bad for the spread of disease, and the very limited space that could be spared for movement, would make it difficult to allow this to more than a few people at a time. Quarantine would probably then be unnecessary, since the computers of the System would have an exact record of every action and of every contact made by each person during his entire life. If anyone were found sick, therefore, all of these contacts over any desired period could be immobilized for observation.

Apart from the rare outbreaks of illness, continuous computer observation would anyway be essential for the maintenance of ordinary living. Thus the System would enable the food and drink – if it was found desirable to separate them – supplied to each outlet to be matched to each individual who used it. Exact records of when and what each had eaten during his or her entire life would be available to the computers, so that they would no doubt be able to estimate extremely accurately what would be required, without necessarily inducing any feeling of regimentation among the consumers.

Indeed, I have some confidence that the consumers would not merely be unresisting, but would be actively appreciative of their directed lives. A lot of freedom could be allowed to develop originality and creativeness, in such matters as hair style and the quieter, lighter forms of art, but never since babyhood would anyone ever have been allowed to disobey the System's computer-supervised rules.

Even in trivial matters, small children are never very good at thinking for themselves of the activity they will most enjoy at any particular moment. With complete records of a thousand million million children, the System computers would be very good at it indeed. Well before they were six, children would have learnt that whatever they did, and whatever they looked at, and whoever they played with, was always more enjoyable and satisfying if they accepted the System's choice rather than their own. The food which they had received at every meal would have been delivered in the optimum quantity, and with the exact degree of sameness or variety which was best adapted to their temperaments.

Even when we are ill, and know that it is for our own good, we in the twentieth century do not like being treated like this. We should find life in the society I am considering utterly intolerable. But if we tried to express the reasons for our dislike of the system to the natives, we should meet with complete incomprehension. 'How', the native would ask, 'could I choose for myself what to eat, if I didn't know what the System had decided was best for me?'. And if pressed to consider the novelty and interest of eating for once in his life something other than the System's choice, he would reply: 'But the System's choice for me is perfect. If I choose something different, it would be less than perfect. You must be mad to think it better to have something imperfect when you could have had perfection.'

I do not want to imply that the inhabitants would regard the System as God. They would be more likely to feel a vague pride in it as 'theirs', as a man is proud of a well trained dog or a well tuned car. Mostly they would take it as we take the law of gravitation; as a permanent part of the environment that cannot be cheated or persuaded; which has no favourites and bears no grudges, but which you ignore at your peril.

But to return to the living accommodation. Apart from the rather low ceiling, there would be no need for any feeling of constricted space; within the bulkheads of each unit there would be no need for any continuous walls at all, so that long vistas might be seen between the food, excretion and ventilating shafts, with every thirty metres or so the steady untiring motion of a continuously running elevator. This might be popular in some areas, but in others each floor of each unit might be broken up into very large numbers of separate rooms by light, soundproof screens.

In either case, sleeping accommodation would consist of tiers of folding bunks or similar structures, so that one could get several sleepers per square metre, leaving extra space for the active (but not too active, of course) remainder. There would obviously be no need for any time differences in different parts of the globe, and those areas in which people preferred to sleep all at the same time could be synchronized over the whole world to make communication easier. A useful extra amount of space would be made for the waking ones, however, if people slept in regular shifts, about a third being in their bunks at any one time, giving nearly half as much space again per head for the rest. It is likely that no normal person would ever want to be alone; but bunks could be isolated from the rest of the community by sound-and-light-proof screens if anyone wanted them. Most people, however, would feel happier with plenty of others around. This would not be a novel situation. When I was a boy I lived for a time in a country area of Kent, next door to a small cottage whose tenants had thirteen children. I well remember that when one of the older girls got married, the thing about her new state on which she commented most, was how odd and cold it was to have only one other person in the bed.

Thermal output would be reduced if people were kept lying down as much as possible, so that taped television entertainment would be displayed on the ceiling, best viewed from a position flat on one's back. With only one person per three square metres even at the limit, each one of the million in the unit could be looking at a different show at any one time, and since by this time some forty million people with the dramatic capacity of Shakespeare, or the skill in musical composition of Beethoven, would have lived and worked on the planet, not all of the million

The Blazing Limit

simultaneous programmes would need to be less than first class in quality.

Education and Way of Life

The planners would have to put at least as much thought into fitting the minds of the people to the System, as they had put into catering for the needs of their bodies. Unconditioned young people will indulge in a great deal of heat-producing activity. Unconditioned people of all ages also like to enlarge their 'own' territories wherever possible. Both of these tendencies could seriously reduce the number who could live in each Unit.

Early education would therefore have to be universally controlled, to eliminate these types of behaviour. As soon as children could walk, they would have to be effectively discouraged from running or jumping. Like our present training of children not to excrete in public, this would in most communities be mainly the responsibility of the parents. Just as our nursery schools now get a percentage of children who are not yet pot-trained, the nursery schools of the System would get occasional children who were liable to run, or even jump, unless closely supervised. These would have to be quickly and permanently quieted, both for their own sakes and to avoid the risk that they might damage the satisfactory conditioning of others. The psychologists of four hundred years in our future who helped to set up the System, would know very precisely what mixture of rewards for mental or physical passivity, penalties for physical activity, and tranquillizing drugs, would most quickly cure such problem children, and would programme the schools to provide them.

Education, like other important services, could not safely be left to individual teachers, since over a few generations of lazy teachers, grave perversions could develop. A blind eye turned to the surreptitious passing of obscene pictures of people playing violent games like bowls, or even cricket, would quickly lead to the spread, first of 'blue' films for adults, showing such illicit activities, and finally to a complete breakdown of public morals – when television could show even scenes of athletics meetings without arousing a blush on the cheeks of the watchers.

Basic education would certainly be carried on with the help of permanent taped programmes, worked out at the beginning of the System. People would readily believe the genuine truth that these programmes had been carefully prepared by the best teachers that a million million people could produce. Compared with this, the quality of any local effort could only be hopelessly inferior – and who would wish their children to have hopelessly inferior instruction, when the best education ever received by humanity was freely available? A complete feedback system would enable pupils to answer questions, or to ask questions of their own. The System computers, with records of the questions of a thousand million million children, would always be able to recognize or supply the appropriate response. Naturally, the nursery schools at least, would need some local staff to deal with children too small to understand the instructions given by the System, or the consequences of disobeying them. Normal, well-adjusted adults would find such a job intolerable, constantly surrounded by the disgusting activity of the tinies whose processing had only just begun. To maintain self-control in such circumstances would require special training, and would best be in the charge of a special branch of the police. Alternatively the work could be carried out by robots, which would be neither revolted by their task nor lax in carrying it out.

Although little actual physical movement would be permitted, or indeed desired, multi-stereo-video-telephones would be available to anywhere on the planet, giving the illusion, if desired, of the actual presence of the person to whom one was speaking. A uniform culture could hardly be maintained, with so many effectively isolated social groups, and televideo exploration of some of the hundred thousand million other units, all identical in structure and operation, but infinitely variable in culture and tradition, could be quite absorbing. Competitions could be arranged for every conceivable pastime, from chess to tiddlywinks, each competitor operating in his own environment, but surrounded by the life-sized images of the others.

Team games could even be arranged, each player of which could remain stationary at home, controlling the movements of a piece of real appearance but synthesized by his computer. He would see the corresponding pieces of the other competitors as though he were on the field of play himself, and could operate his own at any speed that the players chose. Non-playing viewers would be able to watch the entire synthesized scene, as though they were watching a live match. If the pieces were to move at any speed, each player would be represented by an animal, or vehicle, or space ship – all equally fabulous to the operators – since vigorous physical activity by human beings would be disgusting to any normal person. Even so, older people would probably find the faster games unpleasantly suggestive.

Although everyone would have been brought up to believe that actual physical activity of any other heat producing kind was wickedly wrong, love-making – which of course they would be brought up to think it immoral to control – would be excepted. Hence it would be likely that far more groups would programme their screens to block the showing of such obscene activities as running or dancing, than would programme them to block the display of the interesting variety of sexual customs available over the planet.

It would seem unlikely that any human beings could be permitted to interfere, even slightly, with the delicate balances of the enormous energies and fantastic flow of raw materials which kept the planet alive and operational. The reliability required, to avoid breakdown anywhere in a hundred thousand million units, could be obtained only with an extravagantly redundant number of overlapping and interconnected computer systems, cooperatively controlling every machine and every person on the planet.

At the same time, the planners of the System would have recognized that people like to have power over their environment – and perhaps each other – and to have some responsibility for their future. Consequently, there would be a large number of tasks of apparently vital importance, which could be undertaken only after a long training, and from which only a few would be chosen for the highest grades. Each such job would then represent an important status symbol, and if enough different jobs existed, and if hours of work were short, a large enough proportion of people could feel themselves a vital part of the System, to give a useful built-in stability.

The sort of job which I have in mind, is the supervision of

power, air-conditioning or food production. Food production would involve a very complex series of processes, from the collection and transport of excreta and other organic wastes, through their homogenization and testing for chemical balance, their supplementation with specific chemicals, and their treatment with a succession of artificial high-temperature enzymes, to their final distribution and adaptation to the needs of specific individuals. Every stage in fact would be monitored and controlled by a multiplicity of sensing devices, backed up by a comparable multiplicity of computers having functions analogous to the ganglions in a simple invertebrate animal. Continuously patrolling robot machines, equipped for fault location and repair, would be capable of welding, sealing or completely reconstructing the pipelines, including cleaning up of the mess after such processes.

A supernumerary set of monitoring machines could be so effectively connected with associated human 'directors' that each of these could see and feel, and even taste or smell, exactly as though he himself were moving along the tangle of pipes in the 'digestive' system, even though this was a kilometre below him, in a boiling hot and poisonous atmosphere. The entire set-up would of course be an illusion of the nature of the driving simulator of our own time, the actual maintenance being done by the fully automatic systems. This would not however be apparent to the operator so long as any errors of judgement on his part were recognized by the System, and followed after a natural-seeming interval by a change for the worse in the flavour of the food of the group for which he was 'responsible'. A proper pride and a sense of achievement would then accompany a consistently good performance, together with the associated social approval.

I have no idea what would be the optimum ratio of such apparently important tasks to the obvious kinds of entertainments and relaxation. But the planners of the System would know this rather well, and would anyway establish a constant slow variation of the amounts of 'work', to enable the System to monitor its own success as well as that of individual humans. If a small increase in 'work' showed a slight increase of contented passivity in the group, it would be increased a little further before it was decreased again and vice versa. But I think I have said enough to show that no-one conditioned to the environment from childhood, even if he or she lived a long life without ever even visiting another unit, would ever need to feel bored or frustrated – whatever we might feel like in the same place.

I could not presume to guess, either for this situation, or for the easier one represented by the under-sea cities of the last chapter, what would be the political organization of the system. Since, for the reasons already described, humanity would be divided into units of the order of a million, subdivided into a hundred floors of ten thousand each, an exceedingly democratic organization of each floor or even of each complete unit, would be perfectly practicable – so long as no unit were capable of interfering with any other. People are not too bad at co-operating with the genuinely inevitable.

Two hundred years or so would elapse while the Ultimate Building slowly spread over the planet, displacing section by section the more primitive twenty-to-hundred storey buildings preceding it. As each section was completed, it would be occupied by perhaps a tenth of its final population, giving an easy run-in period with all the power, mechanical and chemical systems running at a tenth of their final rating, and offering over a hundred years of growth at the standard rate. Then each thousand people – doubtless for convenience including a high proportion of young adults without children – would have an enormous living space compared with the region from which they came. If this space were not too big, which would give a feeling of insecurity, the immigrants would be easy to find on a voluntary basis. Each floor load would normally be taken from a single origin with common customs, and would certainly be willing to accept any small extensions of the familiar computer controls that might be necessary to ensure their non-interference with either the working of the System, or the 'quarantine' arrangements. With every 'tribe' of people living artificially in a box supplied entirely from outside, any popular revolt would be highly unlikely, whatever the régime, so long as this made no positive attempt at interference with their continuation of the life to which they were conditioned and accustomed.

The instinctive component of potential aggressiveness in some human beings, especially the younger males, would certainly not have changed by a few hundred years of non-selective breeding, and might not be possible to eliminate entirely by conditioning the children. The System would make provision for the diversion of any such residual aggressiveness into harmless channels. Computers might systematically establish uninhibited public arguments between communities too distant for any possible physical contact, and whose social customs were suitably different; that is to say, different enough to be disapproved but not enough to be incomprehensible. This if done correctly, which it would be, would lead to enough popular verbal violence to keep both units cheerful, and with a pleasant feeling of purpose in life, and would help a lot to deflect attention from subversive issues.

Although people's physical actions would be rigidly limited, there would be no need to prevent them *talking* about almost anything, except in the one vital field of reproduction. If this were nowhere to be interfered with, a highly effective censorship would be essential. To get into this situation at all, people would have had to neglect for thirty generations the regular cries of Wolf! Wolf! by the prophets of imminent destruction. And so far the people would have been absolutely right. But the simultaneous maintenance of a humane and rational rejection of war, with a humane but irrational refusal to consider a change in the birthrate, would need very skilful conditioning of each new generation. Inevitably, even after thirty generations, there would be ill-adjusted characters, who would want to change one or other of the dogmas. In the final thirty years, the prophets of doom would be able to put a lot of solid arithmetic into their gospels, and the criers of Wolf! could give detailed experimental measurements of the size and rate of approach of the wolf. It might then be difficult to avoid much spontaneously generated ill-adjustment among even the most stable population. Even so, since every action of every person would obviously have to be monitored for his own health and well being, there would be no difficulty in jamming at once any discussion of birth limitation. Alternatively and more probably, it could be directed into a computer sub-group specialized in interminable argument, and

The Blazing Limit

capable of producing this through the mouths of perfect simulacrums of other human beings. If this proved ineffective, it would at least give plenty of time to use hypnosis, or in serious cases to have tranquillizers added to the food, of the individual concerned, by the computer circuits responsible for his welfare.

The complex of engineers, biochemists, sociologists, everything-else-ologists and computers, which worked out the grand design for the first part of the Ultimate Building, would be particularly proud of the permanent stability of the System which they set up to run it. They would, of course, have failed to look for trouble two or three hundred years ahead. Even without four hundred years of expert conditioning to avoid doing so, it is even now possible to find engineers, biochemists and sociologists who do not look two hundred years ahead, and no computer of my acquaintance shows any sign of wishing to do so.

Their immediate future being assured by their own efforts, the System-planners would have had no pressing need to question the reproductive mores of their time. Even if a few of them did momentarily listen to the current prophets of doom, they would probably think that their own generation need not be concerned. They would have given their descendants several hundred years to consider changes when these should become necessary, and could easily overlook the fact that they had built an insurmountable barrier against any consideration of any change whatever.

The main part of this barrier would of course be the censorship, established in the easy and spacious times when the world of 2400 AD held only fifty million million people, set up to control any and every one of the many possible but utterly immoral forms of artificial limitation of births. It would easily seem to those who set it up that there was a quintessential rightness in maintaining an outlook and a way of life that had succeeded for so long, and any objections to its continuance would seem unworthy of practical consideration and contrary to human nature – the usual cry of those who fail to see that the most important characteristic of human nature is its fantastic adaptability. They would have been used to rigid control, and would have seen only necessity, and no moral problem, in its extension from things of the body to things of the mind.

And so, in 870 years from now, we should come to the blazing limit of the population of our planet, when there really is a wolf, and the prophets of doom will die honoured by all.

Eight

Anticlimax

I had thought of calling the last chapter the Ruddy Limit, but that would be nothing like hot enough. Seen from the Moon, the earth-shine would be twice as hot as the radiation from the sun itself, and only when the sun was close beside it in the sky would one see that the earth was yellow by comparison, and gave twice the amount of heat only because it covered almost sixteen times the area of sky. The earth-bound human race would have its little blaze of glory before it went. But although we can foretell with some certainty that if we continue to multiply at our present rate, we have less than a 999-year lease on our planet, we do not have to remain on it. Like the use of the mirrors in the sky described in Chapter Six, the Ultimate Building of Chapter Seven represents a dead end, but only for those who would not use the emergency exit.

Colonization of the Planets

Long before the Doomsday men had had their gloomy prophecies confirmed at last, in triumphant immolation, the optimists (the *real* optimists, not just the anti-pessimists like me) would have been pointing out that, when earth became too crowded, we could go to other planets of the solar system, or even to the planets of other stars.

This is indubitably true. It would be very troublesome, but it would give us quite a bit longer to go on multiplying. Long before we get dangerously overcrowded, we can be quite sure that we shall have extensive colonies on the moon and probably also on Mars, Venus and Mercury. All of these should not only be self sustaining within a hundred years or so from now, but would be capable of forming nuclei for rapid expansion. Mars, Venus and Mercury will for a long time have only small colonies, almost entirely engaged in scientific work, since they take several months to reach for every day required for the journey to the moon. Mars has a useful if unbreathable atmosphere to keep off the meteorites, and would be easier to live on than the moon, but Mercury would need a very large shiny umbrella over the colony, to keep off the sun in the months-long day. Venus, with its enormous atmospheric pressure and possibly red hot surface, would be definitely difficult. The moon alone would be likely to have an economically, as well as technically, self-sustaining community in the foreseeable future.

Within the next fifty to a hundred years, most new major astronomical instruments are likely to be built on the Moon, and the air-filled underground towns built to serve these will have enormous attractions for very diverse groups of people.

The fact that a girl who weighs fifty kilogrammes on earth, would weigh eight kilogrammes on the Moon, would make a lunar ballet an impressive spectacle. This, with the added fact that anyone, fitted with a set of wings and willingness to learn, could fly in a kind of underground Albert Hall, and play a most telegenic series of possible aerial games, would gain much solid cash from the entertainment industry.

People with weak hearts, bedridden here, could run upstairs on the moon faster than they could ever have run when well and young on earth. They would be expensive to transport, in heavy water-beds to reduce the effects of acceleration, but the rich and sick are often willing to accept expensive treatment.

Good as all this will be, however, it does not make emigration from earth a permanent solution. As in other cases mentioned earlier, a little arithmetic shows that the value would be exceedingly limited. The first difficulty is that the heat liberated on earth, in taking a passenger to even the nearest of the planets, would be comparable with that required to keep the passenger on earth for his whole life. To keep level, 2 per cent of the population would have to be exported each year, and the resulting load on the power and constructional facilities could well be several times the load due to the entire permanent population.

Anticlimax

This would be most unlikely to be accepted until the matter became extremely urgent.

Nuclear fuels should of course be well established, but the cost in effort would be great. If we were trying to export only a million million people a year, long before the final limit, and if only one rocket in a hundred thousand crashed on earth, it could be inconvenient.

It is possible that these problems of detail would be solved by the time the solutions were needed. There is, however, a much more serious and fundamental problem. The planets are not nearly big enough. Venus, the nearest, is about the same size as the earth, and has the advantage that there is as much carbon dioxide in its atmosphere alone as there is in the whole earth's crust, so that the first element likely to run short on earth would be in plentiful supply.

But if the population of earth is doubling every thirty-five years, and we stabilize it by sending the increase to Venus, in thirty-five years Venus will have the same population density as earth – and of course, if neither is yet at the blazing limit, both will increase at the same rate and reach this limit together. Venus and the earth between them, would then cover with people an additional area as big as either in a further twenty years, which would mean that Mercury, Mars, the Moon and all the moons of Jupiter and Saturn, would be filled up to the same density. Uranus and Neptune would be very difficult to reach in less than several decades, and Pluto would take longer still. If they *could* be reached, Uranus and Neptune are usefully larger, giving some eighteen times and fourteen times the surface area of the earth respectively, so that it would take nearly 120 years before they too reached the same limit.

Jupiter and Saturn are very much bigger still, but offer formidable difficulties, as they have extensive poisonous atmospheres, at the bottom of which the pressure is far greater than at the bottom of our oceans. No known materials could be used to build structures which would support such pressures, and still maintain air pressures inside them at which we could live.

In principle, one could construct big balloons a few kilometres in diameter, filled with hydrogen at a pressure of fifty tons per square metre, and warmed to a comfortable 20°C by a nuclear power unit. Then, since the outside atmospheres are only partly hydrogen, and are at temperatures at least 100°C below zero, each balloon five kilometres diameter could carry the weight of a town of a million people – allowing a hundred tons of equipment, including the balloon, per person, which should be adequate. The problems of setting it up in the first place, and of keeping it supplied with mineral requirements such as calcium or iron, which would certainly not be found in the atmosphere, would however still remain to be solved. Presumably the elements required all exist on Jupiter, but our present ignorance of the planet is rather comprehensive, and they may be rare. On some theories of planetary formation, it would seem quite reasonable to suppose that Jupiter and Saturn have much the same amounts of such elements as does the earth itself, and that most of their extra weight is built up of hydrogen and the lighter elements. Jupiter is 314 times heavier than earth, so that the heavy elements may have less than 1 per cent of the frequency of occurrence on Jupiter that they have here. Saturn is only ninety-four times heavier, but the difference is too little to be important. Furthermore, even if common, it is unlikely that the metallic elements are found on the surface, and they might need mines 30,000 kilometres deep to dig them out. It would probably be easier to fetch them from our moon or from Mercury – the local moons may well be largely composed of ice.

As the reader may have noticed, I do not like saying that things are impossible, but I will certainly go so far as to say that we *might* not be able to colonize Jupiter and Saturn on any large scale, even in 800 years' time.

If we could do so, although Saturn has a surface gravitational pull much the same as earth, and would be comfortable enough so long as we kept ourselves warm, Jupiter would have a further drawback. We should weigh over 2.5 times as much as we do here, even floating high in the atmosphere. This would mean that the weight of our building structure would be 2.5 times as great, and the internal air or hydrogen pressure would have to go up more than 2.5 times as fast, as we went down from floor to floor, so that we could probably manage fewer storeys. Only a fairly strong man could even stand up unaided, and either people would have to live their lives in powered suits like those

Anticlimax 161

used by the US Army's 'amplified men', or else everyone would have to live their lives in water up to their shoulders, as the giant herbivorous dinosaurs were once supposed to have done. The weight of the water would reduce the possible number of floors drastically, and technical industry would be difficult in such conditions.

If we *could* solve all these problems, we should gain about another ninety years at the standard rate of multiplication. Thus, although the surface area of all the planets, including Jupiter and Saturn, adds up to 250 times the area of the earth, we should bring the whole lot to the blazing limit in less than 300 years, and should then be faced with a problem 250 times as big. A lot of extra problems, some of them insoluble by techniques imaginable at the present day, would have to be solved, but they could only defer the ultimate heat limit.

Emigration, whether in space or on earth, postpones the problem; it doesn't solve it.

Colonization of Other Solar Systems

There remain the stars. Moon-based instruments should long since have shown us which of the nearer ones possess planets. The difficulty is that they are a long way off. Chemical rockets are entirely unusable. The theoretical physicist F. J. Dyson has suggested using a very large vessel and propelling it by letting off a series of A-bombs behind it at perhaps one a second. A method more likely to be feasible would be to use a deuterium fusion chamber running at say 200,000,000°C. The exhaust velocity of the helium-hydrogen mixture left in the plasma from this, would be around a three-hundredth of the velocity of light. Remembering that the global supply of deuterium in the oceans is limited, and that the space ship must be able to land its cargo when it reaches the other end, it might be difficult to send a two-stage space ship itself faster than 1/150 of the velocity of light. Light takes 4.3 years to reach the nearest star, Proxima Centauri, so that our space ship would take 645 years. In 645 years, doubling our numbers every thirty-five years, we should multiply 350,000 times, so that for each young couple embarked, the ship would have to be built big enough to take 700,000 when it arrived – with all the power supplies, and life-support equipment, to enable them to conquer whatever major difficulties the new planets might present. This would clearly be impracticable. And if the basic human freedom to be fruitful without artificial interference were to be abrogated, and it were suggested that the young couple embarked should establish a new tradition of limiting their families to replacement level, the same people under the same conditions could have been kept on earth, which would have saved a great deal of trouble. Similarly, if it were possible to put into deep freeze half the yield of people for each thirty-five years, until they arrived at a suitable distant star, they could be put into deep freeze for increasing periods on earth, again much more cheaply. Finally, even if we did discover how to nullify gravity, to travel almost at the speed of light, or rediscover the old Arabian principle of the Magic Carpet – which seems to me the most likely of the three – the occupation of a complete new solar system as big as ours would give us only another thirty-five years.

Living in Space Ships

A faintly less improbable procedure would be to put people in spaceships and *not* send them off to the stars. If the moon were made into a vast number of ceramic spaceships instead of being colonized, the heat problem would be finally and genuinely solved. If they were made the right size, the power and other heat production inside each could be radiated at a reasonable temperature into space from a blackened hull, with no special equipment apart from an aluminium foil screen to keep the sun off. If living in free fall proved to be unsatisfactory, it would be better to provide the minimum necessary pseudo gravity by tying spaceships together in pairs by a long cable, and to swing them round their common centre of gravity, than to spin each separately. Then one's weight would remain nearly constant throughout one ship and there would be no giddiness in moving around.

The limiting factor would then be the availability of critical

Anticlimax

elements such as carbon in our own bodies. By this time, however, we would have developed the techniques of transmuting hydrogen and helium into heavier elements on an industrial scale. We can now do this atom by atom in the laboratory, with a quite enormous expenditure of energy per gramme of material produced. Using nuclear fusion at high enough temperatures, which we should soon be able to do, it would be possible to do it with an actual release of useful energy, so that it could simultaneously form the basis of our power supplies. Twenty kilowatts for a year would be provided by the total synthesis of one gramme of carbon from hydrogen, and rather more by the synthesis of heavier elements. Production of the twelve kilogrammes of carbon needed to make one extra human being would provide 720 kilowatts for thirty-five years so that this alone would give each member of the previous generation 720 kilowatts throughout the standard doubling time. This would give a very adequate surplus of power for ships, 'to mine' the atmosphere of Jupiter for hydrogen; during this process we should get quite a lot of carbon and nitrogen directly from the methane and ammonia which are already there. Hydrogen and helium form between them over 95 per cent of the solar system – most of it in the Sun, and most of the rest in Jupiter – so that there would be no need to use other elements, though this is also possible in principle if it should be needed.

With economy, it should be possible to get the total weight of a space ship down to ten tons per person so that, by the time we had used up the whole solar system except for the sun to make people and spaceships, we should have about 3×10^{23} or a third of a billion billion people (old-fashioned British billions; not the cheaper transatlantic kind). This would have given us 735 extra years after we should have been finally cooked if we had all stayed on earth, and would have given us a useful breathing space to work out the best way of getting at the useful quantities of raw material in the sun itself. In the process of using up the planets we might, if we (uncharacteristically) looked providently ahead, have arranged for the space ships to orbit the sun in the opposite direction to the present planets. By feeding the angular momentum back into the sun magnetically in doing so, we could speed up its rotation so as either to burst it outright or at least to spread it so nearly into a disc as to make abstraction of hydrogen from the rim a great deal less difficult and hazardous.

Using up the sun completely would involve some formidable logistical and heat-dissipation problems, and would give us only a rather disappointing 350 further years. The extra time gained since the abandonment of earth would have been too little for most of us to reach the stars.

But if anyone still wants a real absolute limit: within 4,000 years from now, expanding in numbers at our present rate, we should have used up every atom in every star or planet, out to a radius of 4,000 light years. To go on multiplying at our present rate, we should henceforth have to exceed the speed of light, which is not possible. So in space as well as on earth, the ultimate limit is a physical law of nature; on earth the laws of thermodynamics, and in space the laws of special relativity.

The Dangers of Relying on Computers

Some sincerely religious people do not believe that our brains were given to us to find humane ways of limiting our population. But few would hold that they were given to provide the engineering skill for the programme that I have described. As I have said before, I do not readily claim that something can never occur, and I would prefer not to claim that this astronomical débâcle is actually impossible. I do feel, however, that it is unlikely; both technically unlikely that we could solve all the practical difficulties in a few thousand years, and psychologically unlikely that the whole of humanity would continue to support a policy that made it inevitable. The only faintly probable way of achieving it would be to develop complete dependence on the interlocking computer complex, which I showed would be necessary at an early stage in the multiplication process.

The demonstrably false forecasts of inevitable and imminent disaster by the prophets of doom, as each in turn was predicted to be false by the engineer-computer alliance, and then indeed proved to be false, could just imaginably lead to a dangerously complete reliance on the engineers and computers to go on finding solutions. And as the computers became more powerful and versatile, the engineers might understand the implications of their technical programmes less and less. Even in our present simpler world, a lot of problems – such as pollution – have arisen because the technologists and the politicians have not worried about the implications of their work thirty years ahead; let alone three hundred.

In a world of the complexity it would necessarily reach, even before the Ultimate Building on earth, it would be impossibly dangerous to leave much power or responsibility in the hands of individual leaders. In the organization of a system to ensure that no-one had too much individual power, it would be difficult not to ensure at the same time that nobody had enough power to feel responsible.

The computer complex would at all times use the world's technical resources and its own planning resources in the most effective possible way – including the necessary extensions to its own designing and computational capacity, and would provide a reliable technical answer every time a worried customer fed in a question about the latest prediction of immediate disaster. If the computers had early been given a set of limits to their operations, including one which forbade them to interfere in any way with human reproduction, they could still estimate the likely changes in the population, and would plan for its safety and comfort.

A set of computers of adequate power, armed with the laws of physics and engineering, could well pursue the path I have sketched; evacuating the earth for a swarm of ships when necessary, and continuing to the really final inter-stellar disaster four thousand years from now.

The computers wouldn't care.

Just as I do not believe that we shall reach the blazing limit on earth, I do not believe either that we shall ever hand over the control of our destinies to a group of computers, and degenerate into a race, however upright and kindly, of what would be essentially playboys and playgirls. All I am doing is to say, in an involved sort of way, that we had very much better not do so.

Now that I have sketched the series of physical limits to our numbers that could replace in the future the biological limits that we have defeated in the past, it may be well to consider some of the non-technical factors and accidents that might set earlier limits than the purely physical ones.

Possible Accidents

There are plenty of Micawbers who will say that the last three chapters are entirely irrelevant, since something is bound to turn up, as it always has in the past, that will limit our numbers without thought or effort on our part. This I don't believe. A large part of my purpose in writing this book, is to illustrate our enormous and quite unprecedented capacity for dealing with things that turn up. There are still, in 1972, possible accidents with which we couldn't cope. For example, we *probably* know all the asteroids big enough to wreck the earth, and know they are not going to collide with it at least in the next few thousand years. But it is perfectly *possible* that a hundred-kilometre-diameter asteroid was diverted long ago by Jupiter into a long elliptical orbit going out several thousand million kilometres from the sun, so that it has been too far away for us to see. If this should return in the next few years and hit us at sixty kilometres a second, it is doubtful whether anybody on earth would survive. We should probably detect it three years or more before it arrived, but could hardly get enough people and equipment to the moon to form a viable settlement in time.

In thirty years' time we would be able to do this, and with telescopes on the moon, would have a good deal longer warning. Inside a hundred years we should be able to detect it twenty to fifty years in advance, and could send up an adequate crew of mining engineers armed with H-bombs, to blow it into calculated fragments which would pass us by harmlessly on either side.

Of course, if a lot of little green men from the planets around Sirius turned up with a far higher level of military technology than we had, we could do nothing about it, and they could adjust our numbers to suit their little green convenience. But even if we knew that this was going to happen, we would still do well to demonstrate our ability to control both our numbers and our aggressiveness before their arrival, or they might decide that we were too dangerous for any of us to be permitted to survive at all.

Psychological Problems

More serious is the question of possible psychological disturbances, which might appear as populations become greater or denser, and which might make successful reproduction difficult. Many people cite the experiments of Calhoun on rats, which were described at the end of Chapter Two, as evidence that we, too, should suffer a breakdown in our family patterns of behaviour with a resulting drastic fall in our net reproduction rate. It is always well to learn as much as we can from any of our fellow mammals, and it is certainly safer to consider the possibility that human beings might have some similar instincts or reactions to stress. On the other hand, it is also important to remember that no other species will have quite the same reactions as we have, to stress or anything else, and finally it is not in the least certain that rats with identical instincts, but with human intelligence, would behave in the same way as they now do.

Some of the rats' reactions are paralleled by human beings under certain kinds of stress. In big cities, there is certainly more non-standard sexual behaviour, but while part of this does not lead to babies, another part leads to more unwanted and abandoned babies than occur in villages. The extent to which this is due to population density as such, and the extent to which it is due to other, controllable, factors in the upbringing and ways of life of their mothers, is not known. What is known is that rather few of the abandoned babies are left to die or be eaten by the adults, as happens to infant rats in similar circumstances. The babies, almost all of them, are rescued and put into children's homes, and brought up to be able to have some more babies themselves.

A large part of the disorganization of the rats was not directly due to the high density, but to the forced communalization of living, with the resulting constant harrying of females by hyperactive females, and the disruption of normal rat family life by the destruction of privacy. We control fairly strictly the raping of females by emotionally disturbed males, and, even in the densest areas of modern cities, we make considerable efforts to provide more privacy than most of our race has ever enjoyed before. Local densities of human population in the past have been higher than the highest overall density I have so far described, and have had much higher reproduction rates, without obvious mental or social disturbances. There is plenty of working space around a traditional Chinese village, but the actual living space has often been tightly limited. Twenty-seven people, including two or three married couples, sleeping in a single room would not have been unusual, and while this required a lot of mutual tolerance, it did not lead to extensive abnormal behaviour. The fact is that, whether by instinct or training, we are better at communal living than rats are.

A large part of this is certainly due to our capacity for developing helpful inhibitions. It is currently popular to regard inhibitions as evil, and uninhibitedness as a virtue. In fact, of course, inhibitions are an essential requirement for living at all, let alone living in a complex society. Babies will usually cry at any loud noise, and everyone jumps at the sudden and unexpected appearance of something large close by. Our first reaction is a preparation for flight, and the second is an urgent call for help. In the course of our upbringing, we learn to inhibit both the yell and the flight, for an extensive list of large but familiar objects.

We can eliminate completely any reaction to the familiar noise of traffic outside, and may be unable, when asked, to remember whether it was there or not. Yet every sound has been recorded, checked against a list of sounds learned to be unimportant, and the natural reaction to sudden sounds has been inhibited.

If a grizzly bear were to growl a foot behind your chair, even though the noise you heard might have been considerably less than that of a lorry going past, the sound would not be on the inhibited list, and you would be well down the street before you felt any inclination to work out why it was that your head whipped round so fast that it nearly came off.

Similarly, we learn in childhood to inhibit a great many simple and natural reactions; in excretion, in taking what we want when we want it if it happens to belong to someone else, and above all in the natural reaction to other human beings who happen to be in the way of what we want to do. Whether or not someone completely uninhibited would be otherwise happy, I do not know, but he would certainly be very lonely, unless he could find someone who was herself inhibited on a pretty massive scale. Inhibitions, like everything else, can be overdone, but they are the basis of our social life. Parents may even enjoy their children better if they concentrate on trying to save them from a few injurious and de-humanizing inhibitions, such as those preventing the expression of emotion in the proper conditions, or the acceptance of help when it is seriously needed, rather than on trying to achieve the impossible and highly destructive course of preventing them from having any inhibitions at all.

Animals are not so easily able as we to develop complicated inhibitions. Most animals, when they meet a strange member of their own species, have to carry out a well defined protocol which involves close attention. Among territorial animals the protocol will usually consist of warnings, followed by threats from the landowners, with appropriate signs of submission from the interlopers. On both sides there is considerable physiological stress. Such animals find it very hard to neglect strangers, and if the density of population becomes too large they may be unable to stand the nearly continuous state of stress produced.

We have the capacity to change or inhibit our reactions quickly in response to changing circumstances. In a village it will be normal to greet appropriately everyone you meet, and, if not in too much of a hurry, to stop and chat a little. On the main street of a big city, if you said good morning to everyone you met, it would be assumed that you were drunk or advertising something, and you would have an excellent chance of a discussion with the police about what exactly you meant by it. An elderly countryman who comes up to town, finds the townspeople rude and inconsiderate, and is often badly disturbed by what seems to him a complete lack of normal human reactions. But he soon learns to stop greeting everyone, and quite quickly he can inhibit his own 'natural' human reactions as easily as can the natives.

This is definitely an inhibition of reaction, rather than a switching off of the attention so that he does not see the other occupants of the city pavements at all. If a familiar acquaintance happens to be among the approaching throng, he or she will usually be recognized at once; often at quite a distance away. Every face in the approaching multitudes, therefore, is being checked against the whole list of familiar memories, before being rejected as of no interest and requiring zero reaction. This ability to inhibit reaction certainly requires some effort; walking in such conditions is more trying than walking down an empty village street; but it requires nothing like the effort that it would, if even the slightest overt notice had to be taken of each and every individual in the crowd.

Much of our social education is adapted to teaching us whom we can neglect to notice among those around us. This is vitally important, and without it, and without our ability to develop new and modified inhibitions at short notice, we should probably be unable to live in cities at all, where the frequency of meeting strangers must be tens of thousands of times as great as the frequency during the main period of our evolution. It is unfortunate that the code of neglect differs widely in many complex ways among different social groups, so that group X find group Y stuck up and standoffish, and group Y find group X impertinent and over-familiar. But this is a minor trouble compared with that which would arise if none of us had any codes of neglect at all.

Hence we are immune to many of the pressures that disturb the behaviour of animals very seriously. The human beings who suffer from the internal ulcers, and the other stress diseases, are not the peasants who live in crowded huts, or the housewives who spend their mornings in the busy crowds. They are the personnel managers, and the trades union officials, and the big business men, who avoid the crowds and see nobody of unimportance to them, but who have to give an accurately judged response to every person they do meet, even if there are only a few of these each hour.

The local densities of population in the vast city structures which I have discussed in the last two chapters, are lower than in many existing towns. In parts of Hong Kong, there is literally not room for all of the inhabitants to get into the street together at holiday times, and the number per room in most Eastern cities is far greater than any that I have needed to assume. I am not claiming that the situation in such crowded areas is satisfactory, let alone admirable, but it does not lead to a vast demand for mental hospitals, and neither does it seriously reduce reproductive capacity. It does not even lead to any important number of people trying to get away from it all; essentially none of the inhabitants of such areas will be found voluntarily to have walked even a couple of kilometres out into the nearby countryside at holiday times, for the joy of being alone.

The people who want to get away from people include nearly everyone who writes books, but are drawn only from those who have a great deal more living space and privacy already than has ever been possessed by the mass of civilized humanity.

With over 100,000 schizophrenics in Britain alone, I am not claiming that life in our present civilization does not stress many people to breaking point. It clearly does do so. What I am saying is that this has more to do with our way of life than with the population density at which it is lived. Probably we shall soon find out how to diagnose the causes and cure the effects of emotional and mental strains, but even if we didn't, they are not now controlling the growth of population and there is no reason to suppose that they will necessarily increase. In the spoon-fed, computer-directed, responsibility-free conditions which a major growth of population would force upon us, there could well be fewer schizophrenics than we have at this moment. The limitation of travel, imposed upon us by lack of space for roadways, as we came up towards the blazing limit, might lead to an atmosphere much more like that of a small walled mediaeval town – without the stench – than like the atmosphere of a major modern city. There is no evidence that gastric ulcers or schizophrenia contributed much to the manifold horrors of a mediaeval town.

If I turn out to be wrong in my optimistic way about the dangers of stress in the future, there are plenty of positive measures that could be taken to reduce it. Tranquillizers will no doubt continue to multiply even faster than we do ourselves, and where the continuous use of these showed signs of impairing physical health, might well be backed up by hypnotic suggestion. If, as a result of skilful hypnosis, one did not believe that anyone else was there at all, it would be difficult to build up stress by a constant interaction with the non-existent crowds. Of course, care would be taken that the hypnosis should not be so complete that individuals really believed themselves to be entirely alone. This would reduce the efficiency of reproduction and would hence be regarded as gravely wrong.

As usual, I am not prophesying, and I could not possibly prove that we shall *not* be limited by psychological factors before we are limited by physical ones. But in view of the evidence we have, it would be even more difficult to prove that we certainly *should* be limited by psychological factors, and that these would necessarily vanquish the world's entire resources of medical skill. Such resources would certainly be fully mobilized for their defeat, well before any kind of mental disturbances could become a serious menace to the highly stable class of married women under thirty-five on whom our rate of growth depends. It may well be, that in investigating the causes of the stress diseases from which we are now suffering, we should take into account the Case of the Crowded Rats. But it is unlikely that we are sufficiently rat-like to be caught in the rat trap, when we know it exists and the need to avoid it is clear.

Some Real Impossibilities

Two final, entertainingly off-beat, suggestions that are sometimes made are worth a mention. The first is that under the pressure of numbers, we might evolve to a smaller size so that the world could hold more of us. It is arithmetically true that if our rate of reproduction and our life-span stayed the same, and if our average weight were halved every thirty-five years, the total weight of human beings on the planet would remain constant. The number of atoms of each element required to make them all would also remain the same and it would indeed, if continued, represent a permanent solution. By the time we would otherwise have polished off the planet as an abode for man, we should be six millimetres high: about the size of a medium ant. After a further 1,050 years, when we would otherwise have used up most of the solar system, we should be the size of a not-too-large bacillus.

The later steps of this process are technically impossible, and even the first reduction by a factor of two in average weight could be attained only by a sustained and systematic selection of those permitted to mate. This would be quite incompatible with the freedom of procreation which alone could give rise to the situation of concern in the first place. If only the shorter half of the

Anticlimax

human race were permitted to breed at all in each generation, the desired result could doubtless be obtained in a few generations, but since this criterion would obviously lead to nearly all of the survivors being Japanese, it would be unlikely to appeal to Europeans or Africans. And since the Japanese have anyway solved their problem by more conventional methods, it is unlikely that they would then see much point in continuing after the other major races had vanished. So this 'solution' need not be taken seriously.

The second is that we might evolve into spiritual or otherwise insubstantial beings, which could survive in space and live on radiation. Not in a million years. After that, something might, for all I know, live in space on radiation, but it would not be us.

Nine

Traditional and Practical Means of Artificially Controlling our Numbers

In the last eight chapters two things have been demonstrated. The first is that we have reduced to impotence all past and all existing natural checks on our rate of multiplication, and that there is a serious likelihood that we shall be able similarly to cope with any natural checks that may arise in the future, apart from those arising from the basic physical laws of the Universe. The second is that if we do not operate any checks at all, we cannot avoid an extremely comprehensive disaster when we finally come up against these laws. Since most of us would think it right, and almost all of us would think it preferable, to avoid this disaster, we must now consider the various possible alternative checks that we could operate. There is no shortage of suggestions for these, and for the purposes of discussion I shall divide them into three main groups: the reintroduction of one or more of the one-time natural controls; war; and individual limitation of numbers or sizes of families.

Reintroduction of 'Natural' Controls

I find that this is often advocated in indirect as well as in direct ways. So far as I know, no-one but Hilaire Belloc has suggested the reintroduction of control by the larger predators. Belloc fans will remember the poem on the tiger in his *Bad Child's Book of Beasts*:

> *The Tiger, on the other hand,*
>   *is kittenish and mild,*
> *He makes a pretty playfellow*
>   *for any little child.*
> *And mothers of large families*
>   *(who claim to common sense)*
> *Will find a Tiger will repay*
>   *the trouble and expense.*

Plenty of people, however, express regret that improved medical facilities have so quickly increased the expectation of life in the poorer countries, by reducing the effectiveness of control by disease. Some of these people go so far – though not always in public – as to suggest that medical supplies and assistance should be provided only for countries which are taking effective steps to control their populations.

Others doubt the desirability of supplying food to India and other countries in similar need, again until other methods of population control have been established to replace the natural method of control by famine.

I shall come back to these suggestions in the next chapter; here I want to point out that such controls, natural as they once were, are no longer natural but artificial. Deliberately withholding an available defence against a killing disease is just as artificial an operation as would be introducing a new disease against which no defence existed. A moral difference may be discernible by an expert casuist but it will not be discernible by the victims of the resulting epidemic, and the political effects are unlikely to differ at all. I shall therefore include such measures with the other more novel and numerous methods which are already generally regarded as artificial.

Control by War

The second form of check is war. It is difficult to classify this as either natural or unnatural. When war between tribes was the only possible means for the sharing out of indispensable food or territory, it could properly be called natural. In so far as it helped to mould our present natures it could be called natural. Yet it was natural to have recourse to war only *because* it was indispensable; *because* the food supplies could not be artificially increased, so that one man's gain was inescapably another man's loss. War was dangerous and uncertain, and a tribe which attacked surrounding tribes of comparable size at random, might find itself both weakened and occupying an enviable amount of rich territory when times were hard – a combination unlikely to help its permanent survival. War was natural when it was used as a last resort; as the final arbiter in times of major stress. War used now, when there is no material gain that it can give which could not be obtained more cheaply and more safely by the use of modern technology, can no longer be regarded as natural. In the future, however, if no other means of control of population could be found, we might find that space to expand was itself as vital a necessity as food supplies could ever have been, and we can say with confidence that the directly threatened populations would quickly come again to think it natural. It is this confusing situation that leads me to regard war as in a separate category by itself, not reliably to be classed either as natural or as unnatural without knowledge of the circumstances in which it is to be waged.

With this introduction, let us see whether, and if so how, war could work.

The major objective of war would shift from the pattern usual in recent times. This has been to control strategic territories and populations, in such a way that they could no longer build up and deploy effective armies in the future. Wars arising from direct population pressure could be expected to revert to more primitive objectives; to eliminate alien populations, and to occupy permanently their territories.

In pre-human times, when communications were rudimentary and apemen were loyal directly and only to the group with which they grew up, this led to a stable result. A successful tribe could destroy or evict its neighbours, but as it multiplied to fill the space and use the resources that it had gained, the exigencies of food gathering over a larger area would inevitably lead to the fission of the extended tribe into separate parts, and the more distant of these would have become strangers and enemies in one or two generations. The process could thus repeat indefinitely

Means of Artificially Controlling our Numbers

as local multiplication outgrew local food supply, without any great change in the number of independent tribes.

The modern equivalent would not be stable. Any country which successfully wiped out another and expanded over the ruins, would be able to maintain its political unity however geographically dispersed its new territories might be. There would also be a very strong incentive to do so, since its combined strength would obviously be greater than the strengths of any of the separate parts when further growth made further wars necessary. The bigger a unit grew, the more effectively could it ensure its further growth at the expense of weaker powers. This is not a stable situation.

Many interesting strategies might be evolved to ensure final victory for a particular power, but the most important single factor would certainly be the degree of understanding of what was happening. To see this, let us suppose that it had been proven in an absolute mathematical sense that no other means but war could continuously control population. This might be first seen by anyone, but wherever the proof originated, knowledge of it would rapidly pass to the largest powers. This would happen even if it were first proved in a small pacific state such as Sweden. It would be obvious to the originator that what he had proved others could prove independently and that no imaginable action by Sweden could enable her to eliminate the rest of the world for the sake of her descendants before the bigger powers had got the idea. The only sensible plan therefore would be for the originator and his family, and any friends he still retained after explaining his conclusions, to migrate forthwith to the USA or the USSR or China, and to educate the government of his new homeland in the shortest possible time to understand his proof. What would happen then would depend on the military calculations of this government. To do nothing indefinitely would *certainly* lead to someone else doing something drastic first, and on the principle that best armed is he who gets his blow in first,* the only problem would be whom and when, not whether, to attack. Ideally, if it could be done, it would be best to wipe out first the strongest rival. It would be worth while to accept con-

---
* 'Thrice armed is he that hath his quarrel just,
But four times he who gets his blow in fust.' Josh Billings.

siderable losses so long as these did not leave the attacker too weak to ward off an immediate pre-emptive attack by Power No 3, or by a temporary combination of this with one or two others.

If conditions when the light dawned – or perhaps I should say when the dusk fell – were similar to the present balance, Power No 1 could not hope to eliminate Power No 2 without gravely weakening itself.

It is not therefore likely that either would attack the other. Rather, they would do well to combine forces to eliminate Power No 3, together with any others which had any long-range weapons. This could be done, in the foreseeable future, with quite acceptable losses. (By acceptable losses I mean only losses which would not destroy their hegemony. Thus a loss of half their populations could easily be made up in thirty years or so, and would therefore be acceptable so long as they retained the strength to block the development of major weapons elsewhere.) With the ruthlessness that comes readily to most human beings when their futures are really at stake, this would not be too difficult. Power 1 and Power 2 strategists would then, with little hope for either of 'safely' destroying the other, settle down to spread competitively over the rest of the planet. When, eventually, they alone remained, any losses whatever would be acceptable that left *some* survivors on the attacking side in the final débâcle.

I do not want to imply that the winner would *necessarily* be one of the present or future Big Two. If they both played their cards correctly it would be, but the capacity of leading generals for blunder is beyond the range of quantitative prediction, and it is quite possible that one of them would get itself conclusively wrecked in a premature or ill-judged campaign. The point is that sooner or later one power would win – or lose least – and would then, since the world population at this point would not be excessive, have plenty of time to develop pest-spray techniques which really would be effective in destroying the rest of the population of the planet.

The difficulty is that the situation is still not stable. Suppose that the USA had won, and that the entire population of the globe was American. Then it would inevitably occur to the more farsighted Americans that there would come a time when even Americans would overcrowd the world, and that if they acted drastically and at once, before the rest thought of it, they could ensure the proper survival of their own higher and more farsighted type for a considerably longer period. And then among the farsighted there would be some ever farther sighted characters . . .

We can see that if war really is, and is recognized really to be, the only way of limiting our population, it is unlikely to produce the long-term stability of the natural checks which we have learnt to evade. It is unlikely that war could wipe out humanity completely at the first try, unless at this time our technical level is very much higher than now, but if it did not, all we could do would be to run through the pattern over and over again until it did. If it really were the only means of population control available for a technically educated population, there would of course be no chance ever of avoiding it. Properly used as I have described, it is evidently an extremely effective way of preventing overcrowding, which the rather aimless wars of the last few centuries have been unable to do. Nevertheless, it does not represent an attractive alternative, and could easily wipe out the human race even sooner than would the heat death resulting from uncontrolled multiplication. On the other hand, the process might repeat a large number of times; at short intervals if a tenth or more of humanity survived each débâcle; at long intervals if a millionth or less did so. But sooner or later, the human race would either disappear or would learn some alternative method of permanent control. It would save a lot of grief if we could do this the first time.

The only way to make wars work without seriously overdoing them, would be to control them so tightly that they were really large scale gladiatorial shows rather than wars at all – with a kind of league table requiring the densest country to fight the next densest – with full television coverage – every weekend, and with weapons adequate, in efficient hands, for the combatants to satisfy the umpires that sufficient total population reduction had occurred before it was necessary to return to work on Monday morning. A useful incentive could be introduced by a penalty clause requiring them to fight new and fresh opponents the following weekend if the total combined reduction were inadequate. If the wars were fought entirely by unmarried young women, with cheap weapons and no hospital services, they could really be quite efficient. Disputes concerning the rules would tend to be frequent, and might not always be amicable, and although people who had been killed by foul play would of course be declared to be officially alive again, much ill feeling would be aroused, leading to unnecessary and excessive damage to property. Hence, although this represents a potentially stable and permanent control, even well-organized wars seem to have little to commend them.

Traditional Methods of Control

For people who prefer the old, tried, methods hallowed by years of tradition, there are of course several techniques a good deal cheaper and more predictable than wars. The Aztec plan of sacrificing some ten thousand people on holy days was locally effective, but a probable lack of consumer-co-operation might make this difficult to organize on the seventy-million-a-year scale which we should now require. Infanticide, which has been used by many people for extensive periods of time, could much more easily be made acceptable. The highly sophisticated Romans and Greeks, and many primitive peoples, used it. We often ascribe this practice to superstition; but it has sometimes kept populations at a steady level appropriate to their resources for long periods. This would seem to require an extraordinarily lucky coincidence in the quantitative components of the superstition. Any unprovable belief which we do not hold ourselves is liable to be described as superstitious and it might be at least as reasonable for the infanticidal Spartans for example to regard as superstitious the beliefs that prevent us from achieving a steady level appropriate to *our* long-term resources.

Infanticide seems to me to be very much the most stable and effective, and also the least undesirable, of the older traditional methods of control, but still has little appeal at the present day.

There seems no reasonable question whatever that the methods developed by the very scientific technology which has made control so vitally necessary in the first place, are morally, aesthetically and humanely superior to any of the traditional procedures.

Means of Artificially Controlling our Numbers

For the rest of this chapter, therefore, I shall discuss the methods of limitation which are available now but which were not known in the past.

Availability is not sufficient by itself. As in so many fields of life, what people *will* do needs much more consideration than what they *can* do. Nevertheless, even if not sufficient, availability is an absolutely essential factor, so I shall deal with this first, by discussing briefly the main methods now in use.

Control of Conception

I shall begin at the beginning with control of conception. The most complete and definite method is surgical sterilization, which is easy and safe for men but involves a significant surgical operation for women. For obvious reasons this is used almost entirely by parents who regard their family as quite large enough or too large already. So far, except in India, it is little used.

Less drastic methods of preventing conception may be either behavioural, mechanical or chemical. Each has its advantages and disadvantages. The most effective of the behavioural methods is to forbid marriage for an adequate fraction of the population, or to delay marriage till well on in life, and to maintain effective social sanctions against extra-marital alliances. The big convents and monasteries of mediaeval times implemented the first of these; in devout periods effectively, in others less so. The convents alone are important, though it would annoy Women's Lib if symmetry were not maintained by the establishment of an equivalent number of monasteries. While every little helps, it is not believable that this could furnish our main means of control in the present era. Delay of marriage has sometimes been effective in the past, but only with a particularly rigid social pattern and under very severe economic stress which made youthful marriage impracticable, as in rural Ireland in quite recent times. The rapid improvement in absolute, if not relative, economic standards all over the world makes it most unlikely that this will spread appreciably, and it is much more likely to disappear.

The only behavioural methods which are of any current importance are cruder; withdrawal (*coitus interruptus*) and the rhythm method. Withdrawal has had an appreciable influence on population growth in some areas, but it is inefficient and rapidly becomes unpopular when alternative methods are developed, so that it is not worth extensive consideration.

The rhythm method on the other hand, although it also is inefficient, is important for two reasons; first it is the cheapest of all widely used methods, and second it is the only method permitted to strict Roman Catholics and some other smaller groups. It consists simply in avoiding coitus during the part of each month when the woman has an ovum available for fertilization. Each menstrual period begins about 11-16 days after ovulation. Sperm may remain alive and effective for some time after ejaculation and the ovum may be available for a day or more so that for safety some ten days around ovulation must be avoided, if conception is not to occur. The practical drawbacks are that for some people ten days seem too long, and that if periods are at all irregular, ten days are too short since the time is related to the period yet to come rather than to the period already past. Periods are not always regular. Given good sense and self control, however, it can be very effective for subfertile couples, and can materially reduce the birthrate for others. A possible long-term disadvantage therefore is that, if it were widely used, it could lead to a serious degree of natural selection against the possession of good sense and self control; qualities which are not notably in excess in any human population. In its favour, it has no undesirable long-term physical effects on its users,* is aesthetically acceptable, offends none and may be the method of choice by enough couples to have a real effect on the rate of population growth in advanced populations.

For illiterate and innumerate peasant populations who do not possess calendars, it is necessarily less effective. In some parts of India women were supplied with necklaces of red and green beads, one of which was to be moved on each day. The green beads represented safe days and the red ones unsafe ones. Various difficulties have been reported, apart from the obvious one that

---

*It has been suggested that when the method fails it may give an unusually high proportion of malformations among the embryos produced, since these may often result from eggs which have remained unfertilized for unusually long periods. As yet the evidence for this is inconclusive.

only a fraction of peasant husbands are predisposed to allow their rights to be restricted by the colour of their wives' necklaces. For example, it was quickly pointed out that in homes without artificial light the beads could often not be seen at critical moments. This problem was solved by making the red beads square and the green ones round. Some women could not remember in which direction the beads were to be moved, so necklaces in which they could be moved only one way were produced. Some women, though, regarded the necklace as a powerful charm and, when the need arose, would move the beads on until a green one was reached and then go ahead, relying on its protective power.

I do not actually disbelieve these stories but I doubt very much whether they represent long-term difficulties. Ignorance is often confused with inability to learn, and, when there is really a will on both sides of the family, the bead necklaces have no doubt a useful effect, at least in spreading the family out a bit. Gaining the goodwill of both sides in a community where it is socially shaming for a married woman to have a period at all, and gaining the acquiescence of the husbands everywhere, are likely to be much more important.

Limitation of Births by Mechanical and Chemical Methods

Mechanical methods currently used include the condom or sheath for men, various kinds of cap for women, and the coil or intra-uterine device, also for women. As for the rhythm method, problems have been reported in educating illiterate people to use any of these. It is probably more important, however, that the rubber protectives are far too expensive for mass use by primitive populations. They have also a considerable failure rate due to breakage of the condoms in use or to misplacement of the caps, which is much more likely to be unnoticed in unskilled than in technically educated populations. They are however harmless to health, and have almost certainly been the main material factors in reducing the birthrates of the industrialized countries during the first half of the twentieth century.

The coil has a number of drawbacks. It can be used only by

women who have already had a child; it may not remain in place, and it may have uncomfortable side effects such as the production of irregular bleeding. It is however extremely cheap; one insertion may be effective for a time of the order of years, and no practical measures need to be taken by the husband. In poor populations therefore it may well be the method of choice.

Chemical methods consisted at first mainly of spermicidal liquids or jellies, used at least as much to supplement mechanical methods as they were to do the job themselves. Within the last ten years or so, however, the contraceptive pill for women has risen to pre-eminence among all methods used in the West. This works by simulating the hormone system of oestrogens and progesterones of pregnancy itself. Under natural conditions these prevent the destructive interference which would occur if a new embryo started to grow, when an earlier one was already well on its way. When regularly used the pill can be 100 per cent effective. In some cases it can have undesirable side effects, but these are fewer and its dangers are very much less than those of pregnancy. Nevertheless its dangers are not zero; with some formulations there may be several deaths from thrombosis in a hundred thousand. While every one of these might also have died if they had become pregnant instead of taking the pill, and while the actual danger is of the same order as that of smoking one or two cigarettes a week, the scale on which the pills are taken makes attempts at further improvement well worth while.

At a cost of between ten and fifty pence per week according to the variety used, they may be cheaper than rubber condoms for some couples, but remain very expensive for the big peasant populations of the East. Since they need to be taken regularly, it needs both effective motivation and good housekeeping to ensure uninterrupted supplies. Oddly enough at first sight, in practice this seems to make it less efficient among the rich than among the poor. Thus in the early trials the Pincus pill was 100 per cent effective among the largely illiterate Puerto Rico women, but well below this among white Californians, although there was and is no evidence of any difference in physiological response. It is likely that the poor have much more practice than the rich in worrying about future supplies of other things.

Under rapid development at the time of writing is a new class

Means of Artificially Controlling our Numbers

of chemical agents, the prostaglandins, or 'the morning-after pills', which can be used to prevent the development of an ovum even after fertilization. The cost of these is not yet known but might well be less than that of the usual contraceptive pill for older couples, and its effectiveness would certainly be greater for the poor housekeepers and others who act without effective premeditation.

If conception has not been prevented, there remains the possibility of abortion, before returning to the traditional solution of infanticide or human sacrifice.

Chemical abortifacients exist but the most effective ones are dangerous and the safe ones are not very efficient. Various agents of the latter kind may be sold as cures for 'menstrual disorders' when pregnancy tests have proved positive. For obvious reasons, the facts required to establish the percentage effectiveness of these are very difficult to obtain reliably. It is clear however that in a large proportion of cases such agents are *not* effective.

Surgical abortion consists in removal of the foetus either mechanically or by vacuum suction. Both, especially the latter, in experienced hands, are safer and easier than is going to full term and giving birth to a baby, but, as with the pill, even a few deaths in a hundred thousand would be worth a lot of trouble to prevent. Far more than the contraceptive methods, however, the incidence of abortion is controlled by law rather than by individual prejudices or concern for health.

The pros and cons will therefore be left for the next chapter in which I shall explain and discuss my own beliefs as to the methods to be preferred and the ways in which we can most effectively encourage their use.

Ten

Possible Solutions

The best solution to any problem is one that will work. I am a physicist, and I have some training in choosing the easiest of several technical answers to a technical problem. I am not a social scientist, and have no training in the selection of the best of several answers to a human problem. I am therefore putting forward what seem to me to be some possible solutions, with the full realization that some of my solutions may not be socially practicable at all, and that even if the others are, there may be better and simpler ones.

Just as the good engineer is one who can do for one dollar what any fool can do for two, the good social scientist may be the one who can see how to do in fifty years, with popular support, for the hundred thousand million pounds the world could well afford, what any committee of fools could do in a hundred years by dictatorial methods, for the hundred million million pounds, the world could not afford.

World population growth has an enormous inertia, and is travelling at unprecedented speed towards an unattractive goal. As with a train doing the same thing, the only way to stop it instantaneously is to blow it up or run it into a cliff. Neither of these is likely to be acceptable to civilized people or to the travellers in the train. We cannot even change its velocity or direction instantaneously without catastrophic effects. The best that we can do is to build up a tolerable deceleration capable of bringing it to rest in a foreseeable period, and to take all necessary measures to avoid disaster during the inevitable further travel that must yet take place before it stops.

Any viable solution must therefore provide simultaneously, both for the urgent retardation of population growth, and for an

Possible Solutions

inevitable rise of numbers for decades ahead. To believe that we could escape the imminent necessity of feeding thousands of millions of extra mouths by the universal limitation of births, is as foolish as to suppose that we can avoid the long-term need to limit births by adequate provision of new sources of food.

In the long run we have to balance our books, and to attain a state in which we can live on the world's income rather than its capital. This admittedly may be exceedingly difficult if we do not try seriously and soon, but is absolutely impossible to achieve overnight.

In the first eight chapters of this book I have given the reasons for supposing that our present population growth *could* continue for many hundreds of years, without giving rise to insoluble technical problems or material privation. My conclusions, as I have already admitted, are often regarded as irresponsibly optimistic. This is unfair. There is nothing irresponsibly optimistic in believing that I could win the Irish Sweep. It *would* be optimistic to think that I have a large chance of doing so, and irresponsible to the point of lunacy to start spending the proceeds before even buying a ticket.

I have given a sustained exposition of the best that we could achieve with a planned, uninterrupted and concentrated application of technology, with continuous and worldwide co-operation lasting for hundreds or thousands of years. The fact that this best turns out to be quite unattractive is hardly important in view of the obvious fact that the best is almost incredibly unlikely to be attained, and that all the more likely alternatives are a great deal worse. Unlike Professor Ehrlich, I do carry insurance, and I do often make plans for a number of years ahead, but though my time scale may differ from his, I am sure that he and his co-thinkers are absolutely correct in believing that unchecked population growth must lead to disaster. In fact, if such growth does continue, I think that *he* is the optimist, in believing that we shall soon reach a form of nemesis familiar on a smaller scale, in worldwide poisoning and starvation. The end that seems to me more likely if we once become certain that we cannot control our multiplication, and that we are limited only by the presence of each other, looks so diabolically horrible, that although I have quite a high threshold of boggle, my mind boggles at considering it in detail. *Any* alternative would be preferable.

My object in showing at such length the highly improbable *best* that we could do is to show conclusively that we couldn't do anything better, and that since even this best is not tolerable, we really do have to choose a different route. An important secondary object is to show that we *have* got time to think, even though the price of time comes high – every year's delay costs an extra seventy-five million people or perhaps seventy-five thousand million pounds. But even if we dither and argue for twenty years, the cost is less than that of blowing the world up to get an instant result. Twenty years of inaction would do untold and unnecessary damage to many amenities, and to the wild life of the planet, and would heighten the political and economic difficulties, but would present no insuperable technical problems. The fact that I cannot put forward an instantaneous panacea is not important. I am showing how to make a start, and if a start can be made on slowing down our multiplication without building up such opposition that the deceleration cannot be maintained, we can work out improvements as we go along.

The first point that I want to make is that we should not look for a single universal plan which should be best for everybody. The optimum population depends upon one's way of life. A country of city lovers with twice the British population density might feel that they could still improve their freedom of choice of complex ways of living, and cheapen their productivity, by some further multiplication, while a country with a tenth of our density, inhabited by enthusiastic gardeners and fishermen, might feel itself already too dense. Practically, the former attitude is rarer than the latter simply because all of us have multiplied in the last generation, and all of us are thus adapted by early training to a lower density than that in which we live.

Even where some increase of population is desired, however, there is an advantage in increasing more slowly. There would be advantages in some considerable degree of multiplication in parts of Africa. I do not say this for the suspiciously racialist reason that the yellows and browns and whites – especially the whites – have all multiplied by large factors in recent centuries, and that it is therefore the turn of the blacks. The reason why I think they have a good and real case for expansion, is that over much of the hitherto epidemic-ridden continent, the populations are so sparse that the raw material of human skill and effort is too small to build the infra structure of roads and railways and power supplies and hospitals and schools and factories on which high living standards depend.

Ghana, for example, could be a rich and comfortable country with eight times its present population, which it would not reach for seventy years at its present rate of rise of around 3 per cent per year. Even in such an area, however, there can be almost as strong a case for the limitation of births as there is in overcrowded Western Europe. One cannot produce people for seventy years and then stop to build factories. The initial build up of industrial capital, and of an adequate store of the needful wide variety of industrial skills and experience, is inevitably slow. If the whole of the increase of output is swallowed up by new mouths, and the whole of the newly educated are needed to keep up with teaching an explosive increase in the children at elementary school, the build-up of capital may be so slow as to stop altogether. Increase is needed, but where an increase of 3 per cent per year could only just be fed and clothed, an increase of 1 per cent would make possible a concurrent expansion of the technical fabric of civilization, as well as some of the increase of living standards which is essential to make people feel that their efforts are worthwhile. Thus while the motives for population control may not yet be the same as ours, and the long-term objective may be quite different, it is equally urgent and compelling.

The Example of Japan

If I had desired twenty years ago to discuss the most socially and politically practicable plan for stopping, or even greatly slowing, the rate of population growth, I would have had to start with an extensive series of arguments designed to show that there were any proposals that could possibly work under any conditions. Now I don't. We have direct experimental evidence that control can work – and control without compulsion at that – in appropriate circumstances. This evidence has been provided by Japan.

The Japanese indeed have given us lessons on a broader scale.

Well before the war, they recognized quite clearly that their rate of multiplication was such that their small islands would soon be unable to maintain them. The semi-feudal but responsible Government saw the need for action, and adopted a simple and traditional solution; if one's territory is too small to feed one's growing population, take over some more territory. The Tanaka Memorandum envisaged a long-term plan over several generations, for taking over first China, then the rest of eastern and southern Asia, the Pacific countries and eventually the world. The takeover of the first half of China went according to plan. The rest of the plan might have followed equally satisfactorily if the armed forces had not made the strategic error of trying to jump a step by attacking the United States, the importance of whose industrial power they did not understand.

Luckily for all of us, the Japanese not only lost, but understood clearly that the cost of modern war had risen so high that even if they prepared for and won a new war later, it would cost more than it would be worth. After the war therefore, when the population began to rise even faster than before, attaining a net reproductive index of two (see Appendix I) they abandoned the traditional solution, and set themselves, with characteristic effectiveness, to limit births instead.

Before the war, the sale of contraceptives was illegal, and abortion permitted only when there was serious danger to the mother or, under the Eugenic Protection Act of 1938, when there were mental or physical defects among close relations which might lead to the birth of inferior descendants.

Extensions to the Eugenic Protection laws, from 1948 onwards, also permitted abortion where the economic situation of the family would be made impossible by the birth of a further child. This part of the law was very liberally interpreted by the medical profession, and the number of registered abortions in Japan rose to a million or more per year* by 1954. The number remains high but, especially since 1959, a major effort has been made to reduce the abortion rate by intensive propaganda for the use of contraceptives instead. These are made by private firms, under the control of the Minister of Welfare and the Prefectural

* *Home Doctor, Medical Science for the Home* by Dr K. Kazama, Head of Daiwa City Hospital, Kanajawa Prefecture, Japan.

Possible Solutions

governors and are very extensively advertised; the most popular being foaming spermicidal tablets and pessaries.

As a result, in fifteen years the net reproductive index was reduced from two to just under one. The population is still very young, and the total number will increase for some decades if the birthrate simply remains steady at the replacement value (see Appendix I). Japan would be less crowded if the same events had taken place thirty years earlier. Nevertheless, the Japanese success is of inestimable importance. It has been shown by example, not by theory, that a recently-industrialized people can change drastically their reproductive pattern, from one giving a rise far faster than the world average to one which, if maintained, will give complete stability.

What we have to do, therefore, is not to worry about whether this can be done at all but about the best way to do it. Vital as is the Japanese example, it is still necessary to show that other countries are capable of following it, and if at the moment they are not, how they may become capable.

The Factors Involved in Successful Control

In examining this capability, we have to consider three separate factors, which are often confused, with seriously misleading results. The most important factor, and the least easy to change, is whether the people of the country *wish* to limit their birthrate. In every country some will, and some will not, some will not wish to limit it enough, and some will wish to limit it more than would on the average be necessary. The important point is not that there should be no-one who wants children by the dozen, but the *average* of the desires of the whole population should not exceed the appropriate level. To achieve this is a matter of education and propaganda.

The second factor, also essential but easier to change, is the availability of the material and the know-how to carry out their wishes. To achieve this is a matter of education, money and research.

The third factor is the extent to which the chosen methods of limitation are legally, religiously and socially permissible. This degree of permissibility usually, though not invariably, represents the state of public opinion a generation or two earlier. In times of rapid change, such as the present, it may well still represent quite fairly the opinions of the older people who are no longer producing children themselves, but may differ widely from the wishes of the younger fertile generation whose behaviour alone will determine the birthrate. To achieve legal, religious and social sanction is a matter of education and political action.

Methods Appropriate to the Industrialized Countries

Different countries differ in their needs. It would be inconvenient to go into detail for a large number of countries, so I shall deal only with a few representative groups, starting at home with Britain and Western Europe (omitting southern Italy, which is a special case). Although its numbers are less than those of Asia, Western Europe is an important region. Its influence is out of proportion to its size, and, as has already been pointed out, its total usage of world resources is actually greater than that of the more numerous Asians. The rate of natural increase of the area is well below the world average; certainly less than 1 per cent per year. Furthermore, the average age of the population is rising, so that an appreciable part of the increase is a 'transient' phenomenon as defined in Appendix I; that is to say, even if birth and death rates at each stage remained constant for a long period, the natural increase would get smaller over the next few decades as a bigger proportion reached old age. Only a small change in birthrate therefore is required for long-term stability.

It is exceedingly difficult to get reliable figures for the number of unwanted babies born. A rough estimate can be made by supposing that all illegitimate children are not wanted and that all legitimate children are wanted. Quite certainly neither of these suppositions is true, and there is no particular reason to suppose that the two figures are the same. Sample questionnaires are unreliable, as there will be a systematically greater reluctance to admit the unwanted pregnancies than to admit the wanted ones. Questionnaires at a later stage will similarly be unreliable, because a large proportion of babies which were not wanted – whose

Possible Solutions

advent was viewed with real dismay – will be accepted and loved a few years later. This is very fortunate for the children themselves, but makes it impossible to tell what would be the 'free' birthrate of Western Europe; i.e. the birthrate which would result if no undesired conceptions occurred. There is no reasonable doubt, however, that at least in Britain, the number of babies born who were unwanted at the time of conception is very appreciably greater than the excess over the replacement value. In other words, if no unwanted children were born, the population of Britain would soon be slowly falling instead of slowly rising. The same is almost certainly true of Western Europe.

The implication is strong, that in Western Europe it is more important to improve the availability and efficiency of the means of limiting births, and to reduce the social and legal hindrances to this improvement, than to persuade more people to want to limit their families. It seems both unreasonable and inhumane to try to persuade people not to have children that they do want while a lot of people are still having children that they do not want.

I shall return to this point, but before that will discuss the ways by which the number of unwanted children can best be reduced.

Japanese experience suggests that by far the most practically important measure is the easing of the abortion laws. This is partly for the simple technical reason that abortion is 100 per cent efficient and contraception is not. Furthermore, a mechanical contraceptive which is 98 per cent efficient each time of use, or one which is 100 per cent efficient but is forgotten 2 per cent of the time, will not reduce the birthrate by anything approaching 98 per cent. An unrestricted and healthy young couple may well copulate several times in each fertile period, and if so the total effect of the contraceptive may be merely to postpone conception on the average by about a couple of years – useful in a rapidly multiplying peasant community, but not in an advanced one where completed families of two and three are the likely targets.

Many couples of course achieve considerably higher efficiencies than 98 per cent with rubber devices plus pessaries, by a combination of sustained good housekeeping in maintaining supplies with careful advance inspection for faults of the devices themselves. Averaging over all couples, however, a very considerable number of unwanted babies will result from reliance on such a system alone, unless its occasional failures are backed up by readily available abortion. It is likely therefore that the most practically effective method of reducing unwanted births is to make abortion free of charge and available on demand. It is encouraging that, after many decades when no visible progress at all was being made against rigid opposition, there has since 1967 been a sudden change in the legal position in many parts of the world. For example, in USA alone, where before 1967 no single state permitted abortion except to preserve the health of the mother, by 1971 a dozen had modified their statutes and four, New York, Washington, Hawaii and Alaska, had removed abortion from the criminal code altogether, thus in effect freely permitting abortion on demand.

If none of those who wished to avoid parenthood disliked the idea of abortion, this measure alone would be sufficient, although expensive and less safe for the woman than most contraceptive methods. In fact however, many people who regard contraception as right believe that abortion is wrong, and furthermore believe it so strongly that they would much prefer the birth of an unwanted baby to having it aborted. An even larger number of people – this time including the author – regard contraception as to be preferred for a mixture of material, moral and aesthetic reasons, even if abortion should be freely available as a last resort. It is therefore important that the know-how and the material equipment for safe and efficient contraception should also be made fully available. Here there is considerable room for improvement. The rhythm method is of course perfectly safe as far as the health of the mother is concerned, but is ineffective when the woman concerned has irregular periods; where her arithmetical accuracy is poor; or where the self-control of the couple is inadequate. Between them these three limitations can let through a lot of unwanted babies; not necessarily those with the best chances of being well brought up and educated. For the older couples for whom the arrival of a child would not be a disaster, it can however be perfectly satisfactory, and to many people it is morally or aesthetically the best of all. Like other methods which are only moderately efficient, however, it is not sufficient by itself to control the growth of population.

Possible Solutions

Condoms are widely available both in slot machines and in retail shops, and are therefore at present making the largest single contribution to family limitation in Britain and most of Europe. They also give fair protection against venereal disease, but they occasionally leak, come off, or tear apart in use.

In a survey by 'Which' of brands on sale in Britain, between 3 per cent and 20 per cent leaked or tore apart under stress. It is difficult to relate this to the probability of conception when no other method of protection is used. On the average it is unlikely that they will permit as many as 10 per cent of the conceptions which would occur if no contraceptive precautions were used at all. (As we have seen above, this is quite compatible with a failure rate of much less than 1 per cent per occasion of use.)

As we saw in the last chapter the contraceptive pill is very considerably the most efficient method now available and the less expensive kinds may indeed be a good deal cheaper than condoms, even if a further 4-6p per week is paid to the family planning clinic which provides the pills, for regular health checks. The main limitation is the fact that the pill can be obtained only on prescription, and hence for practical purposes is available only to that fraction of the population that will plan ahead, and is prepared to pay consistent and regular visits for years on end to a doctor or clinic for further supplies. As with the rhythm method, it is therefore less effective for the feckless and un-self-controlled.

The Pill is at present avoided by numbers of women as a result of the publicity given to the danger of thrombosis resulting from the use of some formulations of pill. As we have seen, this danger is very small compared with the dangers attending most of the regular pleasures of life. The regular use of the 'dangerous' type of pill is about equivalent in immediate danger to driving about 500 miles a year in a private car. Over a long period it reduces one's expectation of life by about as much as smoking two cigarettes a week, or, if you are a little overweight already, increasing your excess weight by three or four grammes. It is clearly desirable to encourage the development of equally reliable and even safer materials, but meanwhile a quantitative statement of the actual size of the risk on each packet might reduce the number afraid to use it.

There are several less widespread methods, which should not be condemned because they are less popular than the ones which I have mentioned. People differ widely in their likes and dislikes and in the motives which lead to action, and between them the minor methods may prevent the birth of an important number of unwanted babies which might without them have been born.

Sterilization in particular is worth mentioning, since it is different in kind from the others, although at present it is used only on a small scale in Europe. This is thoroughly efficient if properly carried out; and requires no further trouble, and hence for many people is by far the most reliable system. As we have seen, for men it is completely safe and very simple, while for women it is safer than abortion and much safer than childbirth, and of course has to be done only once in a lifetime. It would seem both desirable and economic for this to be provided free on request – the cost of the operation is less than the cost of even one more confinement. The main and very serious disadvantage of sterilization, apart from the normal and natural prejudice against anything new, is that it is not reliably reversible and therefore may make it impossible to change one's mind. For men, fertility can be restored in rather more than half of the cases in which it is desired, but a long period of sterility may lead to atrophy of the severed tubes, after which no restoration is possible. Much the same proportion of reversibility applies to women although, as before, a bigger operation is required. Many and perhaps most people who wish to avoid having more children than they already have, may be uncertain whether they will *never* want another, and may well feel that if a catastrophe should destroy one or all of the existing family, they would want to start again. It is therefore highly desirable that research on a considerable scale should be done on reversible methods of sterilization. It would not be important whether this was done surgically as now or by, for example, the implantation of a kind of long-lasting pill. If a really reliable method of any kind should be found which did not affect potency or libido, it could well become the best method of all. Of course, if by some rather unlikely chance a reversible means of sterilization were found which actually increased male libido or enjoyment, the prospect of overpopulation would vanish overnight. So it would if an effectively aphrodisiac contraceptive were developed. However, I would not myself be anxious to see such a device produced; I would like to see the world population stop increasing, and in Britain actually to fall somewhat, but I would not like the human race to vanish altogether.

In principle, a trouble-free and really effective method of contraception either for men alone or for women alone would be adequate. In practice both are needed. Organizations such as Women's Lib would object strongly to the unfairness of having the whole responsibility forced upon the women – they object already to the fact that a pill has been developed for women and not for men – and would probably object more strongly still should the situation be reversed, and all contraceptives be controlled by men without any practical control being given to women. More importantly, in a field involving such strong feelings as does reproduction, a method which appears ideal to one couple may be anathema to another, and however obvious it might be that a particular method was 'best' in the purely technical sense, it will always be important that people should have, and should feel that they have, some real choices available.

To summarise, then, it seems likely that the number of unwanted children born in Britain, and many other industrial countries, could be quickly and greatly reduced by easing the sale of the Pill, by making sterilization simple to arrange, and by making abortions easy if other methods have failed. Increased research on a male Pill, on improved and perhaps longer-lasting female ones and on methods of reversible sterilization would improve matters further but more slowly. All of these methods appear to me to be both desirable and urgent, and between them likely fairly rapidly to change a serious rate of growth of population into a comfortably gradual fall.

Compulsion?

To many people this gradual approach is quite inadequate, and to some it seems highly unlikely that it would ever reduce the growth rate to zero at all, let alone reverse it, even if it succeeded in its main aim of reducing the number of unwanted babies to a negligible value. It may be that they are right. I will therefore discuss some of the proposals which have been made to accelerate matters. As most of these proposals involve some degree of compulsion, we should think first about the possibilities of this. I am myself totally opposed to compulsion, but want to explain why I believe that such compulsion would be ineffective as well as wrong.

The technical problems involved do not lie in chemistry or physics, but in the methods of enforcement. Thus, one of the simplest proposals is that any couple wishing to have a baby should be required to obtain a licence, and that not more than two such licences should be issued to any couple until the population had dropped to an appropriate value. Oddly enough, this proposal is often put forward by people who have shown no interest in the easing of the laws on abortion and on the sale of contraceptives to give voluntary action a chance.

A licensing law would be expected to lead to an initial increase in birthrate to young couples who would otherwise have postponed having a second child for a time, but who might fear a stiffening of the law to limit the number even of licences for two. This would be a transient effect if the law could be enforced. I find it extremely difficult however to see how exactly this could be done – at least until voluntary methods had been tried and failed, and the situation had become a great deal more desperate than it is at present. The only really effective methods of enforcement would seem to be forced abortion or the execution of unauthorized infants followed by compulsory sterilization. The idea that either the Government or the public would accept forced abortion of those who wanted their babies, before even accepting the right to free abortion on demand for those who do not, seems utterly ludicrous, and the proposal for infanticide of wanted children even more so.

An apparently more practicable procedure would be to keep contraceptives continually placed in the water supply. This also seems to me preposterous, but needs mention because it is very frequently suggested, especially by educated but (technically) ignorant people. Antidotes could be obtained only on licence, and until the permitted number of children had been produced. This proposal has three main drawbacks – it would be expensive,

Possible Solutions

it would be unpopular, and it would lead to an explosive increase in the birthrate. The first two drawbacks are obvious; experience has shown me that the third needs a little explanation.

First, then, we should presumably not wish to sterilize the entire sheep, pig and cattle population of the country, so that farmers would have to be allowed a supply of the antidote, and might find it paid them to find their cows unexpectedly infertile and to sell a lot of home-made drinks on the side. Then the sale of water butts would go up; most countries have a rainy season, and some have few non-rainy seasons. Then there is the likelihood of black market enterprise in the antidote.

I do not know how many contraceptives would still be effective after being boiled for an hour, filtered through a water softener and then made into ginger beer, but this would no doubt soon be found out, and if homely methods with filters of earth or toast or even mouldy sawdust failed, an inefficient but adequate distillation apparatus could be assembled from ordinary kitchen utensils which would do the job. The actual *rise* in birthrate which I forecast would arise partly from the natural and automatic reaction of most people to outside interference with their affairs, and rather more from the highly reasonable fear that if they didn't have a baby while they could, the Government might find some method that could not be so easily fixed.

An initially more effective procedure than putting contraceptives in the water supply, would be to insert a slowly-dissolving long-term contraceptive surgically into every adolescent; to permit its removal only on licence, and automatically to reinsert it after every childbirth. This could in principle be applied to either sex alone. It is almost always assumed that women would be chosen – probably because those discussing the scheme feel that more people will be shocked by the idea of forced surgical operation on young girls – but possibly for the obvious practical reason that an occasional man who escaped the net could do a great deal more harm than an occasional woman. Treatment of both would clearly be much more effective in preventing the consequences of occasional failures than treatment of either alone.

This method would not lend itself to so many do-it-yourself evasions after application, but would be difficult to apply. I find it absolutely impossible to visualize the average surgeon, his anaesthetist and nursing staff, forcibly anaesthetizing a struggling and screaming teenager in order to make the surgical implant in the first place. After all, quite a lot of medical men at present refuse to sterilize either men or women who have actually asked for the operation. At first not all of the teenagers would scream and struggle, but if the screamers and strugglers were reprieved they all very soon would. The numbers involved make it quite impossible for treatment to be given by the very small number of doctors who would obey Government orders in such circumstances. If no such surgeons could be found, and an adequate number of unqualified operators under army control were pressed into service instead, this would not enhance the willingness of the rest of the medical profession to acquiesce, and those that had been treated would find no difficulty whatever in finding a surgeon to remove any structure that had been implanted – even if he had to introduce an ineffective dummy to escape detection and imprisonment.

The technique of implantation might be very useful as a form of *voluntary* birth control lying between the Pill and voluntary sterilization, and, once fully-developed and tested, could become quite popular for its trouble-free reliability, but as the base for a compulsory method it would not be satisfactory.

A proposal for compulsory action on a smaller scale that is often advocated is sterilization of the feeble minded. There could be some social advantage in limiting the reproduction of people incapable of bringing up children, and many who have now to be strictly confined in institutions might be allowed far more freedom to work outside, and to be freed from forced sexlessness, if they would accept sterilization, which would give a real and useful increase in individual freedom. But the numbers involved are too small for this to have much numerical importance.

So far it may seem that I do not favour methods more rapid and positive than the removal of existing obstacles to contraception, and am relying on an unsupported hunch that spontaneous voluntary action would do the rest. At the moment, this is so. But I should be quite prepared to consider the use of further measures, if and only if, the milder ones proposed did not work in the generation or so that I would expect them to take. What I am sure of is merely that the mildest measures should be tried first.

Possible Solutions

It is quite obvious that if people and Parliament refuse the voluntary methods, they are most unlikely to agree to anything compulsory. To press for more vigorous methods now, therefore, could well postpone any action being taken at all, even on the removal of legal obstacles to voluntary control. Again, it is impossible to do everything simultaneously, and if the mild measures gave even a partial improvement, at least the urgency would be somewhat reduced, and time gained for assessment of the morality and effectiveness of possible alternatives.

If on the other hand, as may be the case, it quickly appears that a mere decrease in Government interference is by itself inadequate, there is much that could be done without the jump to compulsion, which is most unlikely to be tolerated.

Persuasion

A measure widely supported among the old and rich, and among the young and unmarried, is the abolition of family allowances or perhaps the provision of such allowances for the first two children only. This would undoubtedly have some effect, but could affect in any way only those who plan their lives at least nine months ahead, and would leave the entirely feckless quite uninfluenced. It is, unfortunately, the quite feckless whose children need help most, if they are to grow up healthy and with a chance of social improvement. This is important, because the object of the entire exercise is to give the people that we do have decent lives in a tolerable environment, not merely to ensure that they don't actually die. A reduction of cash benefits, combined with an increase in cheap milk, and perhaps other important foods such as eggs or cheese, would be less objectionable from this point of view.

More money would be saved and perhaps as many births might be prevented, if, instead of cutting the family allowance, the tax relief for children were eliminated. Most parents who are well-enough off to gain the full advantage from these reliefs are in positions where planning ahead is usual. Hence, although the numbers affected by the loss of tax reliefs would be less than would be affected by a cut in the family allowance, the net effect on population might be as great or greater.

This economically superior alternative is rarely proposed in letters to the press, most of which are written by people who would suffer more from the loss of the tax relief than of the family allowance. It is of course a common form of human bias to put the blame for difficulties, and the responsibility for solving them, on anyone other than oneself.

Another simple measure which is often proposed is the shutting down of fertility clinics, or more drastically, forbidding the treatment of infertility. The numbers involved are so small that it does not make a vast difference whether this is done or not, and it certainly seems more sensible at the moment to concentrate on the control rather than on the increase of fertility. I think however, that to abandon the treatment of infertility and even to abandon all research on it, would be a mistake. First, a better understanding of infertility could well help us to control fertility. Secondly, to forbid the cure of infertility is not very different from compulsory contraception – except that it is applied to a helpless minority. Practically, extra resistance would be produced to the whole programme for little gain, and even this gain might be illusory; confidence in the availability of fertility treatment if necessary may encourage people to postpone for an extra year or so the start of their families.

A method which by all analogy could give a far greater effect than any of the methods proposed so far, would be the use of extensive television advertising in depth. People do not much like being done good to if they notice it being done, and direct Government advertising of the desirability of contraception might have little effect, but straight advertising of the Pill and of other equipment by the makers, would not be suspected of aiming at the good of anyone but the manufacturers, and should be well tolerated. Attacks on the immorality of this by opponents of all forms of contraception would aid the publicity, and the Government could indirectly ensure a large expenditure by the firms concerned by leaving advertisements of birth control materials untaxed, while taxing heavily the advertising of other products such as headache cures, which now help so much to keep the names of their makers before the public. Since aspirin kills many

Possible Solutions

more people than does the Pill, this might be in the public interest for other reasons.

Statistics could no doubt be rapidly assembled to show that the average childless couple would attain a colour television set by the time they were twenty-nine, while the couples with two children didn't get it till they were thirty-eight and those with six children never got one at all. Variations on 'you will give your child a better chance if you give yourself time to prepare a better home for it with the help of Stopp...' would also proliferate, and I think that there are few countries which could not make a very considerable difference by this means.

Voluntary societies such as the Conservation Society in Britain could do a great deal to help the public see that the quality of life depends on having fewer children. Practically every way in which technical civilization damages the environment in which we live is either accentuated or caused by the growth of population. Some people dislike the noise of jet aircraft; some regret the disappearance of our wild flowers and butterflies; some wish to preserve our old buildings from destruction; some just disapprove of parking meters and high-rise flats. Every one of these problems would be easier to solve, and many would solve themselves, if the population were going slowly down instead of rapidly up. Only a minority is bothered about any particular one of the few concerns I have cited, or the many concerns which I have not, and hence no one of them is of major interest to the Government. All the minorities together, however, add up to what must be a considerable majority; and correspondingly the societies concerned, although the effect of each may be small, have collectively an important part to play.

There are plenty of indirect ways of influencing the birthrate which it might be useful to consider. Even if the effect of each is small, a large number of methods applied gently are more stable, and likely to be more acceptable, than a small number pressed hard. For example, such trivial procedures as running popular television serials later at night – especially at weekends – could have an effect. An attractive positive plan might be to subsidize fairly heavily a large number of small flats suitable for young couples in the central areas of large cities – perhaps requiring all new office blocks to have a quota of such flats on the top, and associated garages at the bottom. Fitted only with continuously running paternoster-type lifts, these would anyway be very unpopular for mothers with perambulators, and if this were not enough, they could simply be allocated only to childless couples, those producing babies not being fined or punished, but merely moved at once to more suitable and comfortable – and expensive – accommodation in the outskirts. The prospect of giving up the car or the telly would prevent few people from having children at all, but it would encourage quite a lot of them to postpone a family until they had saved up a bit – and family size goes down quite quickly with an increase of the age of the mother at the birth of the first child.

An indirect method of delaying maturity, which would have other social advantages if it could be achieved, would be to reduce the advertising and television pressures on children to grow up as fast as possible. I have heard some Californian parents *boasting* that their daughters began to use make-up and to date boys, at nine or ten years old. Female chimpanzees start to take an interest in boys at seven, and doubtless we could equal them if we really tried, but the human race did not succeed by, if I may coin a phrase, aping chimpanzees.

A reduction in tax on two-seater cars, balanced by an increase on larger ones, would have a similar effect, as well as saving space on congested streets. Free street parking for such two-seaters, in special bays too small for anything else, would have more effect still.

The possibilities are endless, not one of them requiring compulsion, and it is really exceedingly difficult to believe that they would all be necessary, let alone such more drastic steps as forbidding mothers of under-three-year-olds to take outside jobs unless father is staying at home instead.

What are lacking at present are the wills, not the ways. It is perhaps worthwhile to recapitulate the main points which I have made so far. It is true that my proposals would be slow to act, and I am perfectly aware that they might prove inadequate. On the other hand, it is also possible that, mild and individually voluntary as they are, they may still be unacceptable to many populations. Abortion on demand would meet much opposition even in Britain, and both that and the advertising of contraceptives might be quite unacceptable in predominantly Catholic countries. Perfectly true. But is it seriously suggested that a country which refuses to permit the advertising of contraceptives, or their free or cheap issue with a public subsidy, is going to accept their compulsory administration through the water supply, or any other form of compulsion? What people or Governments *could* do is important to know, but far more important is what they *would* do. And I believe that what I have described represents about as much as it is possible to expect that either of them would do in the immediately foreseeable future. It is far more important actually to get something done that will help a bit, than to talk about something that would help much more but will not be done.

Of course the problem is urgent, but this urgency arises much less from the absolute number of people in prospect in the next generation or so, than from their rapid increase in real wealth and from their consequent demands on the environment and on the resources of the world. This demand does not come from the under fives, or from the overworked parents of large families, who cannot rush about the world in cars and aeroplanes, or afford the conspicuous waste which goes with wealth. A sudden dearth of babies would *increase* the rate of rise of standards, and for a decade or more would increase our draining of the world's resources. This could indeed have been avoided – if we had begun to cut our reproduction rate thirty years ago. But we didn't, and whatever we do now is going to take decades to show a real visible gain. This would be true even if we out-Heroded Herod by a factor of two and destroyed *all* babies for five years. But in much less than a decade we can see whether voluntary action is going to work, and just how bad things will be before they get better. And our children can decide on what the next stage will be.

And finally, even if voluntary methods are for some reason inadequate outside Japan, they have anyway to be tried first. At least they will slow down the Gadarene rush to disaster, and give a little more time for education, and their final failure would be the only thing that could possibly give the moral justification for compulsory measures.

The Methods Appropriate to Peasant Populations

All that I have said so far is specifically directed at the rich, industrialized countries such as Britain. For most of these, an actual drop of population could make life a great deal richer, but on the other hand a very moderate change in birthrate would stop the rise. But there are also the under-developed countries which do not yet put such a strain on the capital resources of the world, but which are already in serious difficulties as a result of their rapid rise of population. The Indian sub-continent is already unable reliably to produce the food it is going to need, and South America is within easy reach of a similar situation. The problem has arisen because it is much quicker and easier to spread medical knowledge and equipment, and easier to persuade people to use it, than it is either to persuade peasants to use new methods of cultivation, or to limit births.

First, I believe that *nothing* can be done that will produce a large and immediate effect. The relatively minor measures which are all that Britain needs could be operating within five years (I don't suppose they will be) and the far bigger problem faced by Japan was essentially solved within fifteen. But Japan is an industrialized, united and highly literate country, while India, Pakistan and the South American countries are not. You cannot *tell* an illiterate peasant – at least, you can, but you will not be believed. Over millennia he has learnt that everything that he is told by the slick townsman works out to the advantage of the townsmen, not of the peasants. Over millennia only those have survived who have had families with five or ten spares, and if he is to co-operate he has got to *see* all his children growing up for a generation; not just be told that they are going to do so. This is the answer to those who believe that it is neither sensible, nor even in the long run humane, to supply food and medicines to these countries. Only by the supply of food and medicine can we bring the peasant populations to see the need for, and to understand the advantage of, family limitation. At the same time, of course, they must be educated and given the techniques for birth control. Although too few will use these at first to stop or even greatly slow the population growth – family planning is not

Possible Solutions

population control – the example will be seen, and will be familiar by the time the value of it has been grasped by the many. So the first proposal that I want to make for southern Asia and southern America is that we institute with urgency a twenty-year plan to feed and cure and educate the growing multitudes. This is not enough. By itself it would bring disaster sooner, as the critics of charity have seen so clearly. But without it, nothing can be enough, and eventual disaster would be assured. And the sooner it can be done the sooner the real problem can be tackled.

The main cost and difficulty lies in the provision of food. There is adequate popular pressure in the poorest countries to ensure the internal development and spread of medical facilities, with a very moderate expenditure on external technical help. The cost of education is also largely internal to each country; requiring a diversion of resources from one part of the community to another to make the teaching profession attractive and respectable – possibly needing a revolution and possibly not – but no cash and little help from outside. By education I do not mean the changing of good farmers into bad clerks. In the day of transistor radios and television, it is not even certain that one should begin by teaching children to read and write. Hygiene and basic biology, the principles which lie behind the breeding of plants, and the local techniques of agriculture, are all more important to study first. After the elements of those are established, and when the need for wider knowledge develops, is the time for reading and writing. It may be some time before such matters as the history of Europe, or algebra, or the geography of the United States, become worthwhile.

Much has been done already, and much is still being done, in the development of new crops and new methods for improving food output in the hungry countries themselves. Vitally important as this is, both for its own sake, and to get each country standing on its own feet, it is most unlikely that by itself it can be adequate. On the most hopeful forecasts, the populations of India and Pakistan are likely to double, and those of South America to treble, before they can be stabilized, and for the Asian countries at least, that means food from outside for hundreds of millions of people over two or three decades. The cost of this is not going to be covered by flag days and voluntary collections in the rich countries.

The Cost of an Effective Programme

The war against want will be very cheap compared with the real wars which would follow its failure. But it will be comparable in cost with the present *preparations* for a real war. If the cost is to be acceptable to the USA and the USSR and the other countries which could grow or manufacture spare food, it will have to come off the cost of armaments, not be added to them. Less than half the world's present expenditure on armaments would do the job very comfortably, with plenty to spare for help with the industrial development. The 'miracles' of Germany and Japan are materially founded almost entirely on not spending money on arms while everyone else was doing so.

The form in which most of the money would have to be spent; that is, as subsidies to farmers in the advanced countries, is not politically unfamiliar or difficult to achieve. It should not be impossible to gain the support of the new generation which is protesting against the war in South East Asia, for the replacement of taxes for war by taxes for food to give away. To the sometimes less generous older generations – who have to pay most of the taxes – it can be pointed out that such expenditure could help to reduce the unemployment likely to result – and not only in USA – from the cessation of the war in Vietnam.

The fear of unemployment rather than of unprovoked attack is surely one of the major factors in the vast expenditure on arms for a major war which no-one could possibly dare to start on purpose. It is just imaginable that a series of miscalculations and misunderstandings might lead to such a war, and a little more likely that a technical breakdown of radar or computer equipment might do so. These are quite inadequate reasons for the present scale of armaments. It is also quite possible that an individual may be killed by lightning, but it is not sensible to spend most of one's disposable fortune on lightning conductors. If the USA, the USSR and the other European countries halved their arms expenditure over five years, and spent half the money

Possible Solutions

saved on reducing taxes and the other half on helping the hungry, it is quite uncertain that the risk of being attacked would even be increased. We are obsessed with the risk that Soviet arms might be successful, in a first strike, in simultaneously wiping out on the ground all of the American missiles deployed in the USA and all of those deployed in nuclear submarines over the globe. This would require that every American missile was prevented from getting off the ground during the hour or so that the Soviet missiles took to travel on their way, or that every one of those which did set off towards Russia would be stopped by ABMs. This seems to me impossible as a practical proposition. Its theoretical possibility is not what determines Russian planning. What bothers the Soviets is not the imaginable possibility that such a complex plan might work, but the much more seriously imaginable possibility that it might not work. With far fewer American bombs than there are now, the Russians could still not be sure of destroying all – and very few reaching their targets in the USSR would take all the gingerbread out of the gilt.

There is another point. If the USA and western Europe embarked on a practical long-term plan to raise the food supply and health of India and Pakistan to 1972 European standards by the turn of the century, could Russia or even China afford to do nothing? Gratitude has little influence on politics, but an Asia which knew that it faced immediate starvation if anything happened to Europe and the USA, would be a much more reliable ally than an Asia which had been militarily protected from Communism. A plan to feed the Indians might be a far more effective way of directing Russian budgets away from the provision of rockets, than the building of rockets ourselves has proved to be.

Anyway I do not think we have much choice. I may be underestimating the risk of military catastrophe, though I do not think I am, but it surely is not certain. If Asia and South America cannot be given the critical generations worth of help they have to have, there is no question of probabilities. Catastrophe would be certain. If we don't act first, the Russians will. It would be better if we did it together.

The question of giving food has often been missed in books on population problems. With determination and steadily improving methods of agriculture, probably supplemented extensively with factory-made proteins, there is no technical reason why we should not hold, and indeed much improve, the situation for thirty years. But this merely enables us to fulfil one of the essential conditions which must be met before the problem can be finally solved; it doesn't solve the problem.

Apart from tradition, there are very practical reasons why the peasants in poor countries regard children as of value, and indeed of very great value. The first and minor one is that children who do not go to school can help with simple work such as weeding or bird-scaring at a very early age, and since in good times their food costs nothing in cash, they will make a useful net contribution to the family. This value will automatically drop, and finally turn into a cost; partly because more and more of the children's time and energy will be occupied on immediately unproductive education, and partly as living standards improve and it begins to be socially important to provide even the little ones with clothes, and the larger ones with such luxuries as shoes and perhaps even toys.

Secondly, and more important, children become valuable as supports in old age. Where there are no homes for old people, or old age pensions, having someone young and energetic to feed and care for you eventually becomes a matter of life and death. In bad times, other people's children have all they can do to support their own parents, and it is essential to have surviving children of your own – preferably several, so that the load on each one should not be insufferable.

Nothing will automatically happen to help this situation if the birthrate falls too far, and so this factor alone could have a major influence on population growth. The answer is clear and expensive. The first direct incentive to be applied is the establishment of old age pensions, or other visibly reliable provision for the old, which is independent of their own families. While this is indeed expensive, the expense, like that of the main part of education, represents a redistribution of wealth inside the country; not necessarily aid from outside. As is shown in Appendix I, the total proportion of dependants is usually less in a stationary or slowly falling population than in a rapidly growing one, the larger number of aged being more than compensated by the fewer young. Apart from administration, the total taxation required to support the old would be the same on the average as would be needed from the working generation to support their own aged parents. Since administration costs a good deal, people would in fact have to pay more, and the rich perhaps a lot more, than they would have paid in the absence of public assistance. In a successfully industrializing country, the extra cost could soon be absorbed by the rising output, but there is no doubt that substantial help in cash or kind from outside, conditional on the establishment of effective pensions and tapering off slowly as conditions improved, could make a major contribution to the effectiveness of birth control campaigns.

After this, the main steps still to be taken would differ less from those needed in Europe. This is natural, because with adequate food, good health, and welfare services for the old, we should have established the vital base which already exists in the advanced countries, and which makes it sensible to hope for significant reductions in the growth rate in these within five or ten years, as a result of cheap and simple administrative changes.

India and Pakistan have both started large scale campaigns to reduce the birthrate – India having budgeted a hundred and fifty million pounds for a five-year plan which represents the biggest cash investment that the world has yet seen. The numbers affected so far are numbered in millions rather than in the hundreds of millions required, but it has made a real practical start and has demonstrated far better than could the most impassioned Government pronouncements, that large scale help of the kind I have proposed would be effectively followed up.

Many of the difficulties due to ignorance and illiteracy of the kinds described in Chapter Nine will have been dissipated by the present campaigns by the time that mass action is possible. There is no reason at all to suppose that the pattern of techniques which suit the Japanese or the British would be ideal or even acceptable to the Indians or Pakistanis, with their very different traditions of family life and behaviour. It is vital to push ahead with a major programme of research into the factors which affect acceptability, even while a minority only is prepared to use any kind of birth limitation, both to help by saving as many births as possible now, and to have techniques and teachers available on an adequate scale when the masses begin to respond.

In the many countries in which a far greater importance is set upon sons than upon daughters, the development of a reliable system for controlling the sex of a child, even if it were not particularly cheap, could be very effective. Even in Europe or USA there would be a useful effect. We all know the occasional family of five or six girls and a boy or a long row of boys and a girl where parents have clearly wanted both, and have had a much increased family to achieve it. The availability of treatment would obviate this. The effectiveness in some other countries however could be so great that it would probably have to be controlled. Where in Europe the chief difference might be that the boys would more often than now be born at the beginning of the family, in some Eastern countries there might be a heavy imbalance in favour of boys. This would make a shatteringly effective contribution to the limitation of population, but the social chaos resulting would make this more expensive in human terms than it would be worth. One free treatment for each couple requesting it, with further treatments available only at a high cost, or even as a fairly rare reward for special service, might give a useful cut in population growth without excessive strains. There would then be expected to be a lot more boys among the rich than among the poor, but doubtless before this had gone far enough to produce serious effects, the shrewd operators would switch to daughters in the confident knowledge that the current buyer's market would change to an exceedingly stiff seller's market before the girls grew up. Indeed, it could turn out that little control would be needed for this reason, while the availability of treatment still reduced usefully the growth of population.

In a developing country there might be a big advantage in long-lasting contraceptive systems, whether mechanical or using slowly dissolving chemical inserts, which did not require regular or frequent action.

In all countries without exception, research of one kind or another, technical, social or operational, will be important for a long time to come, to find better and cheaper techniques with fewer side effects, or methods better suited to the needs and preferences of the local population. It will be particularly important, however, in the countries with which we are now dealing,

Possible Solutions

partly because of the scale and urgency of their need, and partly because they are already sufficiently advanced technically, and strong enough financially, to initiate and run the greater part of it themselves. Results thus obtained are always a great deal more likely to gain support than are ideas brought from outside, which can be attacked by agitators on such grounds as that 'They are not merely responsible for the colonial exploitation that brought about all our present difficulties, but are now trying to exterminate us.' Similar difficulties could attend any well-meant foreign efforts to accelerate action by outside pressure.

Technical and financial help given by the USA or Europe to Asian governments can be welcomed. Provision of relief foods impregnated with contraceptives in time of famine might, for all I know, be acceptable to starving peasants if the providing were done by their own government, but if it was sent from the West might easily do more harm than good. Again the opponents of any limitations would not only be likely to attribute every epidemic or crop failure to the poison from the neo-colonialists, but could well build up a nationalist demand for freedom to produce babies to a stage of large scale rioting, which could set back even the present moderate achievement for years. Without popular co-operation, the supply of food containing contraceptives would not even be very effective; the foreign food could be fed to men and children and old people, and the scarce 'pure' local supplies sold at high prices for the use of the fertile women.

The problems of Africa south of the Sahara are different enough from the rest of the world to need some separate discussion. In a few areas, for example in Kenya and Malawi, the population is pressing heavily on food resources, as in India, but this is partly due to maldistribution of land in Kenya and to inadequate techniques of agriculture in both. Over the whole continent, production of food is adequate in quantity if not in quality, and is keeping pace with the population. The death rate from disease is falling but is still very high. Where India needs food to establish the conditions for effective and popular limitation of births, Africa needs piped water and drains and modern preventive medicine. A larger population would be not merely tolerable, but in many regions would be essential to establish the richness of possibilities of living that can go with differentiation of occupation and more efficient methods of production. Nevertheless, they still greatly need to cut their *rate* of growth, so as to make resources available for developing the material base for a high standard of life, rather than for multiplying mouths at present standards. If this can be done, and advantage taken of the cheapness of food production in the tropics, there could be a major and rapid advance, perhaps even without the loss of the capacity to use and enjoy leisure, in which the African is at present so much better than the European.

The main material research required in Africa is not so much on the contraceptive measures themselves, or even into special methods for gaining public acceptance for their use, but rather in the development of less destructive methods of agriculture, and above all on the control of insect pests of both plants and human beings. It is highly desirable to avoid the expensive and temporary expedient of large scale chemical spraying with general-purpose insecticides such as DDT. When this is the only method available for the immediate and direct saving of human lives, as in malaria control, it is entirely justifiable. But even for this, the eventually inevitable development of resistance by the mosquitoes concerned will make the use of DDT or other similar materials effective for only a limited time, and if it is used on the far larger scale required for crop protection, it will become ineffective more rapidly still. Furthermore, the miscellaneous arthropod fauna is so immensely rich that there is an exceedingly big chance of allowing some creature now rare to become a pest, being itself resistant, and at present controlled by insect parasites which would be destroyed. Development of perfectly specific controls such as the sterile male technique, or mutated races showing cytoplasmic incompatibility with the wild ones, or the use of synthetic sex attractants, can be achieved by research on the spot, but cannot be carried on by simple purchase of materials from elsewhere. While every kind of aid may be needed somewhere in Africa, the most important help that must be provided from outside, therefore, apart from pump-priming operations in the form of cash to help with the establishment of old age pensions and hospital services, may be in the advanced training and technical support in the fields of agriculture and applied entomology.

While the technical research is in progress, some major social

Possible Solutions

investigations are needed. Polygamy, and the very different moral responsibilities that go with the extended family, may make the spread of contraceptives easier, or may make it more difficult. The problems will certainly be different, and will certainly need a huge effort for solution. Again, this effort will have to be made inside the countries themselves.

As throughout this book, I have begun by dealing with the programmes that are technically necessary, including the dispelling of simple ignorance. I have also shown that the economic resources required are amply available in the world, but so far I have largely neglected the political problems, since it is sensible to tackle these only after solutions to the more basic problems are known to exist. Everywhere in the world there exist groups with some, or even much, political influence who wish some action to be taken to reduce the rate of population growth. Against them, however, is the dead weight of tradition; the natural objection of human beings to doing anything ever for the first time. When tradition is organized and codified the difficulty is greater. Fortunately the big Communist countries have not set their faces against the limitation of births, in spite of the violent abuse by Karl Marx of Malthus. The problem of overcrowding is not important to the USSR, which has by far the lowest population density of the rich countries, and which could well gain by considerable growth in the long run. Limitation of births has contributed a great deal however to the painful process of transforming an impoverished, illiterate peasant mass into an industrial modern state. The reasons are first that the rapid increase of population which could have followed the improvements in medical care would have swallowed up the resources needed for development, and second that having only small families also released a vast number of women workers. The same two reasons have probably been the main motives behind the big birth control campaigns conducted by China, although here the existing pressure of people on resources may also have been important. The average population density in China is still well below that of Western Europe, but much of the country is mountainous or arid or both, and the easily developed areas are already heavily populated. The empty spaces of Sinkiang, which help to keep the average low on paper, need many decades of expensive development before they can support useful numbers of real people.

Religious Objections

By far the most important traditional sources of resistance to artificial means of control are the organized religions. Major sects of Christian, Moslem and Hindu religions are entirely opposed both to abortion, and to any chemical or mechanical means of contraception.

Some of the difficulties resulting in India and in Pakistan have already been mentioned in the last chapter, but the visible pressure of numbers is rapidly eroding organized religious opposition, at least to contraception, and it is most unlikely that this will be so important as the social factors which I have already discussed.

Far more serious, both in geographical range and in practical effect, has been the opposition of a number of Christian churches, particularly of the Roman Catholic Church. In the developed Western countries these churches may have delayed the recent liberalization of the law by twenty years, and in that time added at a conservative estimate twenty million unwanted babies to the richer part of the world. During their lives these will use as much of the resources of the world as the whole of the present peasant populations of India and Pakistan.

Even more importantly, the Catholics are almost wholly responsible for the fact that South America, the fastest growing area, and potentially the biggest problem on the planet, has done practically nothing to slow the flood of babies without a tolerable present or a hope of improvement in the future. The scale of the effect is shown very strikingly by the first diagram in Appendix I. Like many of the really large scale atrocities committed by the human race, this has not been the result of ignorant people following selfish ends, but of conscientious and intelligent people following rigid rules which once were right.

Fortunately, the wind of change has at last been blowing in Rome, and the effect of Catholicism on the birthrates of populations in the major western countries is rapidly fading away.

Possible Solutions 217

Cardinals in Europe and in the USA have made it abundantly clear, at least to the educated part of their flocks, that the Pope's latest reaffirmation of the traditional prohibition of any form of birth control, apart from the rhythm method, is not finally binding on good Catholics. Those who conscientiously believe that it is necessary to the well-being of their existing families, may follow their own consciences in deciding whether or not to use other methods of contraception. Fear of the Catholic vote no longer ties the hands of the better educated States and their Governments. Indeed, in such countries, the passive inertia of the other Christian churches may now carry a greater responsibility than does the remaining active opposition of the Catholics.

While there has been an enormous step forward, there is as yet no change in the Catholic policy in South America. The last reaffirmation by the Pope was made against the recommendation of the majority of the College of Cardinals, after a six months' discussion. The change in ten years which made this recommendation possible was so enormous, that it seems certain that the next such meeting will lead to official and full acceptance of at least some forms of birth control. But before this there may be added another forty million poverty-stricken and miserable people who by their mere existence are preventing the relief of the poverty-stricken and miserable hundred million already in existence. Every twenty years the problem will be doubled, and the resources of the continent will be reduced. The financial, technical and educational problems are very similar to those of India, but it is difficult to see how even a beginning can be made until the grip of the priests is relinquished or broken. It will be best for all, and would reduce the period of social adjustment by many years, if the Catholics could change their teaching, and use their great influence and basic good will to help their people to adapt. But if this takes too long they may themselves be the losers. Little El Salvador has already started a vigorous campaign for birth control. Sooner rather than later, the government of one of the larger countries concerned is going to see that the first big nation south of Panama to stem the flood of mouths, will have an enormous start on the road to industrial strength. Good money spent on publicizing the fact that the Catholic Church now has one rule for the rich in USA, and another for the poor in Brazil or Argentine, could take the heart out of the educated opposition to contraception, and this government would win the freedom to act accordingly.

Until the change in Catholic policy takes place, there is little that the rest of the world can do. I hope for all our sakes that it will take place soon.

Quality or Quantity?

Before I finish, I want to make my excuses for a glaring omission. Almost the whole of this book has been concerned with quantity; how to match the total number of humans to the resources of the planet. Almost none of it has been concerned with quality; whether we shall even stay as human as we are, let alone improve our humanity. This is not because I think that quality is unimportant. But I do think that there are two rather good reasons for dealing first with the problem of numbers. The primary reason is the matter of urgency. To produce a significant genetic change, without systematic and controlled breeding, takes a very long time. Several millennia of far heavier selection for resistance to disease than for brains or beauty has not made everyone into morons or all girls unattractive. If we systematically selected for stupidity, or for resistance to every kind of inhibition, we might well become on the average a little bit dimmer, and a little bit nastier to live with, in a few hundred years, but we are not systematically selecting for anything, and a harmful random drift would take tens of millennia. If we do not solve the quantitative problems long before that, there won't be anyone left with genes to deteriorate.

The second, even better reason, is that we do not know either what we ought to do or how to do it. There is a widespread belief – especially among people who score well on IQ tests – that the only really vital thing is to maintain and improve human intelligence. I do not believe this. Increases in kindness, cooperativeness and determination are needed far more than an increase in intelligence. We do not know how far kindness is determined by heredity and how far by nurture. But this does not matter very much. In either case, kindly parents are likely

Possible Solutions

to produce kindly children. Of course we want intelligence as well. Well-meaning stupidity can do as much harm to personal relations as can heartless brilliance. But on the larger scale, it would not have helped to have Hitler more intelligent. On the data he had, he made a sensible gamble – and nearly won. It would have helped to have him more compassionate.

More generally, a kindly and co-operative group, with two or three highly intelligent members, will be happy and successful while a clever, selfish and cruel group with two or three kind members will not. It is so abundantly clear that the world is suffering not from lack of know-how, but from lack of will, that the point does not need stressing. When we have got well along the way to solving the problems of quantity, we can come back to the problems of quality, with the time and the freedom from strain that will help us to tackle them with success.

To conclude this chapter, I repeat that I am aware that my proposals for purely voluntary action will seem unambitious and that even if fully implemented their effects would be slow to develop. They are based on increasing the number of things that people are allowed to do, not on increasing the number of things that they are forbidden to do. I am appealing both to the selfishness and to the generosity that lie in all of us, to give help to those in need whenever it will encourage people to move faster in those useful directions in which they are already moving. And I am appealing to our moralists to concentrate their well intentioned efforts on the wickedness of producing an unwanted child, rather than on interfering with the ways in which other people wish to avoid it.

I cannot foretell the future, so I cannot know whether operating my slow methods will be fast enough to save us from disaster. I am not opposing the faster, fiercer methods because I know the mild ones will succeed or because I do not think the need is urgent. Disaster itself *may* not be imminent, but the choices which could make it finally inevitable may have to be made within a very few decades. In the life of a species this is an almost unbelievably short time. And it is because of the appalling urgency that I have confined myself to proposals which have at least a chance of being operated now – and would certainly work to some extent – while the fiercer methods cannot even be tried for a long time and might not work at all. I wish I could be sure that we shall move even as fast as my programme would take us.

Appendix I

Population Growth and Age Structure

If we have a small organism such as a yeast, growing by asexual division in steady optimal conditions, the arithmetic of its growth is very simple. The average time taken by each individual to mature and divide remains steadily the same, and the population follows the growth pattern which Malthus described as a geometrical progression, but which we should now call exponential. This means that if it takes a time T to double the numbers, it will take time 2T to multiply by 2^2 or 4, 3T to multiply by 2^3 or 8 and in general a time nT to multiply by 2^n. When handling large numbers, it is useful to remember that 2^{10} is 1024 or just over a thousand, so that after ten doublings we have just over a thousand times the original number. After a further ten doublings, we have just over a thousand times as many again, or a little over a million times as many as at the beginning; after thirty doublings a little over a thousand million times; after forty doublings about 10 per cent more than a million million times, and so on.

The formula remains true when n is less than 1. Thus if n were one tenth, then in time T/10 we should multiply the numbers by $2^{0.1}$. This we have to calculate or look up in tables; it is about 1.07, since 1.07 multiplied by itself ten times gives us 2. Hence if we had an increase of 7 per cent per minute, we should be multiplying the numbers by 1.07 each minute. This would therefore give us a doubling time of ten minutes. An increase of 1 per cent per minute would give a doubling time of (in round figures) nearly seventy minutes. An increase of 0.01 per cent per year would lead the population to double in 7,000 years and so on.

World population increasing steadily at 2 per cent each year would double in just under thirty-five years.

While this bit of mathematics is firm enough, human populations are more complicated than yeasts, and rarely increase steadily. The simple observation that a population has increased by 1 per cent in a particular year, even when there is neither immigration nor emigration, means only that the births exceeded the deaths in that year by 1 per cent of the original population. If this were a constant rate, the population would double itself in seventy years. But to make any useful forecast of the real doubling time, we need to know a lot more than this. To illustrate this I will take two extreme examples. First, suppose we had a desert island peopled only by young married couples. Then if none of them died in the course of a year, a 1 per cent increase would mean only one child per fifty couples. As they got older, fertility would get less and deaths would begin to occur. If the initial birthrate were never exceeded, the total number of children born could hardly be more than thirty, and the population, instead of doubling every seventy years, would die out in a few generations.

If on the other hand we have a population consisting only of children and old people, we should have some deaths each year, and no births at all, so that the population would obviously be decreasing. But there is no reason at all to suppose that the population would die out. As the children grew up, and the old people died off, the births would begin and the deaths would drop.

The initial growth rates in such unbalanced populations can thus be exceedingly misleading, and are known as transients.

It is not until the population has been maintaining its birth and death rates steadily for the better part of a century – or for a period equal to the greatest age to which a significant proportion of people attain – that one can begin to do reliable calculations from the simple gross growth rates. And forecasts based on these will at once be falsified if either peoples' habits, or the environmental conditions, change.

A useful quantity, knowledge of which can improve growth forecasts, is the net reproductive index. This is the average number of girl babies that each girl baby at birth can expect to produce, in the course of her reproductive life, if no changes occur in death rates or fertility during this period. A constant net reproductive index of one would represent a steady replacement rate and a constant population size.

It is clear that the number of children needed per family, to give a net reproductive index of one, will vary very much with conditions. If only one in two babies grow up, the surviving girls must produce an average of two girl babies each. If only two-thirds of the survivors have families at all, the survivors with families must average three each, and so on. It does not matter how the average is made up. In Britain today, something like 2.3 children on the average are needed per married couple to give a net reproductive index of one, after allowing for the normal slight excess of boys, and for the girls who fail either to grow up or to marry at all. But it makes no difference whether out of ten couples, three have three children each, and seven have two each, or whether one couple have the whole twenty-three and the rest get colour television sets instead.

A constant net reproductive index of one does not mean that the population remains perfectly constant. If in a bad year everyone over sixty were shot, to save food or the cost of old age pensions, the population would obviously drop. But the number of girl babies born would not change, and the total number of people present a hundred years hence would have risen again to be exactly the same as it would have been without the shooting; none of the original sixty-year-olds would have survived the hundred years anyway.

If a population changes quickly from a much higher index, and then settles down to a new but steady index of one, its long term future will be assured, but the population will continue to rise rapidly for a generation or two, as the initially disproportionate numbers of young people grow old and die.

A consequence of this is that, while zero growth may be an excellent target to aim at in some areas, in others it may be much too small. Singapore, in which war-time privation killed off many of the older people before their time, recently had a death rate of five per thousand, or $\frac{1}{2}$ per cent. This is far lower than that of even the healthiest countries of Western Europe. Zero growth would mean reducing the birthrate to the same $\frac{1}{2}$ per cent per year, so that each couple would average a child once in a hundred years. Over a few generations, this would lead not to zero growth, but to exceedingly rapid collapse.

We can gain a far better understanding of likely trends if we look at what is known as an 'age pyramid', rather than at raw birth or death rates.

In Figure 1 are shown five such pyramids. The horizontal axis shows the percentage of the whole population within each five-year range of ages, as shown on the vertical axis. Dependents – i.e. those under fifteen or over sixty-five – are shown hatched, while those of working age between fifteen and sixty-five are shown open.

The first diagram shows the distribution for Brazil in 1950, when the doubling time for this population was a little over twenty-five years. It shows a very close approach to an unlimited exponential growth with a net reproductive index close to two. Contrasted with this are the age pyramids for the United Kingdom in 1970 and for the USA in 1969. These two show clearly the effects of the two world wars and of the 1929 slump. Next there is shown the pyramid for Japan in 1969. This shows clearly the loss of over a million young males in the last war, as well as the effects of birth limitation since 1949. Finally is shown the pyramid which Britain would have if we had a net reproductive index of one and the same death rate at each age as we had over the five years from 1963-68, both birth and death rates being maintained at a constant value over a long period.

The fear has often been expressed, that if births are limited, our standard of living will be increasingly depressed by the burden of maintaining dependent old people. The pyramids show quite clearly that the burden is the other way round. If we take the total number of dependents, old and young, Brazil had seventy-eight dependents for each hundred individuals of working age, while Britain had only fifty-eight and a Britain with a stationary population would have fifty-four. Small babies are certainly less expensive to maintain than seventy-year-olds, but on the other hand a woman with small children is extremely likely to be a dependent herself – in economic terms. A woman whose seventy-year-old mother-in-law is living with her, is even

Population Growth and Age Structure

more likely to go out to work than one whose mother-in-law is not.

A very rapidly falling population might indeed face difficulties, but a population whose birthrate was constant would have no serious trouble for a very long time, even if nobody ever died again. In this case the number of dependents added each year at sixty-five would be just $1/65$, or $1\frac{1}{2}$ per cent, of those below sixty-five. Few industrially developed countries – the only ones in the least likely to have constant birthrates – average so low an annual increase as this in the Gross National Product. Even neglecting the fact that the prospect of going on living itself represents an improvement in standards to most people, the extra elderly immortals would therefore still permit some increase in material standards of living for the rest.

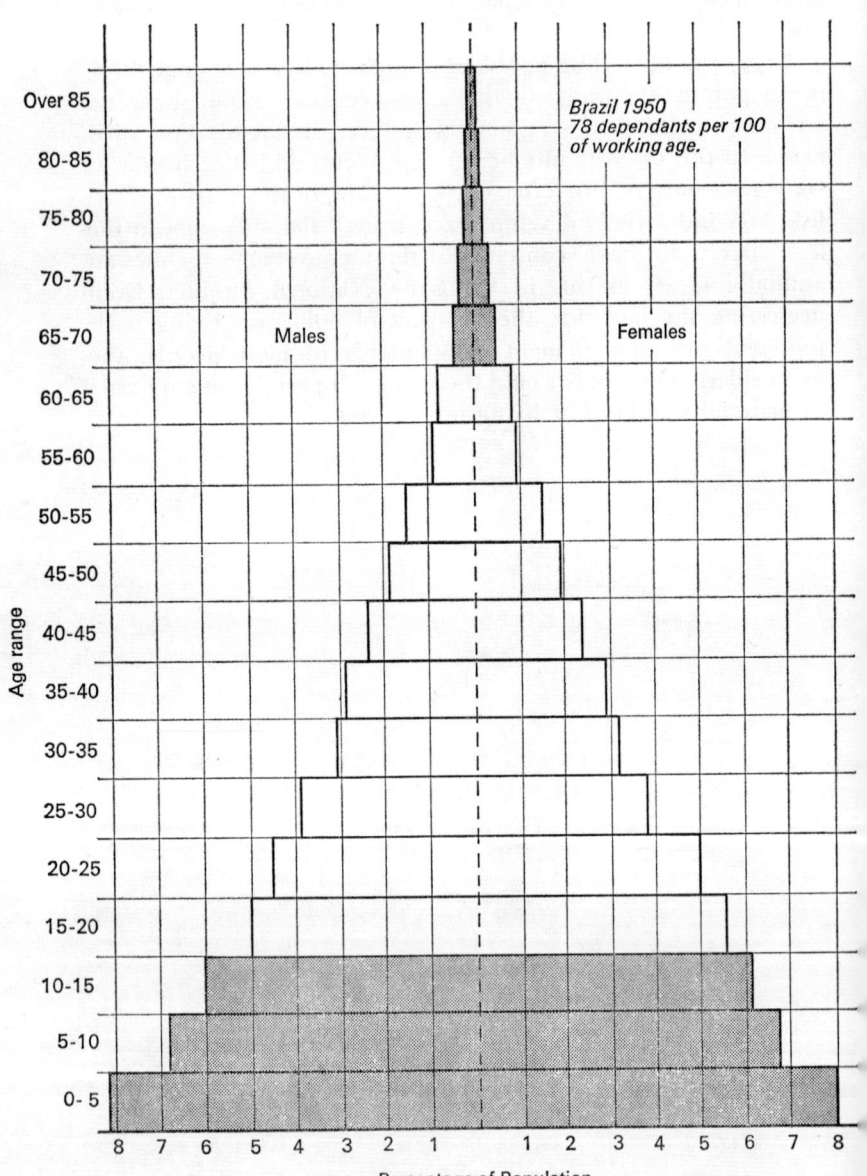

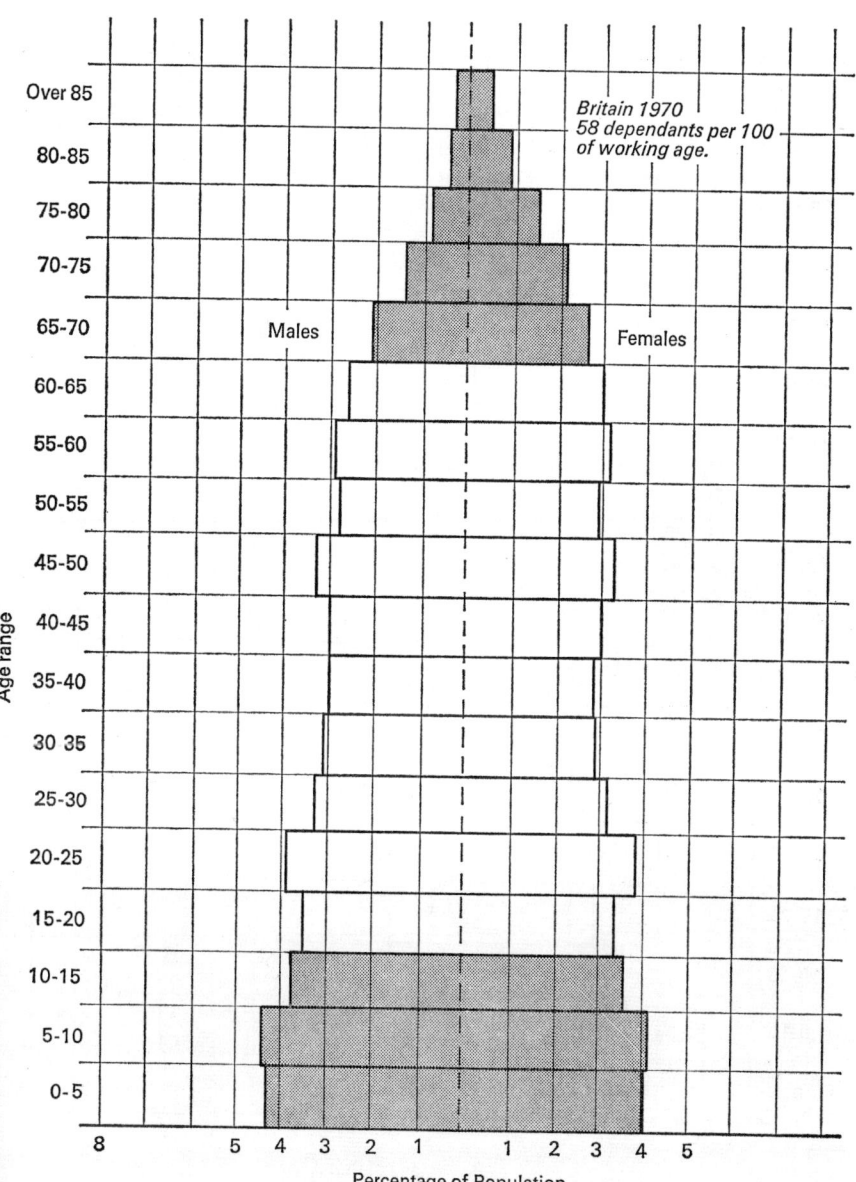

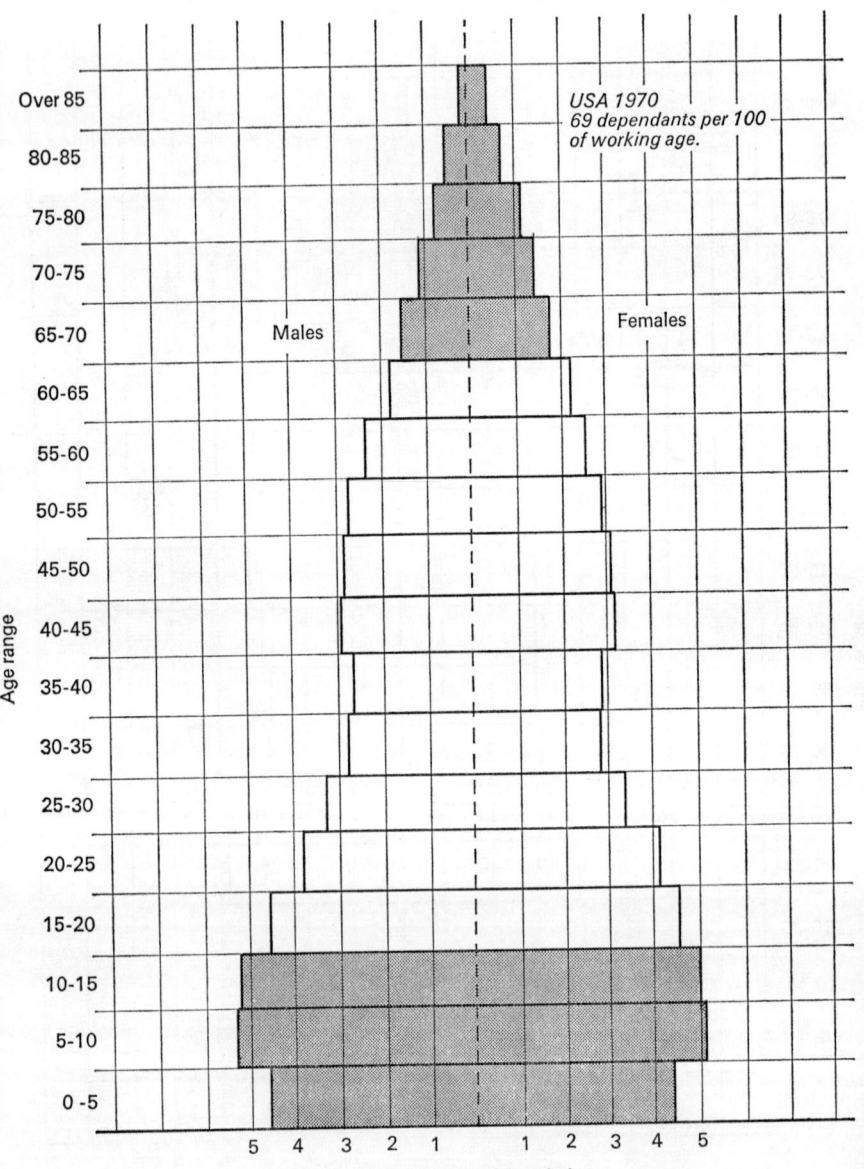

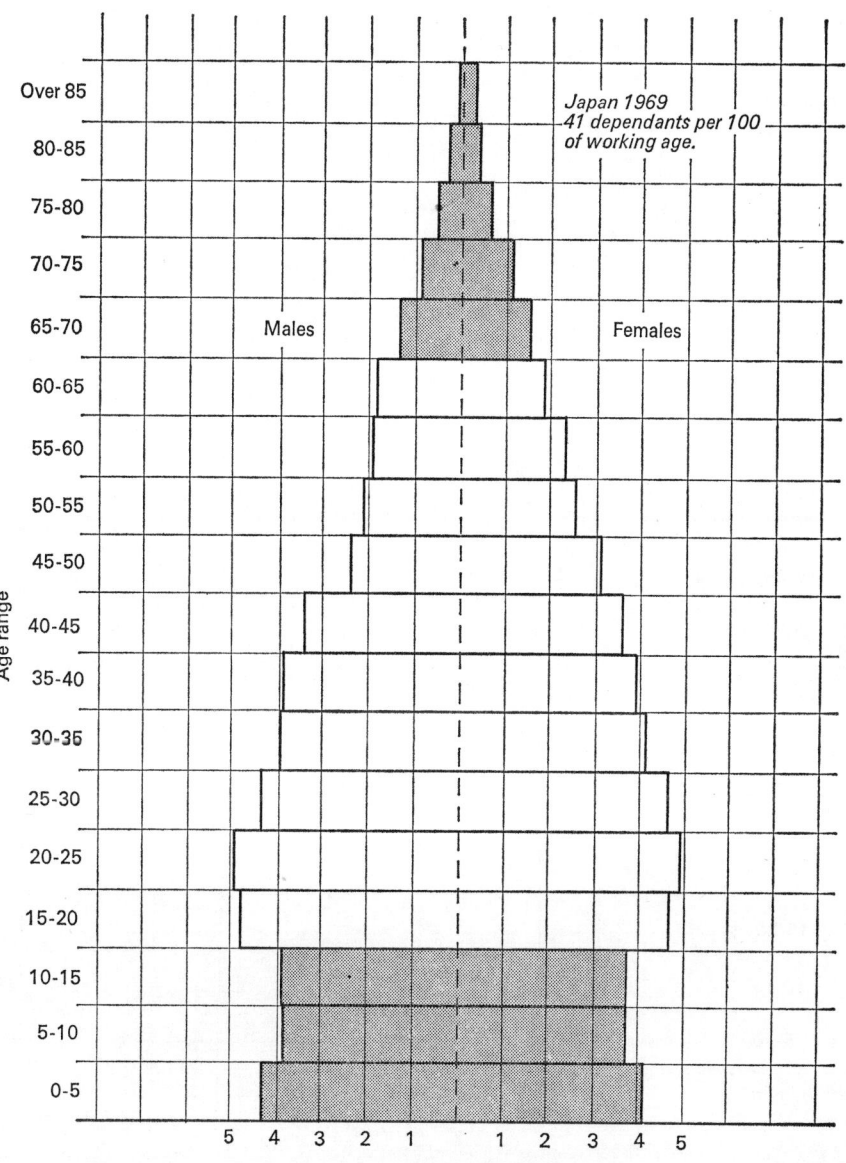

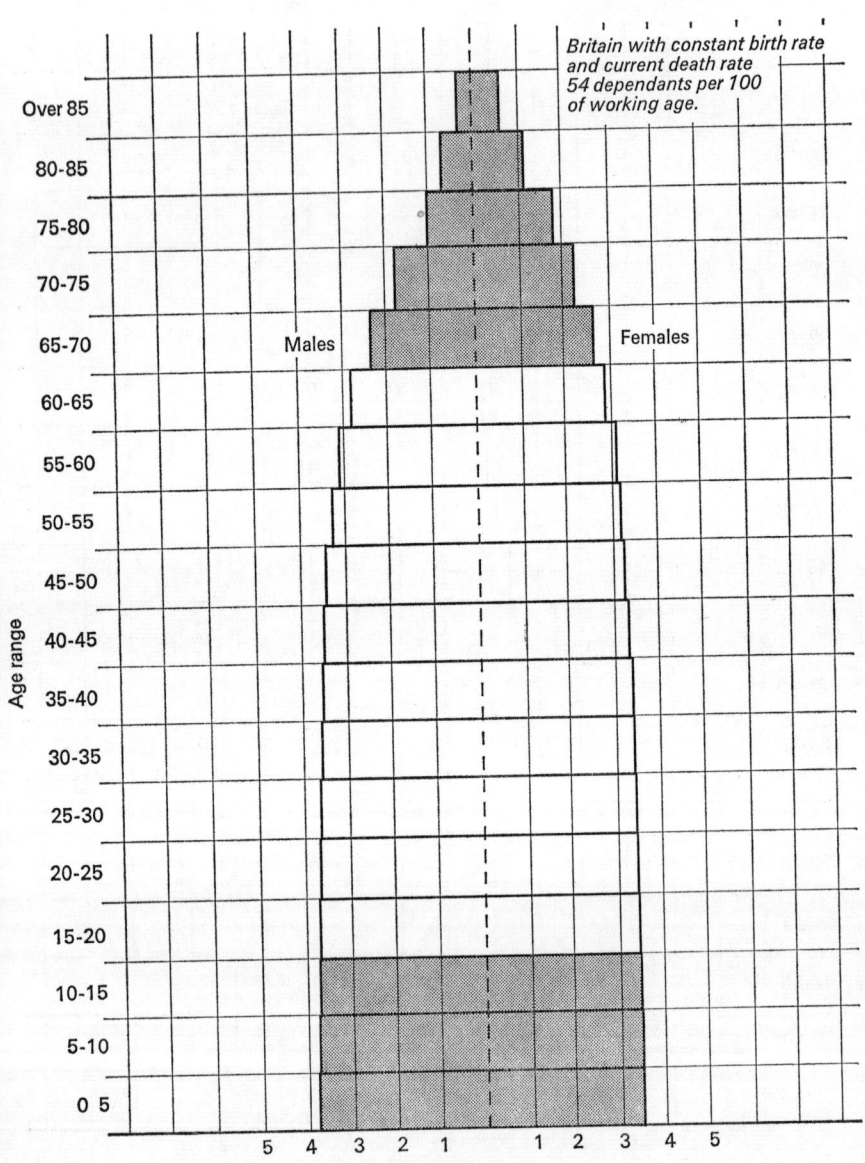

Appendix II

Group Selection for Intelligence

In Chapter Three I have suggested that the extraordinarily rapid evolution of human intelligence could be explained by competition between troops rather than between individuals. I will take an extreme example to make this easier to understand. Suppose that a militarily useful high intelligence on the one hand, and a useful individual asset such as a marked increase in running speed on the other, each depended on possessing every one of six particular genes. Suppose that on the average in a particular tribe with a hundred or so adult males each individual had two genes for high intelligence and two for fast running, only one individual in 3^6, or 729, would have a set of six and be either of high intelligence or a fast runner. (A group carrying only one of the necessary genes would produce only one individual of similarly high intelligence in 46,656 cases, or sixty-four times less often than our two-gene group.)

The fast runner would have a better chance of personal survival than most, and with an average mate carrying two of the needful genes for fast running, his or her children would average four each. Less than one in ten of them would get all six and hence grow up to be fast runners. The advantage to the group of the few extra genes in the general stock would be minute. But if an individual of high intelligence is born, the entire group has a better chance of survival.

If in his lifetime our intelligent individual helped his two-gene group to eliminate only one less gifted group, and if his group could then double its size to fill the vacant space, he would have made possible the addition to the human pool of many hundreds of the genes for intelligence, even if he spent so much of his time thinking that he had no time for girls and never had any children himself at all. Such a wholesale elimination of a duller troop would not have to happen very often to have an important effect. If it happened once in seventy generations, the average rate of increase of the more intelligent group would be about 1 per cent per generation more than among the others. In a thousand generations this would mean a relative increase of over 20,000 times; in fact, for practical purposes the stupider groups would have ceased to exist, and the total pool of genes for intelligence would have doubled over the entire area. Natural selection is very effective when given time.

On the other hand, an occasional fast runner is of little use in hand-to-hand fighting, when it is vital for a fighting force to keep together if they are not to be destroyed separately by a better co-ordinated group. Until a large proportion of the original group has all become fast runners therefore, there will be no gain at all for the group as a whole. The genes for speed can therefore reach other groups only by diffusion rather than, as it were, by convection. With an effective group size of a hundred effective males, the spread of intelligence would be of the order of a hundred times faster than that of a quality of value only to an individual rather than to the group.

Bibliography

A complete list of relevant books would run into hundreds and the 'population' of books and articles may be doubling every three years. The list below gives some of my source-books and one or two representative examples of a different approach to the population problem.

Books: Robert Ardrey, *African Genesis*, FONTANA; Rachel Carson, *Silent Spring*, HAMISH HAMILTON; Conservation Society, *Reprints Vols 1-3*, and *Topics Vols 4-5*; Paul Ehrlich, *Population, Resources and Environment*, and *The Population Bomb*, BALLANTINE/FRIENDS OF THE EARTH; D. V. Glass, *Introduction to Malthus*, WATTS; Garrett Hardin, *Population, Evolution and Birth Control*, FREEMAN; David Lack, *The Life of the Robin*, WITHERBY; Konrad Lorenz, *On Aggression*, METHUEN; Office of Population, *Population Projections, 1970-2010*, H.M.S.O.; United Nations, *Demographic Yearbook*, NATALITY STATISTICS; United Nations, Food and Agriculture Organisation, *Production Yearbooks*; United Nations, *Monthly Bulletin of Statistics*; U.S. Department of Defence, *Effects of Nuclear Weapons 1957*; J. T. Young and Tom Margerison. *The Explosion of Science—from molecule to man*, THAMES AND HUDSON.

Articles: R. C. Bostrom and M. A. Sherif, 'DISPOSAL OF WASTE MATERIAL IN TECTONIC SINKS', *Nature* 228, 154 (10 October, 1970); J. H. Fremlin, 'HOW MANY PEOPLE CAN THE WORLD SUPPORT?', *New*

Scientist, *24*, 285 (25 October, 1964); Edward Goldsmith *et al.*, 'A BLUEPRINT FOR SURVIVAL', *The Ecologist* 2 (1 January, 1972); N. W. Pirie, 'ORTHODOX AND UNORTHODOX METHODS OF MEETING WORLD FOOD NEEDS', *Scientific American, 216*, 27 (1967).

Index

Abortifacients, 185
Abortion, 185, 193-4
  in Japan, 190, 193
  in USA, 194
Abortion laws, 190, 193-4
Advertisement of birth control, 202
Africa, 51, 188, 213 seq
Africans, 51, 53
Age pyramids, 224
Agitators, 213
Aggression, 154
Agriculture, 49, 66, 105
Airconditioning, 83, 128
Airlocks, 145
Air pressure, 135
Aldous Huxley, 91
Algae, 67, 99, 111 seq, 115 seq, 124
Ali, Mahomet, 44
Altruism, 47
Aluminium, 80, 122, 140
American Indians, 17
Americans, 178
Antibiotics, 55
Ants, 11, 46 seq
Aphrodisiacs, 197
Apollo crew, 135
Ardrey, Robert, 37
Arizona deer, 23, 41
Argentine, 24
Argon, 130, 131
Asia, 51, 53, 67, 72
Asteroids, 166

Atmosphere, 64 seq, 119 seq
  removal of, 130
Atomic Energy Authority, 75
Australia, 23 seq
Australopithecus, 37 seq
Aztecs, 180

Baboons, 39, 44
Bacteriological warfare, 102
Balloon cities, 159 seq
Basal metabolism, 132
Beads, 182
Beauty, 218
Beef, 69, 70
Beethoven, 148
Behaviour control, 84 seq, 145 seq
Belloc, Hilaire, 174
Bikini test, 95
Bilharzia, 56
Biological reliability, 87
  warfare, 102, 103
Birth control, 62, 181 seq
Birth rates, 222 seq
Bison, 17
Blast, 92, 93
Bodies, 144
Book of Revelation, 65
Boxers, 44
Braconids, 15 seq
Brains, 218
Brainwashing, 85
Brazil (Age pyramid), 224

Bread, 71
Britain, 62 seq
  (Age pyramid), 224
Bunks, 148
Buttercups, 73
Butterflies, 14, 15, 16, 18

Cactoblastis, 24 seq
Cactus, 23 seq
Calhoun, J. B., 34 seq, 60, 167
Cancer, 56
Capitalism, 102
Carbohydrates, 66, 105
Carbon, 138 seq
Carbon dioxide, 64 seq, 111, 132
Carbon-14, 97, 99 seq
Cars, 81 seq, 86, 88
Caterpillars, 14, 15
Censorship, 154, 155
Ceylon, 102
Chemical spermicides, 184
  warfare, 102
Children, 84, 147, 150
China and birth control, 215
Chlorella, 67
Chlorination, 55
Cholera, 55
Cigarettes, 184
Cinnabar, 14, 18
Cities, drift to, 5, 6
  in balloons, 159
  roofed, 82
  undersea, 115 seq
City design, 82 seq, 121 seq
Cloud, 120, 124
Cobalt bomb, 96
Coil, 183
Coitus interruptus, 181
Communications, 115
Communism, 102, 209
Competition, 41, 46
Compost, 125
Compulsory birth control, 197 seq
Computers, 88, 98, 108 seq, 144 seq, 164 seq
Concorde, 4

Conditioning, 85, 149, 154-5
Condom, 183, 195
Conifers, 13
Conservation of energy, 127, 132
Conservation Society, 203
Contraception, 181 seq, 190
Contraceptives in water supply, 198-9
Control, 12 seq, see limits
Control of sex of children, 212
Convents, 181
Co-operation, 39, 219
Copper, 80
Corals, 13
Countryside, 89
Cowardice, 47
Crime, 87, 106 seq
  rates, 107

DDT, 4, 63, 64
Death rates, 222 seq
Deer, 23, 41
Democracy, 102, 106
Dependent/worker ratio, 234
Desalination, 76, 77, 118
Deterrence
  of predators, 39 seq
  of crime, 108
Deuterium, 140
Dictatorships, 106
Diesel oil, 68
Disease, 10 seq, 50 seq, 140, 145
  defeat of, 53 seq
  in towns, 51
Dolphins, 44
Doubling time, 1, 221-2
Doves, 33
Drains, 54
Duckweed, 12, 67
Dyson, F. J., 161

Edinburgh, 54
Education, 149 seq, 191
  by computers, 150 seq
Ehrlich, 6, 62, 63, 81, 187
Einstein, 100

Index

Electricity supply, 88, 133
Elements in air, *138* seq
  in human body, 137, *138* seq
  in sea, *138* seq
Elevators, 145, 148, 204
El Salvador, 217
End of the world, 65, 156
Engineers, 126, 128 seq, 155, 164
Entertainment, 152
Epidemics, 19, 55, 145-6
Eskimos, 17
Eugenic Protection Act (Japan), 190
Europeans, 51
Evolution of groups, 29, 31 seq, 44 seq
Evolution of intelligence, 231 seq

Factory foods, 67 seq, 124, 131 seq
Fall out, 93 seq
Family allowances, 201
Farming subsidies, 208
Fats, 67
Fertility, clinics, 202
Fighting, 33, 43 seq
Fire, 48, 51, 135
Fish, 66, 76, 111
Fission, see nuclear power
Flats, 85 seq
  subsidized, 205
Fluorine, 72
Food, 63, 66 seq, 207
  deficiencies, 71
  from excreta, 132, 144
  output, 58, 69
  synthesis, 66 seq, 152
Foreign aid, 211, 213
Fossil ant, 11
Frazier, Joe, 44
Freedom, 109 seq, 146, 200
Fusion power, 132, 163

Gangs, 84 seq
Gannet, 30
Garde-lou, 54
Generals, 178
Ghana, 189

Gladiatorial shows, 179
Grangemouth, 68
Great Britain (Age pyramid), 224
Great Pyramid, 65
Grime's Graves, 80
Grizzly bear, 168
Gross growth rates, 222 seq
Gross National Product, 6, 69, 225
Group evolution, 29, 31 seq, 44 seq
Group selection, 231 seq
Growth pyramid, 224
Grouse, 26 seq
Growth factor, 21, 50, 55, 145

Hares, 12, 22
H-bombs, 92 seq, 166
Heaf, 3
Heart disease, 158
Heat flash, 93, 99
Heat limit, 125 seq
Hefting, 3
Helium, 135, 136
Hens, 33
Hereditary damage, 94 seq
High-yield crops, 57-58
Hitler, 219
Homo sapiens
  evolution, 37 seq, 47
Homo erectus, 37, 38, 43
Hong Kong, 170
Hudson Bay, 12
Human nature, 47, 155
  sacrifice, 180
Hunting, 51
Hydrogen atmosphere, 143
Hydrogen fusion, 141
Hypnosis, 155, 171

ICBMs, 92
Ice, 123, 125
  age, 65
Icebergs, 76
Illegitimate children, 192
India, 182, 206 seq
Industrial waste, 74 seq
Infanticide, 180

Infertility, 202
Inhibition, 32, 34, 43, 168 seq, 218
Intelligence, 44 seq, 218-9, 231 seq
I.Q., 44, 218
Ireland, 30, 62, 181
Iron, *138*, 140
Isolation of population units, 145
IUD, 183

Japan, 189 seq
Japan (Age pyramid), 224
Japanese, 173
Josh Billings, 177
Jupiter, 159 seq

Kaibab plateau, 23
Killing each other, 42
Kindness, 218

Lack, David, 28 seq
Lake District, 89
Laverna, 68, 70
Lead, 80
Leisure, 86
Lemmings, 31
Lemonade, 70
Leukaemia, 56, 94
Libido, 197
Licences for babies, 198
Lifts, 145, 148, 204
Limits of population
　by behaviour, 26 seq
　by disease, 18 seq, 50 seq
　by fighting, 41
　by hunger, 18, 23
　by living space, 12
　by parasites, 14 seq
　by pollution, 14
　by predators, 14, 18, 23
　by war, 47, 52, 59
　hidden, 10
　stability of, 38 seq
Little green men, 166
Lions, 39, 40
Loch Ness, 90
London, 63

Longevity, 45
Lorenz, Konrad, 32
Lovemaking, 151
Lunar ballet, 158
Lynx, 12, 22
Lysine, 72

Machinery in Ultimate Building, 142
Magic carpet, 162
Magnesium, *138*, 140
Malthus, 215, 221
Marriage delay, 181
Mars, 158 seq
Measles, 20
Mechanical methods of birth control, 183
Median lethal dose, *95*
Medical aid, 175, 207
Menstrual periods, 182
Mercury, 158 seq
Metals, 80
Meteorites, 121, 131
Micawbers, 166
Micro-organisms, 10, 19, 78, 117, 145
Middle Ages, 51
Mindanao Trench, 130
Miracles, 9
Mirrors, 122-3
Monkey patrols, 32
Moon, 122, 158 seq, 162, 166
Mountain lion, 23
Moving ways, 81
Mussels, 13
Mutations, 19, 103
　by radiation, 94

Natural controls, 10 seq, 174
Natural Gas, 78
Necklaces, 182
Net reproductive index, 190, 222 seq
New York, 128
　blackout, 87
Niciporovic, 112
Nickel iron, 139

Index

Nitrogen, 135, *138*
North Sea, 76
Nuclear
  fusion, 163
  power, 78, 132, 140 seq
  rockets, 161 seq
  war, 91 seq
Nursery schools, 84, 149

Ocean temperature, 124
Old age pensions, 210, 214
Optimum population, 188
Orwell, G., 106
Overcrowding, 34 seq, 167
Oxygen, 64 seq, 135, 136, *138*
Oysters, 117

Pakistan, 206 seq
Parasites, 15 seq, 107, 108
Patagonia, 102
Peasants, 52, 53, 182, 206 seq
Peck order, 33, 41
Penicillin, 55
Penicillium notatum, 67
Perambulators, 204
Petroleum, 79
Phosphates, 113
Phosphorus, 113, *138* seq
Photosynthesis, 112 seq, 124
Pill, contraceptive, 184, 195
  danger of, 195
Pincus pill, 184
Planets, 157 seq
Plankton, 63, 64, 111 seq
Planners, 131 seq, 149, 155
Plasma, 141
Polar ice, 123, 125
Police, 108, 150
Political organization, 153
Pollution, 14, 64 seq, 74 seq
Polygamy, 215
Pop, 70
Population, see world population, limits of population
Population growth rates, 221 seq

Power, 77 seq, 137 seq
  from fusion, 132
Predators, 14 seq, 23, 40, 174
Pregnancy tests, 185
Pressure of sunlight, 123
Prickly Pear, 23 seq
Privacy, 167
Proconsul, 37
Programming of ants, 47
Prophets of doom, 4, 6, 7, 114, 124, 133, 154-6, 164
Prostaglandins, 185
Proteins, 67 seq, 111
Proxima Centauri, 161
Psychological disturbances, 60, 167 seq
Psychologists, 149
Puerto Rico, 184

Quality of humanity, 218 seq
Quarantine, 146

Radiation
  from bombs, 93 seq
  of heat, 127 seq
Radioactive fall out, 93 seq
Ragwort, 14, 18
Rain, 94, 120
Ranks Hovis McDougall, 67
Rats, 34 seq, 167
Raw materials, 79 seq, 137 seq
Reflectors, 122-3
Refrigeration, 125, 127 seq
Reliability, 87, 151
Religion, 48, 104
Religious objection to birth control, 216 seq
Research, 55, 212
Resources of world, 137 seq, 205
Rhythm method of birth control, 181 seq, 194, 217
Rice, 57
Rickets, 4
Risks in education, 85
Rivers, 74, 75
Robin, 28 seq

Rodents, 19
Roundworms, 10
Robots, 150, 152
Roman Catholics, 182, 216
Roof, 82, 127 seq
Rubber contraceptives, 183, 184
Running speed, 231

Satellite, 101, 122
  filters, 124
  reflectors, 122
Saturn, 158 seq
Schizophrenics, 171
Schjelderup-Ebbe, 33
Schools, 84, 149 seq
Seals, 17
Selective breeding, 43, 218
Self sacrifice, 46
Selfishness, 47
Sewage, 54, 118, 144
Sex attractants, 214
Sex control, 212
Shakespeare, 148
Shell Mex-B.P., 68
Sheep, 3, 4
Shops, 84
Siberia, 13
Singapore, 223
Sirius, 166
Size, increase in, 45
  optimum, 45
  reduction in, 172
Smallpox, 54, 55
Social education, 84 seq, 149 seq, 170
Social organization, 113 seq, 153 seq
Sociologists, 125, 155
Solar power, 120
South America, 206 seq, 216 seq
Space ship cities, 162
Space travel, 157 seq
Spartans, 180
Speech, 46
Spermicides, 184
Stability of population, 11 seq
Standard Man, 137-8
Stars, 161 seq

Starvation, 23, 57
Status symbols, 86, 151
Steam, 125
Sterile male control of pests, 214
Sterilization, 181
  compulsory, 198
  reversible, 196
Storage of food, 49
Stress diseases, 169, 170
Submarines, 116 seq
Sun, 163 seq
Sunlight, 111 seq, 122 seq
Superstition, 180
Surgical implants, 199, 200

Tanaka Memorandum, 190
Teachers, 149
Teenagers, 84 seq
Television, 136, 148
Temperature of sea, 76, 124, 125
Territory, 26 seq, 32, 41 seq, 51, 176-7
Thames, 64, 75
Thermodynamic laws, 127, 129
Thermophilic organisms, 125
Thorium, 140
Thrombosis, 184, 195
Tibet, 65
Tiger, 175
Titanium, 80, 140
Tools, 38
Toprina, 68
Traditional controls, 180
Tranquillizers, 149, 155, 171
Transients in population growth, 222
Transmutation of elements, 163
Tulips, 73
Tungsten, 128, 130-1
Tuscarora Deep, 130
Typhoid, 55

Ulcers, 170
Uncertainty principle, 6
Ultimate
  building, 126 seq, 134 seq
  system, 126 seq

Index

Under-developed countries, 206 seq
Underground living, 105
Undersea cities, 115 seq
Unemployment, 208
United Kingdom (Age pyramid), 224
Unwanted babies, 192
Uranium, 140
  in bombs, 97
USA, 92 seq, 101, 177
  (Age pyramid), 224
USSR, 92 seq, 101, 177, 215

Vaccination, 54
Vandalism, 84
Venereal disease, 56, 195
Venus, 158 seq
Virulence, 19
Viruses, 19, 145
Vitamins, 71, 72

War, 47, 52, 53, 59 seq, 175 seq
  against want, 208
  deaths, 59

Water
  closets, 54
  supplies, 73 seq
Weapons, 38, 40
Wells, H. G., 81
Western Europe, 192 seq
Whales, 64
Wheat, 57
'Which', 195
Williamstown Study, 66
Windermere, 89
Wolf, 23, 32, 42, 46
Wolffia arrhiza, 67
Women, size of, 45
Women's Lib, 181, 197
Wood ants, 47
World population
  forecasting, 6
  growth rate, 2, 186
World resources, 137-8, 205
Wrestlers, 44
Wynne Edwards, 26, 29, 30

Yeast, 14, 18, 124, 221

Zero growth, 223

Soc
HB
871
F68

DATE DUE

FEB 25 1974
JUL 28 1975
JUN 11 1979   DEC 23 1993
OCT 23 1991
OCT 11 1992
DEC 09 1992
NOV 03 1993
DEC 07 1994